≈ TEN ≈
Deadly
Texans

TEN
Deadly
Texans

L<small>AURENCE</small> J. Y<small>ADON</small>
<small>AND</small> D<small>AN</small> A<small>NDERSON</small>

EDITED BY ROBERT BARR SMITH

PELICAN PUBLISHING COMPANY
Gretna 2009

*The word "Pelican" and the depiction of a pelican are trademarks
of Pelican Publishing Company, Inc., and are registered in the
U.S. Patent and Trademark Office.*

Library of Congress Cataloging-in-Publication Data

Yadon, Laurence J., 1948-
  Ten deadly Texans / Laurence J. Yadon and Dan Anderson;
edited by Robert Barr Smith.
    p. cm.
  Includes bibliographical references and index.
  ISBN 978-1-58980-599-6 (pbk. : alk. paper)
  1. Outlaws—Texas—Biography. 2. Criminals—Texas—
Biography. 3. Texas—History—1846-1950—Biography. 4.
Crime—Texas—History—Anecdotes. I. Anderson, Dan, 1950-
II. Smith, Robert B. (Robert Barr), 1933- III. Title.
  HV6452.T4.A53 2009
  364.1092'2764—dc22

                                    2009005756

Printed in the United States of America

Published by Pelican Publishing Company, Inc.
1000 Burmaster Street, Gretna, Louisiana 70053

To the men and women of Texas law enforcement

Contents

Preface 9

Acknowledgments 11

Chronology of Significant Events 15

Outlaw Hideouts, Hangouts, and Locales . . . 21

Chapter 1 Cullen Baker: Mad as Hell till Death 29

Chapter 2 John Wesley Hardin: Four Sixes to Beat . . 53

Chapter 3 Wild Bill Longley: Unreconstructed and
Loving It 83

Chapter 4 Pink Higgins: The Gangs of Lampasas . . . 103

Chapter 5 James B. Miller: The Grim Reaper 137

Chapter 6 Scott Cooley: One Angry Man 161

Chapter 7 Sam Bass: Saloons, Horses, Stagecoaches,
and Trains 185

Chapter 8 Marshall Ratliff: Season's Greetings! 223

Chapter 9 Clyde Barrow: Trigger Happy 245

Chapter 10 Joe Palmer: The Deep, Dark Woods 281

Notes 297

Bibliography 319

Index 327

Preface

Our previous popular histories, *100 Oklahoma Outlaws, Gangsters, and Lawmen: 1839-1939* and *200 Texas Outlaws and Lawmen: 1835-1935*, focused broadly on law and order in Texas and Oklahoma during a 100-year period beginning in 1835. The current work profiles ten notable Texas outlaws whose feuds, gunfights, and robberies occurred mostly, but not exclusively, in Texas. The chapters are presented in the rough chronological order in which our ten subjects were "prominent." We begin in the years before the Civil War and end in 1935 with the execution of Clyde Barrow associates Ray Hamilton and Joe Palmer.

No doubt our selection of the ten worst outlaws in Texas will be controversial in some quarters. For the most part, we have profiled the better-known Texas outlaws who engaged in numerous Texas gunfights, or Texas robberies in which significant gunfights occurred. Several of our subjects are included because of the notoriety of their misdeeds.

We have again largely relied upon the scholarship of leading Western writers for the stories told here, focusing upon traditional narratives of events, using standard sources and the works of authors generally accepted as reliable. However, in some instances we have rejected traditional narratives of events, offered variations we deem reliable, or related new interpretations based on recent scholarship. Usually the variant theory is referenced but not expounded, since this is a popular history rather than a work of academic scholarship. Generally, we reviewed books, magazines, and periodicals available to us as late as January 2008.

Robert Barr Smith (*Tough Towns, Tales of Oklahoma Outlaws*) has again inconvenienced his own writing schedule to guide our efforts as consulting editor. Nevertheless, the judgments concerning the relative credibility of competing sources have once again been our own.

Acknowledgments

Research for this project was performed in conjunction with our previous works, *100 Oklahoma Outlaws, Gangsters, and Lawmen: 1839-1939* and *200 Texas Outlaws and Lawmen: 1835-1935*. A number of organizations assisted the authors in the research for these projects over the course of four years. These institutions included, but were not limited to, the Flying Fingers Typing Service, Sand Springs, Oklahoma; Texas Ranger Museum, Waco, Texas; the Haley Library; Harris County Public Library; Dallas Public Library; El Paso Public Library; Fort Bend County Public Library; Houston City Public Library; Young County Historical Commission; City-County Library, Tulsa, Oklahoma; Oklahoma Historical Society; Western History Collection; University of Oklahoma Library; Oklahoma Heritage Association; Oklahoma Centennial Commission; Woolarac Museum, Bartlesville, Oklahoma; Texas Jack Association; Oklahombres, Inc.; Oklahoma Outlaws, Lawmen History Association; Tulsa Police Department; Public Library, Enid, Oklahoma; Beryl Ford Collection, Tulsa, Oklahoma; Oklahoma Publishing Company; Lenapah Historical Society; the University of Tulsa; Kansas State Historical Society; Will Rogers Museum, Claremore, Oklahoma; National Cowboy Hall of Fame, Oklahoma City, Oklahoma; Gilcrease Museum, Tulsa, Oklahoma; Boone County Heritage Museum, Harrison, Arkansas; and the Lincoln Heritage Trust, Lincoln, New Mexico.

Individuals who assisted us in these three projects

include Nancy Samuelson, Bob Ernst, Jan Devereaux, Robert K. DeArment, Rod Dent, Phil Sanger, Ron Trekell, Armand DeGregoris, John R. Lovett, Mike Tower, Michael and Suzanne Wallis, Gary Youell, Phil Edwards, Terry Zinn, Michael Koch, Diron Ahlquist, Willie Jones, Clyda Franks, Emily Lovick, Lisa Keys, Danielle Williams, Irene and Larry Chance, Glendon Floyd, Curt Johnson, Dee Cordry, Rik Helmerich, and Herman Kirkwood. Thanks are also due Helen J. Gaines, Jim Bradshaw, Adrienne Grimmett, Beth Andreson, Mary Phillips, Stacy M. Rogers, Rand McKinney, Jana Swartwood, Gini Moore Campbell, Phillip W. Steele, Dorman Holub, Sgt. Kevin F. Foster, Jane Soutner, Brian Burns, Jim Bradshaw, Ashley Schmidt, Dana Brittain, and Christina Stopka.

Special thanks must also go to Jim Hamilton, Bob Alexander, Donaly E. Brice, Chuck Parsons, Rick Miller, Bill O'Neal, David Johnson, and Jim Knight for their comments and suggestions on the manuscript. Joseph Calloway Yadon, son of one of the authors, is owed a special debt of gratitude for his ardent research.

Finally, without the guidance of our consulting editor, Robert Barr Smith, and patient support of our respective spouses, Julia Anderson and Martha Yadon, this book would not have been possible.

TEN
Deadly
Texans

Chronology of Significant Events

1835   Notorious Reconstruction outlaw Cullen Montgomery Baker was born near the Obion River, Weakley County, Tennessee.

1840   Benjamin Bickerstaff, Reconstruction outlaw, was born near Gray Rock, Titus County, Texas.

1844   Thomas Orr, the nemesis of Cullen Montgomery Baker, was born in Henry County, Georgia.

1851   Lampasas, Texas, feudist Pink Higgins was born in Macon, Georgia (March 28).

1853   John Wesley Hardin was born at Blair's Springs, near Bonham, Texas.

1854   Cullen Montgomery Baker killed his first victim near Forest Home, Texas.

1857   The Higgins and Horrell families migrated to Lampasas, Texas within months of each other.

1865   Union general Gordon Granger declared emancipation for Texas slaves (June 19).

1867   The Baker gang ambushed a Federal soldier and teamster (October 6). James Miller, one of the most notorious assassins in the West, was born eighteen days later in Van Buren, Arkansas.

1868   A reward was posted for Cullen Baker, who reciprocated with a Wanted Dead or Alive poster offering a $5,000 reward for Arkansas governor Clayton (September).

Reconstruction official John Kirkman was assassinated at Boston, Texas, by persons unknown (October 7). Cullen Baker was among the chief suspects.

Wild Bill Longley was hanged for the first time in northeast Texas but rescued by a brother of his associate Tom Johnson, who did not survive the lynching.

1869   Cullen Montgomery Baker was assassinated near present-day Doddridge, Arkansas (January).

The outlaw Bob Lee was killed (May 24).

1871   Hardin killed Pt. Jim Smalley near Waco after being arrested for murder (January 22). He also killed Charles Cougar in Abilene, Kansas, supposedly for snoring (August) and freedman Green Paramore of Gonzales, Texas (October 6).

1873   Mart, Tom, and Merritt Horrell killed three state policemen and mortally wounded a fourth while resisting arrest at Scott's Saloon in Lampasas (March 14).

Hardin killed Irishman James B. Morgan in a bar fight at Cuero (April).

Sutton factionist Jack Helm was killed by John Wesley Hardin and Jim Taylor at Albuquerque, sometime between March 1 and July 31.

1874 William Sutton, supposed agitator of the Sutton-Taylor feud, was assassinated with his associate Gabe Slaughter by Taylor factionists as the pair boarded a steamboat at Indianola, Texas (March 11).

1875 Accused cattle rustlers and cousins Pete and Lige Baccus were hanged by vigilantes near Mason on February 18.

Bill Longley killed William Anderson in revenge for the death of Longley's cousin in Evergreen, Texas, or so the story goes (April 1).

Tim Williamson, friend and mentor of former Texas Ranger Scott Cooley, was murdered on May 13, prompting Cooley to begin the Mason County War by killing and scalping former deputy sheriff John Worley (Wohrle) on August 10. Karl Bader was killed nine days later by Cooley associates.

Leading Taylor factionist Jim Taylor was assassinated at Clinton, Texas, with the collusion of Martin King, who carelessly allowed Taylor's horse to become loose, eliminating his chances for a quick escape (December 27).

1876 Pink Higgins killed Merritt Horrell at Scott's Saloon in Lampasas (January 22).

John B. Armstrong captured John Wesley Hardin on a train at Pensacola, Florida, and killed his associate Jim Mann (August 23).

1877 Sam Bass and other members of the Joel Collins gang robbed a stagecoach near Deadwood, South Dakota, and killed driver Johnny Slaughter (March 25).

The Horrell-Higgins feudists fought a two-hour battle in downtown Lampasas, killing two (June 7).

The Joel Collins gang robbed the eastbound Union Pacific No. 4 train at Big Springs, Nebraska, taking some $60,000 (September 18).

Bass associate Jim Berry was mortally wounded resisting arrest near Mexico, Missouri (October 14).

The Sam Bass gang launched a Lone Star stage and train robbing campaign ten miles west of Fort Worth, robbing the Concho stage (December 22).

1878   Texas Rangers and the Wise County sheriff attacked the Bass gang, killing associate Arkansas Johnson and all the horses, forcing the other gang members to flee on foot (June 13).

Reconstruction outlaw Bill Longley was hanged twice for good measure in Giddings, Texas (October 11).

1882   Former DeWitt County, Texas, resident and Sutton-Taylor feudist John Peters Ringo was killed in the mountains near Tombstone, by his own pistol or otherwise (July 14).

1887   Mannen Clements, Sr., cousin of John Wesley Hardin, was killed in Ballenger, Texas, by City Marshal Joe Townsend in an election-related gunfight (March 29).

1903   Pink Higgins killed his archenemy Bill Standifer near Higgins' Kent County, Texas, ranch, then reported the incident to the county sheriff by telephone, only to be told to make sure Standifer was dead, or so the story goes (October 1).

1908   Pat Garrett was killed near Las Cruces, New Mexico Territory (February 29). Although Wayne Brazil claimed self-defense, James Miller has long been suspected of the crime.

1909   Notorious killer Clyde Chestnut Barrow was born near Telico, Texas (March 24).

1913   Pink Higgins died of a heart attack at home in West Texas (December 18).

1927   Marshal Ratliff, better known as the Santa Claus robber, escaped from a Cisco bank on December 23 with a large amount of cash, only to leave it behind in a stolen getaway car, after mortally wounding two lawmen. One month earlier, the Texas Bankers Association had increased the Dead Bank Robber program reward from $500 to $5,000, today worth about $55,000. Ratliff was lynched two years later following an escape attempt.

1934   Bonnie Parker and Clyde Barrow were ambushed and killed eight miles south of Gibsland, Louisiana, on State Highway 154 (May 23).

1935   Barrow gang stalwarts Joe Palmer and Ray Hamilton were executed (May 10).

Outlaw Hideouts, Hangouts, and Locales

Abilene, Kansas
Kansas mythology says that John Wesley Hardin killed Charles Cougar here on July 6, 1871, in a hotel for snoring, although contemporary newspaper reports make no mention of such a newsworthy motivation.

Ada, Oklahoma
James Miller and three other men accused of murdering Augustus Bobbitt were lynched here, April 19, 1909.

Atlanta, Texas
James Salmon was killed about five miles east of town, reportedly by the Baker gang (October 24).

Austin County, Texas
Dreaded shootist Wild Bill Longley was born here on October 6, 1851, then participated in many Reconstruction-era killings before he was hanged in Giddings, Texas.

Big Thicket
Wooded area where Grayson, Fannin, Collin, and Hunt counties converge, providing a refuge for deserters from both armies during the Civil War and for outlaws in the years following.

Bonham, Texas
Cullen Baker and Benjamin Bickerstaff reportedly murdered a Reconstruction official here in May 1868.

Comanche, Texas
John Wesley Hardin killed Deputy Sheriff Charles Webb here May 26, 1874.

Dallas, Texas
The Barrow family gas station and residence is located at 1221 Singleton Road, not far from the first Dallas residence of Bonnie Parker, 2908 Eagle Ford Road. Deputy Sheriff Malcolm Davis was killed by Clyde Barrow at 507 County Avenue, west Dallas, on January 6, 1933.

Denton, Texas
Motor Mark Garage, 311 West Oak, was burglarized by Clyde and Buck Barrow on November 29, 1929.

Eagle Ford, Texas
Sam Bass and associates robbed the Texas and Pacific here on April 4, 1878, taking $234, today worth about $4,500.

Eastham, Texas
Joe Palmer mortally wounded Major (given name) Joseph Crowson here during a prison-farm break on January 16, 1934.

El Paso, Texas
John Wesley Hardin established a law office at the Wells Fargo Building, 200½ El Paso Street, after serving a prison term. John Selman, Sr., assassinated Hardin at the Acme Saloon on August 19, 1895. The next year (April 5, 1896) Selman himself was killed by lawman George Scarborough

near the Wigwam Saloon before Selman could even draw his weapon.

Evant, Texas
Eight-year-old James Miller was arrested for killing his grandparents here in 1874 but was never prosecuted. Ten years later he killed his sister's husband near Gatesville, July 30, 1884.

Evergreen, Texas
Wild Bill Longley and others killed freedman Green Evans near here in December 1868.

Fort Sill, Oklahoma
Sam Bass absconded with several Indian ponies wagered in a disputed horse race, then refused a request by deputy U.S. marshals to return them.

Fort Worth, Texas
Sam Bass robbed the Weatherford and Fort Worth stage of $400 near here on January 26, 1878.

James Miller killed his real estate partner Frank Fore in a hotel washroom in 1904.

Fredericksburg, Texas
Mason County feudist Scott Cooley died near town after dining at the Nimitz Hotel, possibly of heavy-metal poisoning, on June 10, 1876.

Gladewater, Texas
Temporarily paroled prisoner Wade Hampton McNabb was kidnapped here by Clyde Barrow, Joe Palmer, and Henry Methvin on March 29, 1934, according to Barrow

gang member Ralph Fults. His body was found a few days later about ten miles north of Waskom, Texas, after Palmer tipped off a Houston newspaper reporter.

Grapevine, Texas
The Home Bank at 404 South Main was robbed by Ray Hamilton associates Les Stewart and Odell Chambless on December 29, 1932.

Houston, Texas
Wild Bill Longley arrived here by freight train in 1866, then supposedly killed a freedman.

Houston Press reporter Harry McCormick interviewed Barrow gang members Ralph Fults and Ray Hamilton near the intersection of Hempstead Road and Satsuma on March 18, 1935.

Former Barrow gang member W. D. Jones meddled in a domestic dispute on August 20, 1974, at 10616 Woody Lane and was shot to death.

Hueco Tanks, Texas
Horrell gang adherents Zach Crompton and Edward Hart were killed here by a Lincoln County, New Mexico, posse (February 1, 1874).

Hutchins, Texas
Texas Express messenger Heck Thomas prevented the Bass gang from stealing about $4,000 during a train robbery by simply hiding the money before the train trip even started on March 18, 1878. Heck's cousin, also a Texas Express employee, had been the victim of an earlier train robbery.

Joplin, Missouri
The address of 3347½ Thirty-fourth Street was the site of

an April 13, 1933, shootout between the Barrow gang and local police, two of whom were killed.

Kaufman, Texas
Bonnie Parker, Clyde Barrow, and associate Ralph Fults were forced to flee from an attempted hardware-store robbery in a humiliating mule-back escape after their car stalled in mud. The bandits rode off to nearby Kemp, where Parker and Fults were captured in April 1932.

Lampasas, Texas
Lampasas was the epicenter of the Horrell-Higgins feud, which began in 1873 and ended four years later.

Tom and Mart Horrell were ambushed five miles outside of town by the Higgins faction (March 26, 1877).

Las Cruces, New Mexico
About two miles outside town, former lawman Pat Garrett was assassinated on February 29, 1908.

Lincoln, New Mexico Territory
Ben Horrell and his associate Jackito Gylam were killed in a bordello dispute with Constable Juan Martin (December 1, 1873). Nineteen days later, the Horrells broke up a wedding party in Lincoln, killing four revelers and injuring two.

Loyal Valley, Texas
A town that became a haven for Confederate sympathizers during the Mason County War.

Lubbock, Texas
"Deacon" Jim Miller assassinated attorney James Jarrott near town after Jarrott successfully defended small ranchers derisively called "nesters" by larger ranching interests (1904).

Mason, Texas
This Hill Country town was the epicenter of the Mason County War.

Meridian, Texas
Tom and Mart Horrell were killed in the county jail (December 15, 1878).

Mitchell, Indiana
Sam Bass was born here July 21, 1851.

Oklahoma City, Oklahoma
Barrow gang stalwart Joe Palmer learned about the death of Bonnie and Clyde while lounging in the lobby of the Hutchins Hotel at 16-26 North Broadway on May 23, 1934.

Pecos, Texas
Gunman Barney Riggs killed "Deacon" Jim Miller associates John Denson and Bill Earhart here on March 3, 1896. Riggs himself was killed in a family feud four years later.

Platte City, Missouri
A gunfight between the Barrow gang and local authorities erupted on July 19, 1933, at the Red Crown Tourist Court, then at the intersection of Highways 59 and 71, six miles south of Platte City.

Queen City, Texas
Freedman Jerry Sheffield was murdered about two miles east of town December 6, 1868, after boasting he would collect a reward on Cullen Baker.

Round Rock, Texas
Suspicious lawmen confronted Bass gang associates inside Koppel's General Merchandise Store at the southeast corner

of Georgetown Avenue and May Street on July 19, 1878. Deputy Sheriff Ellis Grimes and bandit Seaborn Barnes were killed in the ensuing shootout. Sam Bass was wounded while escaping. He was captured and returned to Round Rock, where he died of his wound two days later, on his twenty-seventh birthday.

Rowena, Texas
Hometown of the notorious Bonnie Parker.

Train robber Dock Newton capped his career by robbing a bank here at age seventy-seven.

Scott's Mill, Davis County, Texas
A peace treaty of sorts between Cullen Baker and his enemies, self-described as the Famous Six, was concluded here November 3, 1868.

Shreveport, Louisiana
Clyde Barrow, Bonnie Parker, and Henry Methvin stopped at the Majestic Café (now Pano's Café) at 422 Milam Street but were scared off by a patrol car, May 21, 1934.

Texarkana, Arkansas
Thomas Orr served as the first mayor after planning the killing of Cullen Baker.

Towash, Texas
John Wesley Hardin killed Benjamin B. Bradley here on January 4, 1870, following a gambling dispute.

Toyah, Texas
James Miller ambushed and killed Bud Frazer in a local saloon, then threatened to kill Frazer's sister for complaining, September 14, 1896.

Turkey Creek Canyon, near Tombstone, Arizona
Scott Cooley associate John Ringo died here July 14, 1882, by his own hand or otherwise.

Waco, Texas
Bill Longley killed George Thomas nearby on November 13, 1875, during a fox hunt.

Storekeeper Dorrie Vaughn was murdered about thirty miles to the west on May 28, 1878. The Horrells and their associates were identified as the killers by a prosecution witness.

The Bass gang scouted the town banks here on July 7, 1878, but moved on to meet disaster at Round Rock, twelve days later.

CHAPTER ONE

Cullen Baker:
Mad as Hell till Death

Cullen Baker never saw the antiquated Kentucky rifle that blew his brains out. He was dozing away in the grass that Friday morning in January 1869, at the William Foster place near Brightstar, Arkansas, near the Texas line. The noise from the gun blast that killed Baker did at least rouse his last remaining gang member, Matthew "Dummy" Kirby, if only for a moment, just before his earthly journey was also ended by a rifle shot.[1]

Witnesses later mentioned that the "Swamp Fox" died with a scrap of paper in his pocket, whose solemn commitments bound the oath taker to the Ku Klux Klan, one of the many secret organizations that opposed federal forces to one degree or another during Reconstruction days in northeast Texas.[2] Such a discovery was hardly a surprise to anyone on the Arkansas-Texas border, where Cullen Montgomery Baker made his reputation as a killer so cold-blooded that his own former neighbors executed him.

Although much that has been said about Baker's exploits throughout the years is pure myth, he undoubtedly engendered real fear among the people of northeast Texas, particularly the new freedmen he delighted in harassing. A guidebook for Easterners emigrating to Texas in the very year of his death minimized newspaper accounts of lawlessness in Texas but admitted the depredations of Baker and two fellow Texans forever associated with him, Robert Jehu "Bob" Lee and Benjamin F. Bickerstaff.[3]

Baker was emblematic of the Texas Reconstruction

29

A barn stands on the site where Cullen Montgomery Baker was killed. *(Courtesy of Donaly E. Brice)*

outlaws who plagued the Lone Star State even after that movement officially became a dead letter. These outlaws robbed federal supply wagons rather than the banks and trains later raided by the likes of Jesse James and Sam Bass.

He was immortalized in Western fiction by Louis L'Amour, who idealized him as a gunfighter in *The First Fast Draw* (New York, 1959). In fact, most of his gunfights were one-sided affairs, in which Baker faced unarmed innocents or ambushed armed opponents. His modern biographers, Barry A. Crouch and Donaly E. Brice, described him as a coward, bully, and sociopath rather than the mythical figure who supposedly protected the innocent from scores of Unionists, carpetbaggers, and Federal soldiers.[4]

The infamous Swamp Fox crossed into the Great Beyond with the tools of his trade bulging out of his pockets.

His signature extra-large double-barreled shotgun was supplemented by four six-shooters, three derringers, and at least five pocket knives. He also carried a December 16, 1868, article from the Louisville *Courier Journal* reporting that Baker had left the States on an expedition to Cuba. Perhaps this report made Baker think that he might be left alone in spite of all the havoc he had created during the past fifteen years.

His partner left this world armed nearly as well as Baker. A double-barreled shotgun, two six-shooters, and a single pocket knife were found on Kirby after his death. However, his empty wallet showed that working with the Swamp Fox was hardly a road to affluence.[5]

Kirby probably had few such delusions, even if he had the sense to consider his increasingly vulnerable situation in the days just before they were ambushed. The Swamp Fox had quarreled with the rest of his crew less than thirty days ago and could only watch in silence as his principal lieutenant rode away with the bums, bandits, and ne'er-do-wells who comprised the last Baker gang—all but Dummy himself, that is. The Swamp Fox may have been a regionally famous outlaw before Jesse James entered the national spotlight, but now only Kirby remained, tied to Baker by a loyalty that reminded one observer of that shown by a dog to a kind master.[6] Cullen Montgomery Baker was never the larger-than-life, chivalrous Southerner, the tall figure on a white horse feared in the Sulphur River country of his own time and apparently admired from afar by a surprising number of Texans and Arkansans even today. A country fair has been held in his honor at Bloomburg, Texas, in recent times, perhaps reflecting the legends about his crimes and atrocities that still abound in the tri-state area of northeast Texas, southwest Arkansas, and northwest Louisiana.

Baker's sobriquet is just as mysterious as the man. One newspaper article reported that Baker became the "Swamp

Fox of the Sulphur" in a heroic 1887 swim across the flood-swollen Black Bayou under fire from some two hundred pursuers—an amazing feat indeed when one considers that the Swamp Fox had been killed eighteen years earlier.[7]

Still, Cullen was anything but a soft-drawling patrician from *Gone with the Wind.* Instead, one contemporary described him as a chubby, red-faced alcoholic in homespun clothes who rode a black mule rather than a white horse. About two years earlier, one observer described Baker as about five feet, nine inches tall, about 160 pounds, with dark blue eyes, sandy hair, and a yellow complexion probably confirming his alcoholic tendencies.[8]

Undoubtedly, his religious parents had higher expectations. Baker was probably born June 22, 1835, the only son of John Baker and his first wife, near the Obion River in Weakley County, Tennessee, near the Kentucky border.[9] Legendary frontiersman David Crockett lived in that county from about 1822 until his departure for Texas in 1835. John Baker and his young family of five joined the numerous Tennesseans who followed Crockett to Lone Star lands and better opportunities, settling in Red River County, which was created the next year.

The new Baker estate was near Old Boston in present-day Bowie County, which had once been considered part of Arkansas and was separated from Red River County, Texas, in 1840.[10] Settlement in the Bowie County area had begun by 1818 and kept pace with the development of nearby Miller County, Arkansas. Cotton was king in Bowie County, which had more black residents than white by 1850. When the Civil War erupted, Old Boston boasted a population of more than four hundred.

Feuds and violence became the order of the day the very year the Bakers arrived near Spanish Bluffs, a historic Texas site where Thomas Jefferson's 1806 Red River expedition had been blocked by a Spanish army. The 1840 Regulator-

Moderator War, for example, was caused by a dispute over fraudulent land-sales practices along the Sabine River. Charles W. Jackson, an embittered and recently defeated political candidate, claimed he would correct these practices. Instead, he triggered a series of violent exchanges between the Regulators, who sought to expose and destroy the fraud ring, and the Moderators, who tried to restrain the reformers.[11]

Several early biographers suggest these difficulties encouraged the Baker family to move on from Spanish Bluffs to a location some forty miles south on the Sulphur River in Cass County by 1844.[12] When the Civil War commenced, Cass County was renamed for Confederate president Jefferson Davis, then named Cass County again in 1871.

Mrs. Baker apparently died shortly after the family moved to their new home. About two years later, John returned to Weakley County and proposed to Nancy Parker, whom he married on December 7, 1846. Baker returned to Texas with his new bride and claimed land offered to early Republic of Texas settlers.[13] Land ownership did not resolve his problems with Cullen, who had already demonstrated a propensity for trouble by age twelve. One oft-told tale relates that young Cullen stole a horse at Jefferson, Texas, then rode it to death for no reason at all, obligating his father to compensate the owner.[14]

Some Baker apologists relate that at about age eleven, Cullen was harassed at a gristmill for his homespun clothing, prompting him to pummel an antagonist named Atkinson (or Adkinson) and begin a life of crime.[15] Whether this incident happened or not, Cullen's criminal behavior was more likely caused by his drinking and carousing habits.

One story of his boyhood may help explain the irrationality he frequently displayed throughout his life. In 1853, Baker and some friends decided to carouse in the town of Forest

Home, a community near present-day Queen City, Texas, established by South Carolinian John R. Wright and still located on a "soil-surfaced" (dirt) road about four miles west of Winnsboro in northern Wood County. There, in a barroom brawl, he fought with one Morgan Culp over some matter now long forgotten. Culp avoided Baker's knife only by smacking him across the head with a hatchet or tomahawk, causing a concussion that disabled the young Swamp Fox for several months and perhaps accounted to some degree for his frequently displayed mental instability.[16]

Cullen married Mary Jane Petty of Lafayette County, Arkansas, in January 1854, only nine months before the bridegroom killed his first man. According to newspaper accounts, one Wesley Baily saw Baker whip a young orphan named Stallcup within an inch of his life at Forest Home. Baker claimed later that he feared the younger man intended to kill him.[17] Baily evidently thought it was his civic duty to testify about this assault. Baker was convicted and immediately rode to the Baily homestead, where he trapped the good citizen in his own barn and blasted him with a shotgun on October 8, 1854. Baily died two or three days later.[18] Baker fled to Perry County, Arkansas, where, according to 1860 census takers, he lived with his wife, daughter, and two sisters in McCool Township, perhaps for at least two years.

Following the July 1860 death of his wife, Baker virtually abandoned his young daughter, leaving her with his in-laws in Lafayette County, Arkansas. He then returned to Perry County, Arkansas, where he promptly was drawn into a feud with John F. and Mary E. Warthan. The latter apparently had criticized Baker publicly, prompting him to confront her while he was intoxicated. Baker stabbed John F. Warthan to death as Baker attempted to beat her, according to anecdotes accepted by his most recent biographers.[19]

In July 1862, two years to the very month after the death

of his first wife, and while a twenty-seven-year-old resident of Jefferson, Texas, Cullen married fifteen-year-old Martha Foster of Brightstar, Arkansas, a burg about four miles east of the Texas line, near Atlanta, Texas. Her parents were Kentuckian William Foster and Arkansas native Elizabeth Foster, a couple whose lives would be intertwined with Baker, even after the untimely death of Martha four years later. William Foster initially welcomed Baker into his family but ultimately was instrumental in his death.[20]

Baker had already enlisted twice in the Confederate army by the time Martha became his bride. Records show that he joined Company G, Morgan's Regimental Cavalry, at Jefferson, Texas in November 1861. He was paid for his service in August 1862 but deserted that unit by January 1863.[21]

He is also shown in Company I of the Fifteenth Texas Cavalry from February 1862 to February 1863, but he was left ill and incapacitated at the Arkansas River in August 1862. Some writers record sightings of Baker at notable battles in the region, including Wilson's Creek in August 1861 and Pea Ridge in early March 1862, although there is apparently no documentation of Baker participating as part of a regiment.[22]

More certainly, by the middle of 1863, Baker's pathological hatred of blacks began to manifest itself. Stories circulating at the time indicated that, for no reason at all, he killed a black woman in Sevier County, Arkansas, and a young black man.[23]

His principal modern biographers also relate stories that Baker found a unique venue to vent his racial hostilities by joining the Union army as a civilian employee, perhaps to hide from the authorities in plain sight. He obtained appointment as an overseer of black freedmen, one of whom he killed for no apparent reason, thus concluding his Federal service.[24]

Baker also led at least two different outlaw bands during the Civil War. One such gang included the notorious

Benjamin Bickerstaff, who joined Baker by December 1864, according to one early biographer.[25] Some sources relate that during the conflict, Bickerstaff, Baker, and others joined forces to conduct raids on Federal outposts as far away as Louisiana.[26]

Bickerstaff was born in 1840 near Gray Rock, Titus County, Texas, where he joined a company of local dragoons (cavalrymen) before joining Baker in guerilla operations against the Union. Sometime after December 1864, Baker, Bickerstaff, and others reportedly raided Union headquarters at Nacogdoches, Texas, and then ranged into Louisiana, challenging Federal authority.[27] Baker began a peaceful interlude in mid-1865, supposedly mending his outlaw ways for some six months. Reformed or not, Baker lived with his in-laws, the Fosters, from the beginning of an 1865 illness until January 1866, when he went to Line Ferry, Arkansas, to work as a ferryman.

Baker and other former Lone Star Confederates enjoyed a brief period of tranquility because the Texas Reconstruction was quite different than that experienced elsewhere in the defeated Confederacy.[28] Texas Reconstruction began, at least in theory, when Gen. Kirby Smith surrendered his command to Union general E. R. S. Canby on May 26, 1865. Smith was a native Floridian and devout Christian who almost resigned his commission in 1863 to become a minister. He could hardly have been more different from the Union officer who began the Texas Reconstruction effort.

Gen. Gordon Granger was a diminutive, vulgar New Yorker, considered profane even by army standards of the day. Granger was also a highly effective combat commander who proved his mettle, particularly at the Battle of Chickamauga. He informed the people of Texas on June 19, 1865, that all former slaves in the Lone Star State were free, but with strict conditions that essentially bound many blacks to their former owners, at least temporarily.[29]

Further, military control of Texas would be necessary until a loyal (Unionist) sentiment should prevail among the citizens, at least according to Gen. George A. Custer, then stationed at Austin. Custer should have known. His responsibilities in 1865 included northeast Texas, where organized guerilla bands roamed, seemingly with no fear of Federal authorities.[30]

This was so because Texas did not suffer serious physical destruction during the conflict, thus permitting the citizenry to enjoy a relatively stable and prosperous economy after the surrender. These conditions allowed many Texans of Confederate persuasion to maintain that they were unconquered and ready to start a "new rebellion," according to some Reconstruction historians.[31] Indisputably, Texas was the very last state of the old Confederacy in which the Bureau of Refugees, Freedmen and Abandoned Lands ("Freedmen's Bureau") was organized. The Texas bureau was overwhelmed from the beginning by the sheer size of the state and unrelenting hostility demonstrated by much of the Lone Star citizenry.

While stationed in Austin, General Custer noted that three ruffians were the most dangerous outlaws in northeast Texas. Those would be Cullen Montgomery Baker, Benjamin Bickerstaff, and Bob Lee. These three formed a loose coalition dedicated to killing blacks and Union men, according to a Freedmen's Bureau agent in Paris, Texas.[32] Yet another outlaw who claimed to have associated with Baker was Bill Longley.[33]

Bob Lee and Other Associates

Some say Bob Lee rode with Confederate general Nathan Bedford Forrest during the Civil War. More certainly, by the conclusion of that conflict, Lee had settled in the Corners area of northeast Texas, where Grayson, Fannin, Collin, and Hunt counties converge.[34] The deep, immense forests of this area, notably the Big Thicket, provided abundant hiding places for army deserters and outlaws alike.

Bob Lee's Reconstruction difficulties stemmed from his differences with Lewis Peacock, a prosperous farmer who developed Unionist sympathies for commercial or other reasons. The conflict erupted in April 1868, engulfing both men. Lee was killed in late May 1869, and Peacock about two years later.

While Bickerstaff and Lee ordinarily were committed to partisan warfare against Federal soldiers, both before and after the conclusion of hostilities, Baker focused primarily on attacking Unionist civilians and blacks. While periodically participating in such raids in coordination with others or alone, Baker soon confronted an immense personal tragedy.

The death of his young wife, Martha, in March 1866 left the cold-blooded killer inconsolable and even more mentally imbalanced than usual.[35] Some say he built and conversed with a fully dressed effigy of Martha. Eventually, however, he recovered from his grief and proposed to her young sister Belle, who rejected him outright, most likely with the encouragement of Baker's former in-laws, the Fosters.

This rejection became the focus of Baker's remaining years. Thomas Orr, a schoolteacher of Unionist sentiment, courted and eventually married young Belle and thus became Baker's enemy. Orr was born in 1844 in Henry County, Georgia, and moved to the Arkansas-Texas border by June 1866, where he initially boarded with Baker's former in-laws.[36] He became a subscription schoolteacher near Bloomburg, Texas, where the annual Cullen Baker Country Fair is held to this day. Although Orr and Baker were initially friendly, that all changed when their competition for the hand of young Belle began.

Their personalities could not have been more different. Orr was an inveterate joiner who eventually became a judge. Despite their earlier friendship, after being jilted by young Belle, Baker picked a fight with Orr at Line Ferry, a Sulphur River crossing about seven miles from Texas where Baker was working as a ferryman. The Swamp Fox offered the abstinent Georgian a drink, which he surely knew Orr would decline, in spite of the insult that such a refusal represented at that place and time.

During the ensuing fistfight, Baker had no problem at all pummeling Orr, who had a crippled right arm due to rheumatism.[37] Later, Baker appeared at Orr's schoolhouse, demanding the ferry fee that the inconsiderate Orr forgot to pay during the June 2, 1866, fistfight. After collecting the fee, Baker did his level best to run off every single student in Orr's privately run school.

This and other incidents caused Baker's neighbors to meet and consider their options. One William Foster (no relation to Baker's former father-in-law) dissuaded the others from killing Baker, only to be killed later himself by the Swamp Fox, according to one story.[38] Baker was confronted by this concerned citizenry and responded with one of the strangest series of letters in the history of the West.

Baker warned Orr by a letter dated July 20, 1866, not to be absent from his school teachings, then described himself as *"Mad as Hell till Death."* Nine days later, after neighbors intervened in this feud, Baker wrote a remorseful letter to his former father-in-law, admitting that he was a "liar, drunkard and a devil." In an empty gesture of goodwill, Baker promised to defer his revenge against Orr until the end of the school term in deference to the feelings of his neighbors.[39]

Further correspondence between Orr and Baker culminated in a final, public effort by Orr to reconcile their differences. Orr published a letter in the quaintly named

Jefferson Jimplecute on April 27, 1867, offering to settle the dispute. Baker answered with a bizarre series of raids in which he killed several neighborhoods dogs.[40]

Finally, on June 1, 1867, he demanded and received free food at a grocery store while the proprietor, a Mr. Rowden, was away. Nine days later, Baker returned and murdered Rowden, who had complained loudly about the robbery.[41]

Coincidentally, more assertive Reconstruction efforts began that very month in northeast Texas with the arrival in Bowie County of former Union soldier William Kirkman, newly appointed as bureau agent for the Fifty-Eighth Subdistrict of the Freedmen's Bureau. Kirkman made his headquarters at Boston.[42] He was responsible for enforcing the Reconstruction program in an 1,800-square-mile area with nine federal soldiers.

Kirkman could hardly have been assigned to a locale more hostile to Unionist sentiment. The 1861 Ordinance of Secession was supported by all but 15 of the 223 voters in Bowie County. Although Bowie County largely escaped physical destruction during the war years, about 65 percent of the tax base disappeared when emancipation was implemented, undoubtedly an irritant that contributed to animosity against Kirkman and other Unionists.

William Kirkman had been raised by relatives in obscure circumstances after his mentally unstable father had killed his wife. Eventually, William became a telegraph operator and then enlisted in the Thirty-ninth Regiment of Illinois Infantry for a three-year stint before joining the Freedman's Bureau, perhaps with the encouragement of his older brother Joel, who preceded William into Bureau service.

The Swamp Fox came to Kirkman's attention soon after the young agent arrived in northeast Texas. According to Kirkman, Baker killed an area freedman for working his own farm.

The Bureau responded swiftly. Kirkman, three Union

cavalrymen, and others traveled to a location in Cass County, Texas about seven miles from the Sulphur River to arrest Baker and his associate L. R. Rollins, nominally on robbery charges. Kirkman searched throughout the area without finding Baker, who according to folklore actually was close enough to the Bureau representatives to eavesdrop on their conversations. Open hostilities began the next day, when Baker focused harassing gunfire on the Unionists, then followed them into Boston. There, he boldly called for refreshments in a grocery store before a gunfight erupted.

Baker was in a bowling alley adjacent to the grocery store when he was fired upon by federal forces. He promptly returned fire, killing Albert E. Titus, a twenty-two-year-old veteran of the famed Twentieth Maine, commanded at Gettysburg by Medal of Honor-winner Joshua Lawrence Chamberlain. Baker was nearly killed himself, losing his hat to a gun blast, but escaped. Kirkman asked that a $2,500 reward be placed on Baker, but authorities lowered the offer to $1,000.[43]

The threat did not slow Baker down at all. On October 6, 1867, Baker ambushed and killed a soldier and teamster transporting Bureau supplies, then reportedly distributed the goods among his own friends and neighbors.[44] His gang at that time may have consisted of as many as fifteen men, including Ben Griffith, Matthew "Dummy" Kirby, and "Wild Bill" Longley, who later became a notorious killer in his own right. Eventually, federal authorities ransacked Baker's home and rifled through his dead wife's possessions, inciting Baker to even worse banditry, or so the story goes.[45]

Kirkman now joined forces with Hiram F. Willis, an Arkansas Freedmen's Bureau agent. The pair searched the tristate region for Baker without success, impeded and frustrated by bureaucratic conflicts and army ineptitude. Baker, in the meantime, continued to run wild.

Christmas evening 1867 found Baker and some associates

back in Brightstar, where they bought some whiskey, then proceeded to the residence of Howell Smith, who lived near William Foster. Neighborhood stories claimed that Smith harbored freedmen in his home and even slept with a black woman.[46] Whatever the motivation, Baker and sixteen others attacked the South Carolinian's home, according to official government reports. Firing into the residence some thirty times, they killed two black occupants and wounded others in the initial attack.[47]

Then the home invasion began. Baker himself attacked Smith and stabbed Smith's two daughters as they attempted to defend their father. The raid ended with an unsuccessful effort to torch the house. Baker confirmed his role in the crime while being treated nearby by his former father-in-law William Foster. Smith reportedly died of his injuries.[48]

Army captain N. B. McLaughlin learned of the attack three days later, then rode with a twenty-man contingent to the Smith house for firsthand information. He then pursued the gang to a camp about eight miles away. The soldiers surrounded the camp, only to learn that the gang had departed earlier. McLaughlin returned to the Smith neighborhood and persuaded residents to accompany him in further pursuit of the gang.

They found a second camp about three miles away from the first and fared better with a second attack, capturing Meredith McAdams as well as weapons, munitions, and provisions. McAdams was persuaded to name names, fingering Baker, his principal lieutenant Lee Rames (Raines), his younger brother John Howard "Seth" Rames, John Courtney, John Kennedy, and the Nichols brothers, John and Henry.

Buoyed by these successes, McLaughlin persuaded Smith's neighbors to continue the pursuit of Baker. Preston R. Scott formed a group of irregulars for that purpose called "Scott's Company."[49] This outfit meant business.

The vigilante leadership, later known as the "Famous Six," consisted of John S. Jackson, John Williams, Bill Dunlop, Green Allen, Peyton Murph, and John Salmon.

First the "Company" cornered and captured Matthew Kirby, who they learned had been far too drunk to participate in the attack on Smith, then inexplicably released him. They then turned their attention to fifteen-year-old Seth Rames, a more manageable target. The Six killed young Seth, torturing the young man before doing so, according to one of Baker's more partisan biographers.[50]

These developments apparently convinced Baker to seek opportunities elsewhere. He simply disappeared from the Arkansas-Texas border for several months, reportedly taking refuge in Hot Springs or perhaps Perry County, Arkansas, as he recovered from an injury to his right thigh sustained during the Smith raid.[51] Whatever the location, Baker remained secluded, even as violence provoked by the Ku Klux Klan and similar organizations began to rise across the South.

Baker joined the New Rebellion in mid-1868, conducting a series of raids in the tristate area. He may have begun as one of several Reconstruction rebels who pursued and killed a Unionist in Bonham, Texas, in late May. The suspected killers were Cullen Baker, Bob Lee, Benjamin Bickerstaff, Simp Dixon, and his half-brother Dick Johnson, according to one researcher.[52] Other depredations attributed to Baker by his contemporaries suggest coordination of some kind with the Ku Klux Klan, whose oath of membership was found later on his dead body. Baker had also gained a reputation among his neighbors as a free-lance enforcer of sorts for white employers seeking to rigorously control their former slaves.[53]

The next month, Reconstruction outlaw Ben Griffith was killed near Clarksville, Texas, by Freedmen's Bureau official Charles Rand, in the opening salvo of federal efforts to terminate the New Rebellion in the Lone Star State.

Griffith had enjoyed one last act of bravado just before his death. He rode into town, armed with three revolvers and a cocked shotgun across his saddle, then made a speech from his horse about a recent wagon-train ambush. After mentioning that Bob Lee, Baker, and Jack English were waiting nearby, he robbed one freedman in town and was about to kill another on the Boston road outside of town when Rand's posse shot him out of the saddle. Lee, Baker, and Bickerstaff supposedly disappeared after watching the whole episode from a hiding place.[54]

The federal authorities offered "dead or alive" rewards for Baker and conducted intensified cavalry raids into targeted counties during September 1868.[55] Unfazed, Baker immediately posted reward posters offering $5,000 ($69,000 today) for the delivery of Arkansas governor Powell Clayton himself, dead or alive.[56]

Fortunately for Baker and other guerillas, only about six thousand federal soldiers were now in Texas, mostly stationed along the western frontier.[57] Even so, the salad days of Baker and his colleagues, such as Elisha P. Guest, John Pomp Duty, and Indian Bill English, were gradually coming to a close. Such partisans had worn out their welcome, even among natural allies in the region. Worse still for the desperadoes, federal forces carefully avoided the misconduct that had alienated potential allies among Missourians of culturally similar backgrounds at the beginning of the Civil War. Eventually, the success of these forces spelled the end of Benjamin Bickerstaff.

Death Comes for Kirkman

That said, physically isolated federal officials, such as Bureau agent William Kirkman in Boston, Texas, were confronted in the fall of 1868 with one starkly immediate local reality. Reconstruction efforts in northeast Texas were diminishing in the face of increased violence perpetuated by Baker and like-minded outlaws as well as general hostility against Bureau agents.

Kirkman, for example, had only recently extracted himself from murder charges related to the death of John Richardson, a prisoner in his custody. Richardson had instigated a riot against the Orton Circus, rumored to be staffed by Yankees, when it arrived in Boston, Texas and was arrested on November 21, 1867. He was killed by a corporal as he and an accomplice attempted to escape, using guns that had been smuggled into the jail seven days before Christmas. Kirkman was indicted in the death of Richardson, although he never fired a shot.[58]

Kirkman was cleared of the murder charges, but his problems had only begun. He was discharged from his position with the Freedmen's Bureau. While finishing his duties in the early morning hours of October 7, 1868, he heard a noise outside his window. When Kirkman went to investigate, he was cut down by sixteen rounds, one of which was immediately fatal. After the Bureau agent fell to the ground, a voice in the darkness derisively cried, "All is well." Cullen Baker was among the chief suspects at the time but was never charged.[59]

Nine days later, 2nd Lt. Hiram F. Willis, who had served as a Freedmen's Bureau agent in Arkansas for about two years, traveled to the Porter J. Andrews farm with Little River County, Arkansas sheriff Richard H. Standel to negotiate a settlement with Andrews black workers. Rounding a corner on the road, the officials were confronted by six men, presumably led by Cullen Montgomery Baker. Willis barely had time to draw his pistol before he was cut down with Andrews and the black buggy driver. Sheriff Standel ran for the woods. Later, an eyewitness stated that he observed Cullen Montgomery Baker leading three horses, presumably from the buggy, along the Red River bottoms.[60] Ben Griffith's brother Bud and two associates were eventually hanged at Rocky Comfort, Arkansas, for the murders.

Baker was also suspected in a murder that had occurred in the early hours of that same day. James Salmon was one of the "Famous Six" who had allegedly tortured and killed young Seth Rames. The Swamp Fox and his gang had appeared at Salmon's home, about five and one-half miles east of Atlanta, Texas, between two and four o'clock on the morning of October 24, 1868. Posing as federal officials, they insisted that Salmon come out for a discussion. The victim apparently had no illusions about the identity of the group. Despite the pleas of Mrs. Salmon, the gang marched him about a quarter of a mile from his home, then riddled him with bullets.[61]

Prominent farmer D. F. "Frank" Scarborough was the next target about six days later. The gang announced their arrival by killing two freedmen, then insisted that Scarborough serve as the Baker emissary in discussions with vigilante leader Preston R. Scott, according to one source.[62] These efforts were confirmed in the memoirs of Thomas Orr, who suggested that Baker wanted revenge against the "Famous Six" who killed Seth Rames, and peace with everyone else.[63]

These diplomatic efforts resulted in the "Treaty of Scott's Mill," supposedly concluded in Davis County, Texas on November 3, 1868. Baker sent a delegate who insisted that Baker would cease hostilities against everyone, black and white alike, save John Williams, John S. Jackson, and Bill Dunlop, "Famous Six" members still residing in the area. During the past few years, the Swamp Fox was just what his sobriquet described, a bum who lived in the woods near Forest Home, Texas. Yet, during the "treaty" discussions, mentally unstable Baker boasted that he would post a $200,000 bond in Bowie County, to ensure his good conduct.

The surviving trio of the "Famous Six" fled the area, not to be heard of again, or so the story goes.[64] Baker's charm initiative did not deter Arkansas governor Powell Clayton, who was still the target of "wanted dead or alive" circulars Baker had posted in the tristate area. The governor sent Brig. Gen. R. F. Catterson and 500 troops to pacify Sevier (now Howard) County, then in the control of Baker's "perfect Ku Klux Klan organization." According to Catterson, Baker commanded a band of 150 men.

The Swamp Fox was defeated at a largely bloodless confrontation at Centre Point, according to one account, proving once again that Baker succeeded only by trick or artifice rather than personal bravery.[65]

Reeling from this reversal, Baker launched a media campaign for public support. Functionally illiterate himself, Baker procured a ghostwriter and submitted to several tristate newspapers a lengthy letter to local citizenry. The letter was dated November 14, 1868, perhaps the very day Baker met with former Confederate colonel R. Phillip Crump and other citizens concerned about continuing violence. The missive appeared in the *Texas Republican* thirteen days later.

Baker claimed that many acts of lawlessness attributed to him were actually committed by others and even provided an example. Further, he promised to leave black and white citizens alone, with the proviso that he be treated accordingly. Several citizens endorsed these statements, asserting their belief that Baker would abide by his promises.[66] The letter may have resulted from negotiations Baker personally conducted with leading citizens of the area after the Centre Point debacle.[67]

Former slave Jerry Sheffield (Sherfeld) apparently believed that there would be no more trouble with the Baker gang as a result of the agreement, but probably was not told about the proviso in the fine print. Sheffield boasted to anyone who would listen that he knew where Baker could be found and would lead anyone there for five dollars (seventy dollars today). He was shot to pieces on Sunday, December 6, 1868, about two miles east of Queen City, Texas, and was nearly unrecognizable when found.[68]

This episode set the stage for Baker's last significant raids, which began later that day. After murdering Sheffield, the Swamp Fox began to pursue his other enemies. First on the list was Robert Spell, a local citizen who had apparently been among the vigilantes who searched for Baker the prior year. When Spell could not be located, Baker settled for an interview with George W. Barron, who had a minor part in the schoolhouse controversy between Orr and Baker. Soon, Barron found himself swinging from a beam across his own gate. He was saved only by the intervention of Lee Rames, who cut him down as the gang left to find Charles Johnson and "Famous Six" leader John S. Jackson.

Since neither gentleman was available, Baker then had to settle on a series of home invasions. First, he led the gang to the home of I. M. Dempsey, where he burst into the house and proved his identity to Mrs. Dempsey by showing her the wounds he had sustained during the Howell Smith episode. Then he rode to the home of the Dempseys' son, where the gang killed a dog for no more reason than intimidation.[69]

The next night, Baker conducted his final significant raid. About ten o'clock, the gang surrounded the home of William Foster near Brightstar and demanded the surrender of Thomas Orr, who had earlier married young Belle Foster after she rejected Baker. Orr complied, gullibly relying on Baker's word that he would not be harmed. Baker, having no plans to honor this deal, sent several gang members after Joe Davis for a double hanging. First, Orr was hanged from a dogwood tree. When Baker supposed he was dead, he ordered Orr cut down so that Davis could be hanged with the same rope, and so he was, if only for a few minutes. Through the apparent intervention of Lee Rames, both survived the lynching to tell the tale.[70]

When Baker learned that Orr had survived, he swore vengeance on any of his gang members who had conspired to save Orr. Lee Rames quickly identified himself as the culprit, drew his own pistols, then rode off with the entire gang, leaving the Irishman Matthew "Dummy" Kirby behind as Baker's sole companion. Rames, so it seems, escaped with the others to obscurity.[71] About a week after the gang apparently disbanded, the Fourth U.S. Cavalry dispatched federal forces to two Cass and Bowie counties, but in the end, Baker's neighbors did him in.

A cabal evolved from discussions among neighbors in the Brightstar area in early January 1869 as to how the community could be saved from further harm. Eventually, a welcoming committee of sorts was formed. The group consisted of six men. John Chamblee had visited Gen. George P. Buell on Christmas Eve at Jefferson, Texas, seeking assistance from the federal army, but was unable to get Buell's agreement on a specific course of action. Apparently, Chamblee was now ready to take action himself. William Foster, Robert Spell, and I. M. Dempsey had all been threatened by Baker, while Joe Davis and Thomas Orr had actually been hanged by the Swamp Fox. This group decided upon a general course of action on that inevitable day when Baker would again appear in Brightstar.

That day came on January 6, 1869, when Baker and Kirby suddenly appeared at the Lamar residence, less than a mile away from the William Foster place near present-day Doddridge, Arkansas. A new group carried out the actual execution. William Foster, Joe Davis, Frank Davis (no relation), Leonard Spivey, and Howell Smith's son Billy Smith assisted Orr with the killings.

Foster had the most critical and dangerous assignment. First he brought whiskey for both desperadoes and spareribs for Kirby. While Baker and Kirby were sleeping, Foster carefully pulled Baker's shotgun out of his reach. About an hour before noon, while Baker slept, Joe Davis shot him just before Billy Smith killed Kirby.

The rest of the story emerged fifty-seven years later when Foster's son Hubbard revealed what he learned as a young boy on the day of the ambush. William Foster had added a heavy dose of strychnine, a poison normally used for pest control, to the whiskey supplied to the bandits. He had done so during visits in previous weeks, to keep them quiet and subdued.

Now the easy part began. The bodies were loaded in a wagon, covered with cornstalks, and transported to the authorities to claim state and federal reward money. Along the way, the bodies were carefully examined by Edward Stevenson, a commercial ferryman and longtime acquaintance of both Baker and Kirby.[72]

Stevenson and others who actually knew them were quite certain that Cullen Baker was dead, dead, dead. Nevertheless, thirteen years before Billy the Kid and Jesse James supposedly survived their own deaths, the Swamp Fox apparently became the first American outlaw whose demise was staged, if only in the minds of conspiracy theorists in the tristate area.

In the meantime, the good citizens of Brightstar had more interest in collecting reward money than spinning conspiracy theories. Gen. George P. Buell, serving as the commander of Union forces at Jefferson, Texas, methodically approached the issue, gathering affidavits in order to confirm that the dead men were in fact Baker and Kirby.

Eventually, a $2,000 federal reward was collected by John Chamblee and Thomas Orr, who had apparently been designated as the recipients for the benefit of the vigilantes who had at last wiped out what was left of the Baker gang. The state reward was never collected, although affidavits claiming that Orr rather than Joe Davis killed Baker were submitted to the authorities.[73]

The War of Reconstruction in Texas continued long after Cullen Baker was killed that January morning in 1869, even though the program itself was soon a dead letter in the Lone Star State. Baker's associate Frank Rollins was eventually jailed, while Bill Gray, another associate supposedly responsible for some twenty-five murders, was himself killed by the army in late 1869.

Bickerstaff was killed in Alvarado, Texas, the evening of April 5, 1869, with an associate named Thompson. The pair was ambushed by federal forces as they approached a horse rack and prepared to dismount for a night of revelry in nearby saloons. Bob Lee was killed May 24, 1869, by Bill Boren and other Texas Unionists.

As we shall see, the two most famous Reconstruction outlaws both outlived Baker by years. Wild Bill Longley rode on until he was hanged at Giddings, Texas, in 1878, while the legendary John Wesley Hardin managed to outlive Baker by twenty-six years. The world was well rid of Cullen Montgomery Baker. Thomas Orr, on the other hand, eventually served as the first mayor of Texarkana, Arkansas, and died peacefully in 1904.

John Wesley Hardin at eighteen years of age. Inset: The two Colt revolvers he carried until his death. *(Courtesy of The Haley Memorial Library and History Center, Midland, Texas)*

CHAPTER TWO

John Wesley Hardin:
Four Sixes to Beat

Reflecting on his life at age forty-one, John Wesley Hardin, whom the family called Wes, wrote fondly of his childhood as the son of an itinerant preacher. His posthumously published autobiography reminisced about a youth spent among tall pines, swamps, and fields while hunting, fishing, and exploring nature, much as any other teenaged boy of that place and time would have done. In those early, languid days, there was little evidence that Wes would become the most lethal killer in frontier Texas.

Hardin was born of Southern stock. His father, James Gibson Hardin, was a native of Wayne County, Tennessee, born in 1823.[1] James was a devout Presbyterian with wanderlust. He received an allotment of some 320 acres from the Republic of Texas in 1841, but Hardin realized soon after arriving that he was better suited to preaching than planting cotton seeds. He became a Methodist and, at the age of twenty-two, hit the trail to sow seeds of faith. He eventually established a new home at Richland in Navarro County, Texas.

While conducting a wedding for the daughter of Indiana-born doctor William Dixon in January 1847, James Hardin met the bride's sister Mary Elizabeth, whom he married six months later.[2] The couple had nine children, the first of whom died in childbirth.

The second surviving child was John Wesley, whose name reflected his father's reverence for the founder of Methodism. He was born on May 26, 1853, at Blair's Springs on Bois d'Arc Creek near Bonham.[3]

The Hardin family moved in about 1859 from the family homestead near Livingston to Sumpter in Trinity County, near what is today the Davy Crockett National Forest. Young John enjoyed a carefree time in the Big Thicket of East Texas. His most menacing adversary was a family of charging raccoons he once treed, according to his autobiography. During this period, John was schooled in the four *R*s: reading, 'riting, 'rithmetic, and religion. However, according to his writings, he found his most profound childhood experiences in the great outdoors: "I was a very child of nature, and her ways and moods were my study. My greatest pleasure was to be out in the open fields, the forests, and the swamps. My greatest pleasure was to get out among the big pines and oaks with my gun and the dogs and kill deer, coons, and 'possums, or wild cats."[4]

Hardin also wrote of friends with whom he shared experiences in his youth. "If any of those Sumpter boys with whom I used to hunt ever see this history of my life, I ask them to say whether or not our sport in those old days was not splendid. John Norton, Bill Gordon, Shiles and Hiram Frazier, and Sol Adams, all of Sumpter, can bear witness to the good times we had then."[5]

Rev. James Hardin voted against secession, but when the Civil War began, he dutifully helped organize a company of fighting men and was elected its captain. Later, his neighbors persuaded him to resign his command, saying, "You can be of more good use at home than off fighting Yankees."[6]

John Hardin was only nine years old when he decided to join the fight for his beloved South. James heard about the plan and put a wailing end to Wes's dreams of battlefield glory. Still, a favorable opinion of the Southern cause and a poor one of the Northern president loomed large in the boy's mind and never waned: "I had seen Abraham Lincoln burned and shot to pieces in effigy so often that I looked upon him as a very demon incarnate, who was waging a relentless and cruel war on the South to rob her of her most sacred rights." Hardin would later explain, "So you can see that the justice of the Southern cause was taught to me in my youth . . . surely I was but true to my early training. . . . So I grew up a rebel."[7]

Hardin was too young to be a soldier, but he soon started down another path, one that eventually led to fame but not fortune. Incredibly enough, the first victim of John Wesley Hardin was a young classmate in the Academy of Learning, which Hardin's father had founded in 1861.

Charles Sloter was a schoolhouse prankster who did not intend to be outdone by John Wesley Hardin. Later, Wes wrote that Sloter scribbled some rather nasty remarks about a gal named "Sal," one of the few female students in the school and one whom Wes somewhat favored. Sloter also wrote on a school wall, "I love Sal, and Sal loves mutton," and then claimed Hardin was the author. Worse yet, Sloter ridiculed Sal's physical characteristics and then accused Hardin of doing that too, at least according to Hardin, who denied doing these things and turned the blame back to Sloter.

Hardin was seated at his desk when Sloter walked up the aisle, thumped Hardin, and pulled a knife. Hardin quickly produced his own knife. Soon, Sloter was sprawled on the floor with two puncture wounds in his chest and one in his back. Although Sloter's parents complained, the school board and the courts completely exonerated Hardin, who later wrote: "I may mention here that poor Charley was long afterwards hung by a mob in an adjoining county."[8] The lynching of Charley Sloter may have occurred, but it was apparently never verified.

Between 1868 and 1874, John Wesley Hardin killed between twenty and fifty men, if the stories about him are to be believed. Fifteen or so of the killings are sufficiently documented or notable enough to be worthy of discussion here.

In November 1868, a former slave, Major "Mage" Holshousen, was pitted against Hardin in what started as an innocent wrestling match on the plantation of John's uncle, Barnett Hardin, in the Big Thicket country of Polk County, Texas. Since John Hardin was but a wiry teen and Mage was a full-grown adult, John's cousin Barnett Jones readily joined the match to even things up. Hardin and Jones were still outmanned and lost, but not before leaving Mage with a bloody face. Mage threatened Hardin but was ordered off the plantation.

The next morning, Hardin encountered Mage, who was carrying a large stick, at least according to Hardin. After Mage allegedly grabbed Hardin's horse's reins, Hardin mortally wounded him with five gunshots. This was Hardin's first kill. He was fifteen years old.[9]

Hardin's family feared retribution by Federal troops, some of whom were former slaves. Such fears were realized the next month, when Hardin was warned one afternoon of three soldiers snooping about the countryside, asking about his whereabouts. The three-man patrol included a black freedman.

They were in Company B, Sixth Cavalry, and likely had no idea of the danger they were in. Hardin was informed of their every move. He later wrote that since he was aware that the soldiers would have to cross Hickory Creek to find him, he grabbed his double-barreled shotgun and favorite revolver and then chose a spot along the creek to watch and wait. When the trio eventually showed themselves, he blasted both white soldiers off their mounts with his shotgun and then chased after the freedman. The surviving soldier managed to wound Hardin before he too was killed.[10]

Late December 1869 found Hardin betting on the ponies and drinking at Old Boles Racetrack near Towash, Texas, about twenty miles west of Hillsboro. His father asked Wes to return home with him during a visit he made there on December 24, but Wes stayed for a few more days of carousing.

On January 4, Hardin was playing a card game with his cousin James Collins, Benjamin B. Bradley, Hamp Davis, and a Judge Moore. Hardin became drunk and began to abuse Bradley, who pulled a knife and then his gun before Collins convinced him not to begin a fight. Collins then tried to persuade Hardin to leave but Hardin refused, saying he wanted to retrieve his boots and pistol.

Collins himself attempted retrieve the pistol, but when he failed, the intoxicated Hardin went around from bystander to bystander, asking to borrow a gun. All refused. Collins secured one, and then gave it to Hardin, who swapped insults with Bradley and Davis. Hardin then shot Bradley, who yelled out, "Oh, Lordy, don't shoot me any more!" Bradley was asking the wrong teenager for mercy.[11]

Less than a month later, at a circus camp near Horn Hill in central Limestone County, one performer learned that clowning around with Wes Hardin could be fatal. Hardin and yet another cousin, Alec Barekman, stopped at the camp as they rode toward their uncle Bob Hardin's place in Brenham. One fellow took offense when Hardin nudged his arm while lighting a pipe. The man growled that he ought to smash Hardin's nose—this despite a Hardin apology. Hardin told him to go ahead; "I was a bit of a smasher myself." The man hit Hardin, who in turn fired a .45 lead ball through the performer's head, leaving the circus shorthanded by one.

Hardin and Barekman separated and Hardin rode on toward Brenham. He stopped for a night of carousing in Kosse in far southwestern Limestone County. While drinking and gambling, he was encouraged to meet a town girl in her room. Just as young Wes had slipped beneath the sheets with the girl, a man bowled through the door. The intruder claimed to be the girl's betrothed but allowed his loss of honor could be assuaged by a $100 payment. Hardin feigned fear and dropped a gold coin to the floor. The last thing the robber saw was a grin and a bright flash as Hardin's .45 dissolved the boy-girl bandit team. He was sixteen years old, and the kill card read Hardin—7, Opponents—0.[12]

About a year later, State Police lieutenant E. T. Stakes charged Hardin with stealing a horse and four counts of murder, although no victims' names were given. Later that same month, Lieutentant Stakes, Pt. Jim Smalley, and one L. B. Anderson put Hardin on a small black pony and began the journey to Waco, about 170 miles to the west.

After they camped a few miles outside of Waco on the evening of January 22, 1871, Stakes and Anderson left to find grain for the horses, leaving Smalley behind to harangue Hardin with insults and accusations. Hardin walked to the other side of the pony, placed a hidden pistol under his left arm, and then confronted Smalley, who reached for his own weapon but not soon enough. Hardin sent Smalley into the Great Beyond, then stole his sorrel mare and galloped away, reaching his father's home at Mount Calm that same night.[13]

Hardin's autobiography relates that early in February 1871, he and his Clements cousins were riding trail in south Texas when they came upon a Mexican cow camp. A game of Spanish monte was begun. Hardin, erroneously thinking he had won a hand, ordered the dealer to "pay the queen," which he held. The dealer explained that in monte, the queen actually lost the hand. Hardin did not agree with that particular rule and conked the dealer with his pistol. When two other Mexican players drew knives, Hardin shot one through the arm and the other through the lungs, mortally wounding him, at least according to Hardin.[14]

In yet another Hardin story undocumented by any contemporary source, he was riding herd through Indian Territory in May 1871. He had crossed the South Canadian River when an Indian half-concealed in a bush let loose an arrow. Hardin claimed the Indian missed him and he killed the Indian in self-defense.

During the same cattle drive but farther north, in the Osage Nation just south of Kansas, Hardin killed yet another Indian, who supposedly was attempting to drive off a large steer. Later, he wrote that the Osage told Hardin if he could not take the animal he would kill it. Hardin said he replied that if he killed the beef, Hardin would kill the Osage. Hardin explained in his autobiography, "Well, he killed the beef and I killed him." Hardin placed the dead Indian on the dead steer as a warning to others and continued the cattle drive.[15]

When Mexican vaquero Juan Bedino shot and killed trail boss William "Billy" Cohron in early July 1871, along the Cottonwood River in Kansas, he had little thought of the consequences. Bedino apparently disagreed with one of Cohron's orders, so he shot him in the back. After an elaborate funeral arranged by the wealthy California cattle broker who employed them both, several well-heeled cattlemen of the area asked Wes Hardin to track the killer.

While following Bedino, Hardin and Jim Rogers encountered Billy's brother John Cohron and a cowboy named Hugh Anderson, who joined the hunt. They caught up with Bedino on Friday, July 7, at Sumner City, a now long-gone settlement near present-day Wellington, Kansas, later misidentified by Hardin as Bluff City, also now a ghost town. Bedino was enjoying a dinner at the Southwestern Hotel when Hardin strode in, gave him the opportunity to surrender, and then shot the vaquero in the forehead when he went for a gun. John Cohron ran into the hotel and wanted to shoot the dead man again, but Hardin stopped him. Hardin paid twenty dollars to have Bedino buried.[16]

Trouble found Hardin again little more than a year later, in August 1872, as he played an early version of bowling called tenpins with Phil Sublett in John Gates' Trinity City saloon. Hardin produced a concealed handgun and shoved it into Sublett's ear while demanding the return of his losses, a pattern Hardin repeated again and again. Sublett complied, of course, but soon after they parted he reappeared with a shotgun, calling out Hardin. Shots were exchanged and Hardin took two shotgun pellets through the stomach. Two more flattened against a large silver belt buckle Hardin was wearing and did no harm. Sublett took a Hardin round in the shoulder and fled. Hardin's injuries required surgery.

After that shootout, Hardin was recovering at Dave Harrel's place in Angelina when State Police came calling. Hardin claims to have greeted them with his shotgun, killing one of the officers. A coroner's inquest ruled that the policeman had died "at the hands of an unknown party." Hardin was again hit, this time collecting a policeman's bullet in his thigh.

These injuries were serious enough that Hardin realized he needed medical attention. He arranged a rendezvous with Cherokee County sheriff Richard "Dick" Reagan. Reagan met Hardin in a bedroom and accepted his surrender. He then asked the gunman to relinquish his firearms, which he did, even removing a pistol from beneath his bed pillow. This was observed by a deputy who was providing cover for his boss outside an open window. The deputy, thinking Hardin was making a move, fired his rifle through the window and struck the astounded gunfighter in the right knee. The sheriff and his posse apologized to the bullet-riddled shootist as they loaded him into a buggy.

Hardin Rides Again

Sometime afterward, Hardin escaped from jail. In April 1873, he entered a bar in Cuero, had a few drinks, and then won five dollars gambling (about eighty dollars today).

Foolish or inebriated Irishman James B. Morgan rushed up to Hardin and requested a bottle of champagne. Hardin refused and then left the saloon, as Morgan followed. Morgan either had no idea whom he was irritating or was too drunk to care, for he challenged the most deadly gunfighter in Texas, just before Hardin shot him above the left eye, killing him instantly. Hardin wrote years later that, after the incident, he coolly mounted his horse and rode out of town.

However, Texas Ranger T. C. "Pidge" Robinson wrote that Hardin shot Morgan because the Irishman removed his hands from his pockets when Hardin warned him not to. Robinson said that once Hardin had dispatched Morgan, he "went out on the prairie a short distance and peacefully went to sleep." Robinson was well known for writing lengthy, informative, humorous, and exaggerated letters to newspapers describing feuds, forays, and rascals during his career.[17]

John Wesley Hardin killed his last man on his own twenty-first birthday, May 26, 1874, in Comanche, Texas. Brown County deputy sheriff Charles Webb apparently tracked Hardin to collect a $500 reward for his arrest. Webb surprised Hardin and shot him through the side. The painful but nonlethal wound did little to slow down Hardin's gun hand. Wes fired a slug through Webb's cheek, sending him to the ground a dead man.[18] This captured the attention of the Texas legislature, which voted to raise the reward for Hardin's arrest tenfold.[19]

Jim Taylor, one of the witnesses to the Webb killing, had earlier participated with Wes in the Sutton-Taylor feud.[20] Initially, Hardin was neutral in the feud, but eventually he joined his cousin Manning Clements in support of the Taylor faction and then helped kill one of the most prominent adherents of the Sutton cause.

The seven-year Sutton-Taylor feud was one of Texas's longest and deadliest conflicts, claiming twelve lives, or according to some sources, at least twenty more. Although the origins are still uncertain, the conflict may have begun with the 1868 Christmas Eve day killing of Buck Taylor and Dick Chisholm. The pair was in Clinton feuding with William E. Sutton, a deputy sheriff. Threats and accusations of horse theft flew until the shooting began. When quiet returned, Taylor and Chisholm lay face down, dead.[21]

The next year, Brevet Maj. Gen. Joseph Jones Reynolds, commander of the Fifth Military District of Texas, recruited Reconstructionist Charles S. Bell as a special officer for the suppression of crime. Bell in turn appointed John Marshall "Jack" Helm as a special officer in June 1869. The next month, Helm and other special officers, derided by their enemies as "regulators," started a rampage through San Patricio, Wilson, DeWitt, and Goliad counties that lasted into August.

Helm was elected sheriff of DeWitt County, assuming office on December 3, 1869, but still serving his appointment as a special officer.[22] Less than a year later, in October 1870, Helm was suspended from the State Police under allegations of rampant brutality and embezzlement. Nevertheless, his leadership role in the Sutton faction continued. Sheriff Helm rode with Bill Sutton on numerous occasions, the two men leading a posse of killers who worked to rid the country of Taylor sympathizers. In December, Helm was fired from his State Police post as accusations swarmed about his head alleging wholesale killings of prisoners "attempting to escape" or "resisting arrest."

Hard-case John Wesley Hardin met with Sutton faction leader Jim Cox at the King Ranch in May 1872. Hardin led him to believe he was considering joining the fight against the Taylors, and why not? The Suttons, whose ranks included duly appointed lawmen, were fierce opponents of cattle rustling. The Taylors, at that time, were looked upon as cattle rustlers. And depending on who was counting, Hardin had already killed eleven to thirty men. He would have been a welcome addition to Sutton's string of gunmen. In the spring of 1873, John Wesley Hardin was still neutral. Soon, he became aware that Sheriff Helm was looking for him on charges unrelated to the Sutton-Taylor feud. The two met the first time by chance on the road to Cuero on April 9, each man bristling with weapons. Eyeing each other as experienced gunfighters, Hardin and Helm at once dismounted. Now they were free to fistfight, knife fight, shoot, kick, bite, or, least likely of all, simply run away.

Fighting from the saddle was just too risky, since too many variables reduced the possibility of success in close combat. Hardin soon pulled a pistol on Helm, who inexplicably left his weapons on his horse. After a brief discussion in which Helm begged Hardin not to kill him, they rode into Cuero together.[23]

Helm and Hardin met again a week later, this time at the home of Sutton leader Jim Cox. Helm and Cox offered Hardin amnesty from the various charges pending against him, if he would join the Sutton cause. Hardin agreed only to think about their proposition.

Hardin now did a road-agent spin and sided with the Taylors (the spin was a maneuver in which the shootist offered his six-shooter to another, butt end first, and then twirled the gun around suddenly to point at the victim). Wes sent word to the Taylors, asking them to meet him in late April 1873 at Mustang Mott, west of Cuero. There, Hardin, Clements, and three Taylor brothers apparently plotted the death of Suttonists John Christman and Jim Cox, bringing Hardin directly and inalterably into the feud.

The next month, Christman and Cox were assassinated between Helena and Yorktown by a party thought to include Jim and Scrap Taylor and Hardin himself.

On the occasion of their third meeting, Hardin shot Sutton

faction leader Jack Helm to death in Albuquerque, Texas. Curiously enough, Helm had just applied for a patent for a cotton-worm eradicator. He may have intended to visit John Bland's blacksmith shop to check on some details relating to this or some other invention, as well as to sharpen a knife he was carrying as his only weapon. Wes Hardin and Jim Taylor were apparently also interested in eradication that day. Jim Taylor, whom Helm had never met, came up behind Helm inside Bland's smithy shop, according to one version of events. Taylor extended his pistol at the back of Helm's head and pulled the trigger. The weapon misfired, and Helm wheeled around at the sound of the click. Helm pulled his knife and advanced, ignoring Taylor's command of "Hands up, you son of a bitch!" Taylor pulled the trigger a second time, sending a round into Helm's breast.Hardin, hearing the commotion, ran to the shop to back up Taylor. Hardin let loose with a blast of his shotgun. With a bullet in the chest and buckshot in the arm, Helm stumbled back and fell to the ground. Taylor approached the prone Helm and emptied his six-gun into the man's head.[24] The date of Helm's execution-style killing has been variously listed as May 17, late July, or August 1, 1873.[25]

After Bill Sutton was gunned down boarding a steamer at Indianola on March 11, 1874, and Jim Taylor was killed in a gunfight at Clinton on December 27, 1875, the feud began to lose momentum. Hardin lost interest and drifted off to other pursuits. The Suttons continued to use the power of the law officers among their numbers to keep the peace, although their tactics were controversial. The Taylors, it seemed, had been suppressed, yet the violence persisted. Several Sutton supporters were accused of murdering Dr. Philip Brassell and his son George at their Yorktown home on September 19, 1876. Eventually, eight men were brought to trial. Only one was ever convicted, and he was pardoned twenty years later.[26]

Hardin's Fame Secured

Hardin, of course, had become a hard case and a killer years before he joined in the Sutton-Taylor feud. His fame was secured by an 1871, Abilene, Kansas, shooting that became an enduring legend of the West. Charles Cougar died at the American House Hotel on a warm August night.[27] That much is certain. The question is whether John Wesley Hardin killed him just for snoring.

Abilene, Kansas, was one of the wildest, rowdiest cattle towns in the West in the 1870s, and being its town marshal was more than a full-time job. The cowboys' rampant disregard for the law while in town became legendary, so much so that many cattle-drive bosses made arrangements with the town marshal even before any real trouble arose. They did so by paying advance bail in a designated amount, just in case things got out of hand. James Butler "Wild Bill" Hickok and his deputies in Abilene had ample opportunity to enhance their reputations due to the sheer number of shootings, knifings, and brawls that occurred almost hourly when a trail drive was over.

The story that Hardin killed a man for snoring may have originated six years after Hardin killed Charles Cougar in Abilene. A September 21, 1877, newspaper story said of Hardin, "He did not like to be disturbed in his sleep, and so he arose in the silent night and slew the snorer."[28] When this article appeared, the fable had already become the touchstone of the Hardin mystique.

Hardin most certainly knew this and addressed the Charles Cougar legend in his unpublished manuscript, which was sitting on his desk at the time of his death in 1895. *The Life of John Wesley Hardin as Written by Himself* was first published the following year. Hardin wrote that the man he killed was a "dirty, low-down, would-be assassin."[29] Twenty-four years after the event, perhaps near the time of his second marriage to young Callie Lewis in January 1895, Hardin wrote that he and cousin Gip Clements had ridden into town on July 7, following a meeting with Gip's older brother Manning Clements a few miles outside of Abilene. Hardin claimed in his manuscript that Cougar had entered Hardin and Gip's room and then carried away Hardin's pants, presumably to rob him. Hardin awoke and shot the intruder with four rounds from his six-shooter. When the smoke cleared, Cougar was sprawled dead in the hotel hallway.[30] Hardin and Gip then left the hotel through an open window and escaped into the night, because, at least according to Hardin, Hickok would have used the incident to kill Hardin in order to "add to his reputation."[31]

The *Abilene Chronicle* described a much different Charles Cougar in an article published three days after the probable date of the shooting in August 1871. It reported that the murder occurred on the night of August 6, but it likely took place on August 7, after three in the morning.[32] The *Chronicle* called the incident "a most fiendish murder" and claimed that the suspect was one Wesley Clements, also known as "Little Arkansas," both names being aliases Hardin used regularly in Abilene. The *Chronicle* stated that Cougar was "a boss cattle herder, and said to be a gentleman; Clements [on the other hand] is from Mississippi."[33]

The article went on to say that while Cougar was sitting in his bed reading the newspaper, four shots crashed through a partition wall. One of those struck Cougar's left arm and traveled through his third rib before finally tearing through his heart. The coroner, J. M. Shepard, said the bullet killed Cougar almost instantly. Following an inquest, Shepard theorized that the bullet was fired from "Wesley Clements'" pistol.[34] The article ended by saying no motive for the murder had been established.

The *Topeka Daily Commonwealth* reported that a boarder at that hotel was shot to death by two men who entered his room in disguise. The article concluded that the suspects were believed to have been partners of the deceased "and took this method of ridding themselves of pecuniary obligations."[35]

Perhaps Cougar was a trail boss. Since Hardin and his cousins worked as drovers on cattle drives from Texas to Kansas, the three men may have met while on the trail.[36] Given Hardin's temperament, he could have easily killed Cougar for any reason or for no reason, after returning to his hotel room from a night of hard drinking. Whatever the reason, Hardin chose not to wait around to explain things to Hickok.

Hardin's body count grew steadily after he killed Cougar in August 1871, as we have previously noted. Many of his victims were freedmen, appointed as special officers when the auxiliary force of the Texas State Police was created in July 1870. Hardin hated Reconstructionists. One such man was special policeman Green Paramore, who attempted to arrest Hardin on October 6, 1871, in a small grocery store owned by Hardin's future father-in-law Neill Bowen. Hardin pretended to surrender but tricked Paramore with the road-agent spin, then killed him. Reportedly, this murder nearly caused the black citizens of Gonzales County, where Paramore was stationed, to take up arms in an attempt to "depopulate the entire country."[37] Hardin already had the State Police, the United States Army, and various town marshals and county sheriffs on his trail, and now he had also raised the ire of many blacks in Texas.

January 1875 found John Wesley Hardin one of the most wanted men in Texas. He had participated in the Sutton-Taylor feud and killed seventeen men, perhaps more. On January 25, the Texas legislature passed a joint resolution increasing the bounty for Hardin from $400 to $4,000 ($68,000 today).[38] It was time for John Wesley Hardin to leave Texas.

Using one alias after another, Hardin managed to elude capture. He reinvented himself as J. H. Swain and established residence with his first wife, the former Jane Bowen, in Pollard, Alabama, where she had relatives.[39] Occasionally, he traveled to Florida, where he gambled on cards and horses. While Hardin was on one such trip, Jane began writing letters to her Texas kin. She did so under the alias Swain so as not to arouse the suspicion of local authorities.

The State Police had been abolished in 1873 and the Texas Rangers were reinstated as a more professional and less political law-enforcement organization. Capt. Leander H. McNelly was one of the few State Police officers who became a Texas Ranger. McNelly pressed for Hardin's capture, putting Lt. John B. Armstrong in charge of the case.[40] Armstrong was confined to "desk duty" after he put himself out of commission with an accidental gunshot to the groin sometime in May 1877.[41] The injury impaired Armstrong's gait but not his focus. When John Riley "Jack" Duncan entered the fray as a special ranger assigned to Armstrong, Hardin's days as the ever-elusive gunman were numbered.

Duncan was a Dallas city detective and the best sleuth in Texas. He used tactics that would remain a standard part of undercover work for decades to come. Using the name Mr. Williams, Duncan succeeded in becoming a fast friend of Neill Bowen, Hardin's father-in-law. One day, Duncan pretended to have an interest in renting a building the Bowens managed. The conversation continued to the post office, where Bowen was going to mail a letter to Jane "Swain." As Bowen laid the letter on the counter, Duncan distracted him with the business of renting the building.

The men continued their conversation outside the post office, with Bowen saying he would have to contact the owner of the building in question. Duncan let the matter

John B. Armstrong in the late 1870s. *(Courtesy of Chuck Parsons)*

drop, and as Bowen walked on, Duncan went back inside the post office. He approached the man behind the counter and said he needed to retrieve the letter he had just placed there. Realizing that the postmaster would not casually turn over a letter to any who asked, Duncan had managed to mark the letter as it lay unattended on the counter during his discussion with Bowen. When he perfectly described the mark he left on the letter, the postmaster was satisfied that it was his and handed it to him without suspicion.

Duncan opened the letter, read it, and was able to ascertain that Jane, and therefore John, was in Pollard.[42] Duncan later learned that Hardin and a few friends were in Pensacola, Florida, gambling. Duncan decided to alert Armstrong. Once Armstrong arrived, he solicited the cooperation of railroad superintendent William Dudley Chipley. Since Chipley disliked both Hardin and his brother-in-law Brown Bowen, he was easily recruited to assist with Hardin's capture.

On August 23, 1877, Escambia County sheriff William H. Hutchinson and his deputy, A. J. Perdue, were sworn in as Rangers to help in apprehending Hardin in Florida.[43] Hardin and a few friends had just boarded a train that day at Pensacola station and were relaxing in the smoking car when Armstrong sprang the trap.

Hardin was quite taken by surprise. Some twenty shots rang out that day, but Hardin never fired his weapon. Hardin associate Jim Mann apparently spooked and fired at least one wayward shot at the lawmen, one of which sailed through Armstrong's hat. Two other Hardin acquaintances, Sheppard Hardy and Neal Campbell, who were smoking with him at the time of the capture, simply froze. Mann was shot and killed by Armstrong during the fray, taking a bullet to the chest as he dove from one of the car's windows.[44]

When Hardin recognized the threat, he shouted, "Texas, by God!" He then kicked Sheriff Hutchinson in the groin,

Escambia County sheriff William Hutchinson, who was instrumental in helping Texas Ranger John B. Armstrong capture Hardin at a Pensacola train depot. *(Courtesy of Chuck Parsons)*

just before he was splayed out on the car floor. Even then, Hardin continued to squirm, curse, and kick. When Armstrong made his way up the aisle and leveled his Colt .45 straight at him, Hardin looked up and barked, "Shoot and be damned. I'd rather die than be arrested." Instead, Armstrong brought the seven-inch barrel crashing down on Hardin's skull. Armstrong thought at first that he had killed Hardin. He was alive but very quiet for some time.[45]

On September 28, 1878, Hardin was convicted of second-degree murder for the killing of Deputy Sheriff Charles Webb four years earlier and sentenced to twenty-five years imprisonment.[46]

While the most prolific killer in Texas was behind bars, he maintained a busy schedule of working in the carpentry shop, studying law, debating, and acting as Sunday school superintendent.

Although graveyards throughout Texas were filled with the bodies of twenty to fifty men Hardin supposedly killed, he was paroled after sixteen years and then issued a full pardon on March 16, 1894, by then Texas governor James S. Hogg.[47]

In the meantime, John Selman, the professional gunfighter, was pursuing his own nefarious career as a rustler and worse. He was born in Madison County, Arkansas, on November 16, 1839. He was stationed in Indian Territory after joining the Confederate army but soon deserted. By age twenty-four, Selman migrated to Albany, Texas. He married Edna deGraffenried in August 1865 and for the next five years led a rather quiet life in Shackelford County, Texas. A venture with his in-laws trading horses in Colfax County, New Mexico, proved unprofitable after Indian raids depleted their stock.[48]

They returned to Texas, where John and Edna established a home at Fort Griffin. Selman became a deputy sheriff and was moderately successful in the saloon business. His partner was Shackelford County sheriff and gunfighter

John Larn, with whom he soon shared a strong side interest in cattle rustling. He also made the acquaintance of Miss Hurricane Minnie Martin, a prostitute who later became his mistress.

By 1878, Fort Griffin area citizens had grown weary of Larn and Selman.[49] An unwise victim decided to take matters into his own hands. One day in May, while Selman was driving a herd of cattle, the farmer conducted his first and last ambush. He only managed to blast the horn from Selman's saddle before Selman killed his assailant with a buffalo gun.

Larn was eventually arrested at home by a posse. Selman watched the entire affair from the safety of a nearby hilltop, thanks to a tip from Hurricane Minnie. Larn should have been concerned when he saw that much of the posse consisted of his own relatives, although mostly by marriage. His extended-family members may have been among the nine or so men wearing slickers and bandannas over their faces who gunned Larn down in his own jail cell that evening.[50]

Selman fled with his brother Tom "Cat" Selman to Lincoln County in New Mexico Territory, abandoning his four children and wife, who died in childbirth during his absence. The Selmans joined a cattle-rustling ring led by Ed Hart. John shot and killed Hart one morning as the two shared a table while waiting for breakfast to be served. That one well-placed shot gave Selman the control of the gang that he wanted from the beginning of his Lincoln County rustling career.

Now at the helm of his own gang, Selman merged operations with a posse that George Peppin had organized for the Dolan-Riley outfit, during conflicts with lawyer Alexander McSween and Billy the Kid's mentor, merchant John Tunstall. The merged gang did not include Peppin himself but numbered among them such Texas criminal luminaries as John Kinney, Jesse Evans, and others referred to variously as the Scouts, Rustlers, Warriors, Wrestlers, or Seven Rivers. They were much worse than the average cattle-rustling crew, as they proved in a September 1878 Lincoln County rampage, the very month John Wesley Hardin was sentenced to prison.

The Rustlers allegedly robbed and killed a man on September 6, for $40 ($720 today). Twenty days later, they burned the Coe ranch house and then wrecked the Hudgens Saloon near Stanton. For no reason at all, on September 28, Selman and his gang killed three young Hispanics mowing hay, then committed their final September atrocity two days later at the Bartlett Ranch and mill.

A mail contractor named Klein (Kline) volunteered what he knew in testimony recorded later by Colonel Dudley at Fort Stanton. He told of how members of the Rustlers approached Bartlett's mill and, seeing no one around except the wives of two employees, marched the women into the bushes, where they were stripped and raped. Klein said no charges were filed because "their husbands wanted the incident kept quiet."[51]

Selman was so mean that not even a plague could keep him down for long. Some time in the spring of 1879, Selman contracted Mexican black smallpox. His rapidly thinning band of thieves abandoned him at the doorstep of Fort Davis, New Mexico Territory, a civilian fortification designed to protect its inhabitants from Indian raids (not to be confused with the Fort Davis, Texas, post occupied by the U.S. Army).[52]

He cheated death in a tent where he was supposed to have been cared for by a male nurse who preferred to spend his time in a nearby saloon. Selman lay in his tent on the outskirts of town, abandoned to a lonely and deservedly horrid death, when a traveling tailor named Guadalupe Zarate happened by and noticed the flock of buzzards sitting atop the ridgepole of Selman's tent. When Zarate peered inside, he saw a prone man covered in blowflies and maggots, blathering incoherently.[53] Selman recovered with the help of his Mexican friend but forever after bore the disease's pockmarks on his face.

The rustler also survived a bout with jaundice in 1884. The disease was not being treated to his liking in his new home in San Pablo, Mexico, so Selman traveled north and sought medical attention in El Paso. After he recovered, Selman's name was linked for years to cattle rustling and killings on both sides of the border.

Finally, in April 1888, Selman learned that cattle-rustling charges in Texas had been dismissed due to lack of evidence. He then chose El Paso as his new home. El Paso had long been a sparsely populated town of some five hundred souls, whose proximity to the Rio Grande River and the Mexican border prompted early commerce in the usual vices. Then in 1890, the arrival of the railroad transformed the place to a bustling city harboring nearly ten thousand of the West's most rowdy, belligerent, and notorious desperadoes, John Selman among them.[54] Two years later, in spite of his nefarious past, Selman was elected city constable.

Curiously, the ultimate fates of John Wesley Hardin and John Selman soon intertwined with that of Polish cowboy-rustler Martin Morose, who lived in St. Hedwig, east of San Antonio. Newspapers of the time also spelled his name as M'Rose, McRose, and Mrose.[55] Martin Morose was hardly a typical cowboy, since he spoke a disconcerting blend of Polish and English, wore ill-fitting clothes, and favored clodhopper shoes rather than boots.

What Morose lacked in style, he made up for in dexterity with a branding iron. Along with his partners Victor Queen and Dave Kemp, he became a wealthy cattleman, in large part due to the trio's skill in branding over other ranchers' marks. None of that was lost on a buxom beauty named

Helen Beulah, whose last name is lost to history. Her brand of business was found in the brothels of Phenix, New Mexico Territory, where Morose was a regular customer.[56]

Eventually, she became known as Mrs. Morose, although no marriage license has ever been located. Beulah partnered with Martin in matters carnal and fiscal, but not all was blissful. She later complained of unspecified mistreatment by Martin. "His friends also abused me," she said after Martin's death.[57]

When John Wesley Hardin was paroled in 1894, he put his law studies to use and passed a Texas bar examination. He soon was summoned to El Paso to represent his first client, the husband of a relative. It was none other than the noted assassin James B. "Killin' Jim" Miller, who some claim later killed famous lawman Pat Garrett. Hardin soon established his El Paso practice in the Wells Fargo Building at 200½ El Paso Street.[58]

Miller wanted a man prosecuted for attempted murder, G. A. "Bud" Frazer, the former sheriff of Reeves County, who once employed Miller as a deputy. After one mistrial in El Paso and an acquittal in Colorado City, Texas, Frazer swapped his badge and six-gun for an anvil and bellows. He returned to Eddy, New Mexico Territory (near Carlsbad), where he revived his livery business. Dissatisfied with both court rulings, Killin' Jim dispensed his own brand of justice.

On September 14, 1896, Miller entered a Toyah, Texas, saloon where Frazer sat playing cards. Miller walked up to Frazer and leveled a shotgun at the man. One trigger pull later, Frazer his lost life along with part of his head.[59] Thus ended a long-standing feud, which began when Miller had opposed Frazer in an election for the office of sheriff and lost. Although Miller later became city marshal of Pecos, the Reeves County seat,[60] the differences between the two men were reconciled only with the death of one.

Miller continued his assassination business until April 19,

Group of Pecos, Texas citizens, ca. 1883. Standing: Bud Frazer, Tom White, George M. Frazer, Allen Heard, John Rooney, and Tom Babb. Seated: Lee Heard, Herman Koechler, and an unidentified man. *(Courtesy of The Haley Memorial Library and History Center, Midland, Texas)*

1909, when the citizenry of Ada, Oklahoma, lynched him and three other suspects accused of killing local rancher Gus Bobbitt.[61]

In 1895, lawyer Hardin was retained to represent prominent brand artist Martin Morose, who was in the Juarez jail with his associate Victor Queen, just across the Rio Grande from El Paso. The partners were fighting extradition requested by New Mexico Territory authorities on cattle-rustling charges. Beulah also hired Hardin to retrieve about $1,800 ($40,600 today), which Mexican authorities had taken from her when she was arrested with her husband in Sonora.

Hardin, a Mexican lawyer he retained, and the American consul in Juarez eventually convinced Mexican authorities to return the money to Beulah. Hardin also arranged for Morose and Queen to be released from jail, pending approval of Mexican citizenship for the pair. Morose became increasingly hostile as a love affair between Beulah and Hardin apparently developed in late April, while Morose was still languishing behind bars.

Back in El Paso, lawmen sought to collect a reward by getting Morose across the border to stand trial on the New Mexico Territory rustling charges. Their attempts were frustrated. Evidently, this frustration motivated a scheme developed by Constable John Selman, Deputy U.S. Marshal George Scarborough, Texas Ranger Frank McMahon, and Jeff Milton, who lost his position as El Paso police chief in early May. The plan quite possibly included Hardin and Beulah as willing participants.

On the night of June 21, 1895, Scarborough lured Morose across the Texas Central Railroad bridge, where he thought he was to meet Beulah.[62] Morose apparently soon realized he was to be arrested, started to resist, and then was gunned down by at least three of the four officers waiting for him.[63] His death set in motion a Texas whirlwind from which few of the conspirators escaped.

Hardin and Beulah's love affair ended miserably amidst her charges that Hardin abused and intended to kill her. Worse yet, within a very short time, Hardin died at the hands of City Constable John Selman.

While in his cups, Selman had accused Hardin of keeping money taken from the Morose corpse, while paying off Scarborough and no one else. Selman was also outraged at Hardin's habit of taking back at gunpoint any money he lost gambling in both the Acme and Gem saloons. The good constable had quite enough of Hardin and told prominent businessman and saloonkeeper George Look about his frustration. "George, you people may stand for it, but I won't. He has to come across [pay what is owed] or I'll kill him," Selman declared.

Earlier, Selman spread word that Hardin was well heeled with money. George Look wrote in his unpublished memoirs, "John Selman came to me and told me that Wesley Hardin had quite a roll—in fact, had Morose's roll."[64] It was indeed quite a roll. Historians have placed the amount of money taken from Morose as he lay in the weeds at $3,700, worth about $83,000 today.[65] According to Look, Selman said, "I believe he has cut with Scarborough but he has not cut with any of the rest of us. What do you say—shall I get the son of a bitch?"[66] Forgive and forget was definitely not on Selman's agenda.

On the night of August 19, 1895, Selman walked into the Acme Saloon, where Hardin was throwing dice with grocer Henry Brown. Hardin's reputation as a cheat and a dangerous man was well known to the patrons there. A few months earlier, he had recouped his losses by raking all the cash off of the table, then backing out of the place with his pistol drawn. He pulled the same stunt the next evening at the Gem, collecting ninety-five dollars. He once tried a similar tactic in Phenix, the sin city located near Eddy, New Mexico Territory, about the first of August but was confronted with the business end of a six-shooter and took the next train out of town.[67]

Now, eighteen days later, Hardin had his back to the saloon door while standing at the bar. "Four sixes to beat," Hardin taunted Brown, just before Selman drew his pistol, raised it to the back of Hardin's head, then fired. Hardin most likely was already dead when he hit the floor, but Old John was not taking any chances. He fired three more times. His second round ripped harmlessly through the floor as he was bumped by a patron scurrying for cover. Selman's third round went through Hardin's arm, and the final bullet slammed through his chest. John Wesley Hardin was dead at age forty-two. He hadn't fired a shot.[68]

Although the official explanation for the killing was self-defense, the real motivation was probably greed, revenge, concealing the Morose conspiracy, or all three. Whatever the reason for Hardin's death, many of those associated with the Morose affair died violently. During the early morning hours of Easter Sunday, April 5, 1896, Old John Selman was shot down in an alley behind the Wigwam Saloon in El Paso, without even drawing his weapon. He died the next day, following an operation to remove a bullet lodged in his spine.[69]

The shooter was Deputy U.S. Marshal George Scarborough. The two lawmen had met at the Wigwam Saloon, then wandered into the alley for a discussion. Selman supposedly asked Scarborough to help rescue his son John Selman, Jr., from Mexican authorities, who held him on charges of abducting a young El Paso girl for a tryst in Juarez. Others have suggested that Scarborough and Old John argued over the money taken from the corpse of Martin Morose the previous year. Or perhaps Selman was mad that Scarborough received blood money for the Morose killing without telling him and he wanted to waylay the deputy in that alley.[70] Whatever the reason for the gunfight, Scarborough promptly shot Selman four times, leaving Old John wounded in the street as he complained to bystanders that he was afraid of no man but had not even drawn his weapon.

Scarborough was acquitted in Selman's death and then left Texas for New Mexico Territory, where he worked for a cattlemen's association as a detective. Seriously injured in a gunfight with rustlers on April 5, 1900, Scarborough was taken to Deming, where his leg was amputated. Probably contracting blood poisoning, he died the next day, on the fourth anniversary of the death of John Selman in El Paso.[71]

And so Martin Morose was dead; Hardin was killed by

John Selman, Jr., ca. 1894, about the time he joined the El Paso police force under Jeff Milton. *(Courtesy of The Haley Memorial Library and History Center, Midland, Texas)*

Selman, who was killed by Scarborough; and Scarborough was killed by bandits exactly four years later. Beulah disappeared from all recorded history, and John Selman, Jr., escaped from the jail at Juarez but soon left the El Paso area for good. Jeff Milton retired from the immigration service in 1930 to Tombstone, Arizona, and died there in 1947 at the age of eighty-five.[72]

CHAPTER THREE

Wild Bill Longley:
Unreconstructed and Loving It

On the solemn occasion of his third hanging, Wild Bill Longley professed to be sorry for his lifetime of wrongdoing. The event took place on the eleventh day of October 1878 and was heralded with much fanfare. Newspaper accounts of the time reported that as many as 4,000 people witnessed the spectacle.

When this all had started years ago, Bill would never have guessed that his quest would come to this. Too young to enlist during the Civil War, William Preston Longley was a Confederate wannabe who listened attentively as veterans told of their war adventures. Longley was a teenage boy at the time, and he soon began to worship the war-scarred vets and sympathized with the dismal prospects some of them faced in Reconstruction. Soon the starry-eyed kid began a twelve-year spree of often racially motivated killings.

Some say such atrocities were little more than a pastime for Wild Bill, as he came to be known after his death. During his own time he was more often called Bloody Bill, for the worst of reasons. Killing blacks armed or unarmed, soldier or civilian, seemed nothing more than an amusement for Wild Bill, at least in his stories. In one conversation on the subject, Longley reputedly bragged of killing thirty-two men, then scoffed, "Oh, I killed lots of n—s and Mexicans, who I did not count."[1]

William Preston Longley was number six in a brood of ten sired by Campbell Longley. He was born on October

William Preston Longley. *(Courtesy of the Texas Ranger Hall of Fame and Museum, Waco, Texas)*

6, 1851, on Mill Creek, Austin County, Texas. Two years later, the family pulled up stakes and settled on a farm near Evergreen, north of Houston in what was then Washington County, where they raised their children. Campbell and his wife, Sarah Ann Henry Longley, were devout, honest, patriotic people who were respected in the mostly Confederate state, even though old man Longley was a staunch Unionist and voted Republican prior to the Civil War. Campbell Longley was born in East Tennessee, which would have a significant Unionist population during the Civil War. Sarah was a Pennsylvania native.

About 1835, Campbell Longley's family left Tennessee and headed for Texas. He settled in Austin County and fought in the Texas Revolution of 1836.[2] Even though Campbell Longley fought valiantly to gain independence for Texas, like Sam Houston he refused to fight for secession from the Union. While many in the South viewed such an attitude as treasonous, Campbell Longley was never bothered, perhaps because of his service during the Texas Revolution.

Young Bill Longley could not have been more unlike his father where loyalty to the Confederacy was concerned. In the winter of 1866, Longley left the family farm and is said to have taken a train to Houston. The Houston and Texas Central slowed to a stop at the depot and off jumped a wide-eyed, eager, lanky boy named Bill Longley.[3] He was a young man with purpose of mind and heart, according to one author whose unabashed, undiscriminating idolatry of Longley is unique among twentieth-century writers on the subject.

Longley was in Houston to "get help . . . so he could be a man during those heart-trying times," according to Ed Bartholomew in his book, *Wild Bill Longley: A Texas Hard Case.* "He wanted a pistol. . . . He wanted to stand up as a man; he had man-sized work to do."[4] The "man-sized work" Longley "had" to do was nothing short of racist robbery and revenge. To do this he looked for a pistol. Houston was a good place to get such a weapon. There, the teenaged Bill Longley's reverence for the South and hatred for the North would be reinforced. Longley was alone when he entered Houston that winter's night, but he quickly made acquaintances at a camp inhabited by unemployed youths of the war-ravaged South and Confederate veterans whom Longley worshiped.

Ed Bartholomew sympathetically wrote of the young men trailing away from the campfire to steal food. Some were assigned to pilfer vegetables; another made off with a slab of beef. All in all, it was not a bad night's meal for the vagabonds.

During the next few days, Longley "found that everywhere, evidently the negroes were inflated over their freedom and carpetbagger rule made them the more unruly," Bartholomew wrote. "Young men talked of joining the so-called organizations which promised to see that the situation was corrected."[5] Today such organizations are called hate groups. Much later, as he contemplated a death sentence at the working end of a noose, and despite his earlier claims of killing too many minorities to count, Longley sternly denounced the wanton murder of blacks. "The report of my killing negroes for pastime just to see them kick is an ungodly falsehood. It was the Ku Klux Klan bunch that did all the killing among the negroes and laid it out on me."[6] Most newspaper editors doubted Longley's earlier assertion of having casually killed men of color, but a lot of their readers did not. "While most newspapers cast a jaundiced eye at Longley's claims, the boasts nevertheless took hold in the public mind, and he became a notorious figure."[7]

Lee's surrender at Appomattox on April 9, 1865, had done little to ease tensions throughout most of South. In Texas, young Bill Longley joined in the conflict that has since been described as the War of Reconstruction in Texas.

He recruited like-minded young John McKeown (McCowan or McKowen), and the two set out to "disarm some negroes in the vicinity of Evergreen," Longley's hometown.[8] About one year later, Longley was in Houston, camping with a host of former Confederate soldiers, all discussing what to do. They believed that the surrender was bad enough, but they felt that watching former slaves being deputized and occasionally running roughshod over whites was just intolerable. While in Houston, Longley met a like-minded teen, with whom he confronted a black Federal soldier one evening. Words were exchanged and in an instant the black soldier was dead, his kidneys perforated by a knife. The boys rifled through the dead man's uniform and—according to Bartholomew, at least—Longley came away with what he came to Houston for in the first place: a pistol. This was one of only two dozen percussion five-shot pistols manufactured in East Columbia, Texas, by J. H. Dance & Company, then discovered by the Federals in a Houston depot and eventually issued to freedmen-turned-soldiers.

Longley spent the next twelve years campaigning to be labeled Texas's most successful gunfighter. He was ever mindful of the growing reputation of another Texas desperado, named John Wesley Hardin. Hardin likely was not concerned about Wild Bill at all. Longley's need to build his own reputation, however, was relentless. While jailed at Giddings, Texas, in 1877, Longley wrote constantly to newspapers. He said he killed thirty-two men, four more than Hardin, who was two years younger. Longley boasted that having the higher kill rate earned him, not Hardin, the title of "the most successful outlaw that ever lived in Texas."[9] While Hardin was awaiting sentencing at Austin, and Longley was doing so at Galveston and then Giddings, Longley's campaign continued. The *Nacogdoches News* published comments as to Longley's "considerable jealousy of John Wesley Hardin, both on account of the assumed superiority of the latter as a prolific murderer, and that Hardin gets but twenty-five years while Longley is booked for that bourne from whence no traveler returns."[10]

Longley's tendency to exaggerate his actual number of kills likely earned him the death sentence. Wild Bill may well have talked the talk that made him walk the walk to the gallows. Adding injury to insult, he was hanged twice at Giddings, Texas, on October 11, 1878. Apparently the rope slipped on the beam it was coiled around after Longley dropped the expected eight feet. At that point, the six-foot Wild Bill dropped to a knee-banging collision with the ground. Longley was temporarily dazed but not dead. Sheriff James Madison Brown and a deputy hoisted the nearly unconscious Longley back up so that his feet no longer touched the ground. The incident was recounted in the local paper as a ghoulish affair. "Two moans escaped the lips, and arms and feet were raised three times; after hanging eleven and a half minutes life was pronounced extinct."[11]

Longley's first hanging, as told by him but corroborated by no other, came courtesy of a necktie party thrown for suspected members of the notorious Cullen Montgomery Baker gang, probably in 1868, if it happened at all. Longley claimed that he was in northeast Texas awaiting the return of Baker's marauders, who were plundering parts of Arkansas, in order to join the gang himself. He met a young fellow who was wanted by the law and purported to be a member of the gang. Longley's new acquaintance was Tom Johnson, but the relationship did not last long. Sometime in 1869, according to Longley, he and Johnson were hiding out in the river bottoms when they were surprised by a group who believed the pair were members of the Baker gang. The Baker gang had, however, abandoned Baker, who himself was killed January 6, 1869, along with Matthew

"Dummy" Kirby. Longley and Johnson were lynched on the spot without the formality of a trial.[12]

The incident, if it happened at all, probably occurred in 1868, but it was never corroborated or documented by anyone. Most contemporary historians discount the story as just another crow from a young cock looking to further his reputation as a Texas hard case. However, the supposed lynching is no more fantastic than Longley's three tales of his rescue.

One Longley version described how Tom Johnson's little brother shot the rope dangling Longley, dropping him to the ground. Longley also claimed at another time that, as the mob was leaving the scene, one of their number fired three shots at Johnson, all taking effect, and two at Longley. One of the bullets struck a belt in which Longley was carrying gold, and the second went through the rope holding him aloft, cutting two of its cords, Wild Bill claimed. Longley's body weight against the compromised hemp caused it to give way, and Longley dropped to the ground. Johnson's brother then allegedly rushed to the scene and cut the noose from Longley's neck.

A third tall tale similar to the second had one member of the mob turning at some far-off point and emptying his six-shooter at the hanging men. One of those bullets supposedly cut the rope suspending Longley, and he fell to the ground. Here too, Johnson's younger brother rushed to the scene. He attempted to take the weight off his brother's neck by hoisting him from his ankles, until it became obvious that Tom was dead. The younger brother then turned to remove the cinched noose from Longley's neck. In all three stories, Longley received preferential treatment from the rescuer.[13]

Longley claimed that he then became a chief lieutenant of Cullen Montgomery Baker, the Swamp Fox of the Sulphur River. Although Baker's most recent biographers recognized that there may have been some relationship,

Longley's association with Baker is undocumented, and Baker's right-hand man was Lee Rames (Raines), not Wild Bill. One major problem with Longley's claim that he rode with Baker in 1869, as we have seen, is that by January 6, 1869, Baker wasn't riding anywhere.

The Swamp Fox was killed by Thomas Orr in order to avoid being killed himself. As we saw in chapter 1, Orr, a schoolteacher and politician, sought the affections of one Belle Foster, Baker's sister-in-law. Baker also attempted to woo Foster after her older sister, Baker's wife, died. Belle chose Orr, which two years later led Baker to hang him, at least for a few minutes.[14] Although Longley did not ride with Baker in 1869, it is possible he simply placed his association with Baker in the wrong year.

Nevertheless, in spite of all the bluster and factual inaccuracies in Longley's claims, he really did kill people. Though Longley refers to each one as a gunfight—a case of kill or be killed—not all of the participants realized they were in a gunfight until they had been shot. One of Longley's victims was Wilson Anderson, a boyhood friend.[15]

The death of Wilson Anderson clearly demonstrates Longley's predisposition to murder. According to Longley, arresting sheriff J. J. Finney of Mason County had just allowed Longley to escape jail at Austin, seeing as how the sheriff was refused payment of the offered reward money. Not disappointed for long, Finney's pockets were supposedly stuffed by a California relative of Longley's. Wild Bill's travels almost always took him back to one relative or another. This time Longley walked his horse up to the gate of Uncle Caleb Longley's Lee County farm, late in 1874. Uncle Caleb met his nephew with the sad news that Uncle Caleb's son and Bill's cousin, Little Cale, had been murdered. To make matters worse, the man who did the deed, and therefore was lower than a snake's belly in a wagon rut, was walking about as free as a bird just a mile down the road.

Uncle Caleb was referring to a boyhood friend of Bill Longley's and a drinking buddy of Little Cale's. Uncle Caleb said that Wilson Anderson for some inexplicable reason had crushed Little Cale's skull, killing the boy outright. Would Bill please go and kill Anderson? Uncharacteristically, Longley agreed with his younger brother, James Stockton Longley, that if any killing was to be done to avenge Little Cale, it would be proper for Cale's brothers or even Uncle Caleb himself to do the deed. Earlier, a jury had accepted Anderson's claim that he and Little Cale had been pulling on the jug for most of the afternoon. Cale's horse spooked as the two rode together, running his rider headlong into a low-hanging tree branch. Thus the jury ruled that the tragic death was accidental.[16] That, Anderson apparently believed, was the end of that.

Realizing his pleas were not having the desired effect, Uncle Caleb resorted to injuring Longley's pride. He told Longley that Wilson Anderson had also said that Longley was a low-down horse thief who needed killing, and he (Wilson Anderson) was just the man to do it.[17] Those were fighting words.

Even though his brother Jim initially tried to dissuade Wild Bill from reacting, on April 1, 1875, the two rode together to the Anderson place in the Loebeau community, not far north of Evergreen. Jim Longley pulled his horse up in a bank of trees while Bill rode on to meet the unsuspecting Anderson. Bill found him bent over a plow, working a cotton field. When Longley reached his boyhood friend, he dismounted, raised his shotgun, and fired two blasts into Anderson, without any fanfare at all. The first round knocked a stunned Anderson off his feet. The second one killed him. Wilson Anderson was unarmed, taken completely by surprise, and likely did not expect retaliation from Longley. Almost certainly, he would not have anticipated such unprovoked violence from his longtime friend. After all, a local jury had acquitted

Anderson of murdering Little Cale.[18] Eventually, this killing became Wild Bill's undoing.

Thirty-two Men?

Longley boasted that he killed as many as thirty-two men. However, as his appointment with the Grim Reaper was nearing, he realized that such talk was not advancing his call for an appeal. Wild Bill cautiously changed the number to eighteen, as if that made him appear any less murderous.

Longley's efforts to best John Wesley Hardin had been pathetic and arguably were lethal to Wild Bill himself. While both were in jail, Longley and Hardin maintained a battle of words through numerous letters published in various newspapers, in which each man claimed to be the most prolific gunman in Texas.[19] In reality, only six deaths can be attributed to Wild Bill with any degree of certainty. Longley's first documented killing took place on December 20, 1868, when he was seventeen, almost seven years before he killed Wilson Anderson. Anti-Reconstruction sentiment was at a fever pitch and reports of attacks on former slaves were numerous. Gen. Joseph Reynolds wrote to the U.S. adjutant general in Washington, D.C., on December 4, 1868, "The murder of negroes is so common as to render it impossible to keep an accurate account of them."[20]

A few days before December 20, 1868, teenaged brothers Pryor and Green Evans, former slaves of "Captain" Alfred Evans, left the Evans farm to visit relatives in Austin County. The boys were accompanied by an older black man called Ned, and all three holiday travelers were on horseback. Why and how the encounter took place depends on who is telling the tale. One of the most often repeated accounts states that Longley and two others first met the black men in

Evergreen. Longley apparently wanted the horse that Pryor Evans was riding and asked if he would be interested in trading. Pryor declined and the black trio rode out of town. When they were about four miles from Evergreen, they turned in their saddles at the sound of galloping horses.

Longley and his compatriots quickly overtook the men and raised their pistols. The Evans party was coarsely interrogated as to where they were going and searched for weapons. A pistol was confiscated from Green Evans. When Longley, John McKeown, and Jim Gilmore were satisfied that the captives had no more weaponry, they were ordered to follow one of the white riders, with the other two bringing up the rear. According to Pryor, the six mounted men ambled toward Nails Bottom Creek with one of the white riders constantly threatening the black men, saying they "intended to learn them manners."

Fearing robbery and possible murder, Green kicked his horse to a full run. Two of the white captors followed Green, firing their pistols during the brief chase. Green was hit by a bullet in the back of his head and killed instantly. During the distraction, Ned and Pryor broke for freedom and somehow survived, even though one slug flew past Pryor's head. Pryor escaped to the house of a white man named McDaniel, who, along with two freedmen, searched for Green. They found him dead, robbed of about four dollars and his horse.[21] They interred the body in a temporary grave, and Pryor made a hasty withdrawal from Lee County back to the Bell County farm of Capt. Alfred Evans.

Evans was a North Carolina man born in 1810. His first Texas home was in Austin County, where he settled in 1838. A veteran of the Seminole Wars in Florida, Evans also served Texas during the Mexican War of 1848, as an officer. He moved a final time in 1859, when he established his farm near Salado, a town located on a branch of the Chisholm Trail. When the Civil War broke out, Alfred Evans once again took up arms, joining the Bell County volunteers in the fight for secession.

During a trip to Houston, Evans had purchased young Pryor, Green, and the boys' mother. Evans raised the boys, who were given the family name. So it was that this veteran of several wars, landowner, and patriot rode into Washington County to investigate the murder of Green Evans. His reputation alone would have intimidated many men, but he also brought along some escorts. Captain Evans rode with Pryor, his other brother Burril (Burl), and the boys' stepfather, Henry Evans. Each man was armed with a double-barreled shotgun and a mission.

Their sole purpose was to bring the killers of Green Evans to justice.[22] Even though someone quietly slipped a note to old Henry Evans naming the killers as Longley, McKeown, and Gilmore, none of them was ever charged with the murder. Alfred Evans was disgusted with local law enforcement and wrote Texas governor E. M. Pease, imploring him to offer a reward for the three suspects. He thought that the incentive of a reward might lead to the men's capture but recognized the potential for peril for any man who would come forward. While he believed that most of Evergreen's citizens were "opposed to these murderers, and cut throats," those same folks were likely also "afraid to express there [sic] honest sentiments, for fear of being injured in some way by these desperate scoundrels and out laws."[23]

That was a problem, no doubt, as was the leniency afforded perpetrators of violence against blacks. Longley and his kind emulated the organized hate groups of the day. Groups such as the Ku Klux Klan, the supposedly more upscale Knights of the White Camellia, the Constitutional Guard, the White Brotherhood, and many more wore the veil of patriotism to cloak their mission of keeping freedmen from experiencing too much freedom. Longley was never a formal member of these organizations, but his actions against blacks were in lockstep with the Ku Klux Klan.

Threats of bodily harm or death were apparently so prevalent that Captain Evans soon realized the futility of continuing. One cold December day, the four men were seen riding east toward Brenham, probably intending to carry on their quest for justice.Yet the small, discouraged band abruptly turned north and headed back to the farm at Salado. No other attempts to obtain justice for Green Evans were ever recorded.

Longley tried to justify his actions by alluding to the "arrogance" of at least one of the three blacks while they were in Evergreen. He probably hoped to further infuriate his white sympathizers when he wrote that the boys were mulattoes. Wild Bill probably did not have to mention Alfred Evans by name to communicate the intended innuendo.

Longley surely sought the sympathy and support of likeminded Southerners. His version of these events was published in the *Galveston Daily News* in 1877.[24]

Three negroes, two of whom were mulattoes, happened to pass through Evergreen . . . and halted at a bar room to get their drinks. When they returned to their horses one of the mulattoes remarked that Evergreen was the place reported to be dangerous to the well-being of colored people, and added that he would be glad if somebody would undertake to molest him. Young Longley heard him, and at once rallied to his assistance two other young men, and mounting their horses went in pursuit of this party. They overtook them about eight miles from Evergreen, on the Brenham road. No other harm was intended than to disarm the negroes and allow them to go on; but when the pursuers came in sight the negroes drew their pistols and spurred their horses into a running speed. They were ordered to halt, but not heeding the command all three of the young men fired, resulting in the instant death of the negro who had requested a difficulty at the bar room.[25]

Just before Longley's execution, a petition was circulated in Nacogdoches seeking his release. Longley, as usual, claimed that he was simply upholding the law, by disarming former slaves, or coming to the aid of certain citizens who Longley claimed were victims of bullying. He also asserted that the abused citizens were usually elderly and therefore defenseless and easily frightened. Naturally, the victims were always white.

Longley's second corroborated murder came early in 1870, two years after he shot Green Evans in the back of the head. He and his brother-in-law, John W. Wilson, were accused of killing Paul Brice, a freedman residing in Bastrop County.

State Policeman T. P. Woods reported in February of that year that a black woman was discovered dead. Woods reported to the newly formed State Police, a Reconstruction organization, on July 12, 1870, that "Bill Longley and John Wilson killed a freedwoman near Evergreen in 1870."[26] There was also a rumor that Longley had sexually molested at least one woman, possibly this freedwoman, but no record supporting that allegation has been found.

Pressure to capture Longley began to rise in the spring of 1870. Wild Bill and Wilson sprang to the top of Texas's most wanted list when the army offered a $1,000 reward ($14,000 today) for the arrest of each man. Since Texas no longer offered refuge, they resolved to leave. Wilson did not get very far, according to Longley, who claimed he died that spring and was buried in Brazos County. There is also some evidence Wilson may have died four years later, at Falls County, Texas.[27]

Whichever date is correct, Longley had already cut a lonesome trail to the north. Longley traveled to Salt Lake, then moved on to the gold-mining town of Hamilton City, also called Miner's Delight, in Wyoming Territory, by May 1870. He eventually joined a gold-mining expedition led by future judge William L. Kuykendall. In all likelihood, Longley joined the expedition at Cheyenne.

Despite an 1868 peace treaty between the United States government and the Teton Lakota Sioux, that year tensions between miners and Sioux led by Red Cloud ran high. In June, six miners were killed by the Indians. Altogether, eight miners lost their lives to Indian attacks between May and September of 1868.[28]

In 1870, a force of some 275, mostly miners, rode out, undoubtedly expecting to be intercepted by the Sioux. Instead, they encountered an Arapaho party nearly twice their size, at an encampment along the Big Wind River. Although outnumbered, the expedition attacked the Arapaho, believing they held a large number of stolen horses. Later, on April 7, 1870, another party of miners came across Arapahos being led by chief Black Bear and attacked them, killing Black Bear, thirteen of his warriors, three women, and one child. The miners also stole eight children from the decimated party to be taken in and raised by whites.[29]

The Arapaho retaliated with a vengeance. On June 23 and June 24, 1870, three miners, Harvey Morgan, James Mason, and Dr. R. S. Barr, a justice of the peace at South Pass City, were killed after they encountered the Kuykendall expedition and were warned to be on the lookout for hostile Indians. Both Mason and Morgan had been scalped when Kuykendall discovered their bodies. The Indians split the skin on Barr's exposed back along the backbone. Once that was done, they peeled back the hide three inches on either side of the spine and then removed the sinew from inside. Kuykendall believed that the Arapahos were going to use this to make strings for their bows. Morgan's head was split with a hammer from one of the miners' wagons. The hammer was so deeply embedded that the undertaker was unable to remove it and buried Morgan with it stuck in his head.[30]

Kuykendall wrote about this encounter years later. He described his attempt to take the expedition onto the Sioux reservation, which was strictly forbidden by the treaty of 1868. Kuykendall wrote that his party was turned back by 1st Lt. James N. Wheelan of Company B, Camp Stambaugh, Wyoming Territory.[31] Kuykendall claimed that the expedition was followed by as many as one thousand Indians, who inexplicably never did attack.

Despite these and other fully documented, gruesome attacks, Longley embellished his version, perhaps to enhance his own reputation. When Bill Longley was through describing any real event, the story was too preposterous to be believed.

Longley was a member of the Kuykendall expedition of June 1870 and no doubt was present when the expedition found the bodies of the three unfortunate miners. Yet Longley claimed that the expedition was repeatedly attacked by hordes of Indians and that expedition members were killed or wounded all around him. He asserted too that despite such attacks, he and another miner named Miller left the relative safety of the encampments to enjoy mountain views and hunt wild game. This tale was apparently intended to enhance his reputation as a fearless shootist.

Longley also claimed that Indians were not the only peril lurking in the mountains of Wyoming. He reported that a mother Grizzly bear charged him and Miller after Longley killed two of her cubs. Longley's hair-raising tale related how Miller's gun jammed, sending him scampering up a nearby tree, while Longley alone poured lead at the beast. Longley said that he kept firing his Winchester until it was empty and that he managed only to break one of the Grizzly's front legs. After that, he recounted, he promptly joined Miller in the tree. Kuykendall, the expedition leader and a careful diarist, never recorded any of this, nor did any other expedition member.

None of this bravado did Longley any good when the jury at Giddings, Texas, decided his fate in September 1877. The jury promptly chose to rid the country of a prolific and unremorseful killer. Longley was not hanged for his wildly boastful claims of killing black soldiers, Indians, Mexicans, and a few Texas-insulting white men. Instead, Wild Bill Longley answered for the death of Wilson Anderson two years earlier.

Another man Longley killed before he realized things were that serious was one George Thomas. Longley and Thomas got into a fistfight during an alcohol-fueled foxhunt near Waco on November 13, 1875. Wild Bill got the worst of the fight and crept away, returning with a pistol. He shot Thomas three times in the back. Longley was also accused of stealing the dead man's horse to make his getaway.[32]

The only legitimate gunfight of his entire career began as an attempt to get the drop on yet another man he had befriended. William "Lou" Shroyer, alias Sawyer, was a former Union soldier who, like Longley, was reputedly a person to stay clear of. When they met in Uvalde County early in 1876, Longley was operating under the name Jim Webb. Shroyer learned Webb's true identity and planned to collect the posted rewards for the outlaw, but Longley somehow caught wind of the plot and turned the tables. Longley first managed to get himself deputized in order to arrest Shroyer on an outstanding warrant. Now Longley needed an angle by which to ensnare his unsuspecting prey. Shroyer's appetite for free beef did the trick. Longley and a man he deputized, William Hayes, invited Shroyer to help himself to a cow the two had killed in the Dry Frio Canyon. Shroyer jumped at the chance, bringing his pack of dogs with him on January 10, 1876.

Somewhere along the trail, however, Shroyer realized he was about to be waylaid. Just as Longley and Hayes unholstered their weapons, Shroyer spurred his horse and galloped toward a stand of trees. Longley and Hayes were in thunderous pursuit, as were Shroyer's dogs. Just as Shroyer reached the woods, Longley fired a shot, killing his horse. Shroyer managed a return volley, killing Longley's horse. Another round from Shroyer's gun found its mark in the thigh of Deputy Hayes, whose horse then bolted, temporarily removing Hayes from the fight. Shroyer was hit several times by Longley's gunfire, then called out that he wanted to parley. Longley agreed, he said. As he approached, Shroyer raised a gun at Longley, who fired a quick fatal shot. Between the two shooters, thirty-two rounds had been exchanged.[33]

The sixth and last of Longley's documented victims was a man with whom he had entered into a sharecropping enterprise. William Roland (Rolland) Lay was also a preacher. Longley left Uvalde County sometime in February 1876, after killing Shroyer. He took up residence east of Dallas in a small town called Ben Franklin, in diminutive but scenic Delta County. Longley was staying with another farmer named Thomas P. Jack. Jack's sixteen-year-old daughter, Rachel Lavinia, shone brightly in Longley's eye. Longley was using another alias at this time, calling himself William Black. He romanced Rachel Lavinia, whom he called "Miss Louvenia," but Longley was not without competition.

Mark Foster was a nephew by marriage of Longley's sharecropping partner William Lay and had been previously rebuffed by the Jack family. Mark chose the wrong time to try to reestablish himself as Rachel's fiancé. Foster, having no idea he was dealing with Wild Bill Longley, left a series of nasty notes urging him to leave town and forget the girl. The killer must have chuckled at one such message tied to Longley's plow handle, which read in part, "This note is to tell you that if you do not get out of this country at once, your damned hide won't hold shucks."[34] Longley demanded that he and Mark Foster have it out. Uncharacteristically for

Longley, he merely beat Foster with a short-handled riding whip and pistol without killing him. Longley was arrested on charges of false imprisonment rather than assault on June 6, 1876.

That very day, Thomas P. Jack was also arrested for making threats against the Fosters, perhaps in connection with Mark Foster's attempted courtship of young Rachel. Longley and Jack stewed for six days in the Delta County town of Cooper before Wild Bill burned through the jail door, allowing the pair to escape.

Longley chose to place the blame for his troubles on the reverend. Longley later said that Lay had falsely claimed to be a friend, while he secretly encouraged Foster all along to keep wooing Rachel. Seven days after his jailbreak, using the same technique he employed in the murder of Wilson Anderson, Longley ambushed Lay with a shotgun while the good reverend was milking a cow. Lay had been too slow to defend himself with a shotgun he had placed in the corner of the corral, but he lived long enough to reveal his assailant's identity.[35]

Much can be said about the life and times of Bill Longley, but perhaps it was stated best by a soldier, Henry Gross, who knew him when both were stationed in Wyoming after the Kuykendall expedition. Longley was apparently not proud of his military service. He always described himself as a civilian employee of the army, in spite of his enrollment on June 22, 1870, for five years as a trooper in Company B of the Second Cavalry Regiment—which he promptly deserted. Nevertheless, Gross wrote that everyone liked the wild tales Longley told of himself, but "none of us believed him." Gross said that because Longley could spin a good yarn, was good natured, and was a good shot, the soldiers tolerated him. Even so, Gross wrote that Longley was thought of as nothing more than an "idle boaster, a notorious liar and a man of low instincts and habits."[36] The world was well rid of Bill Longley.

Pink Higgins and company after returning from a trip on the cattle trail. Bottom row: Felix Castello, Jess Standard, R. A. Mitchell, Pink Higgins. Top row: Powell Woods, unidentified, Buck Allen, A. T. Mitchell. (*Courtesy of Jeff Jackson*)

CHAPTER FOUR

Pink Higgins:
The Gangs of Lampasas

"Him no beef, him Comanche!" the indignant Tonkawa sputtered.

Young Pink Higgins was taken aback, but after a few moments he understood the remark. The young Texan had complained when the Indian scout allowed some cooking meat to drip onto his own meal broiling over a campfire. On patrol that day, Higgins and other Texans chased a party of Comanche warriors across West Texas, killing several. The Tonkawa scout had cut a small piece from the body of a warrior, in order to consume and thus absorb his opponent's bravery.[1] Higgins, then perhaps only eighteen, did not realize that during his long and daring life he would not only battle the Comanche but would also lead men engaged in one of the fiercest feuds in Texas history, stalk cattle thieves as a range detective, and report his last gunfight to the county sheriff in a long-distance telephone call. His was an adventurous life, indeed.

When the Horrell-Higgins feud was temporarily concluded with a de facto peace treaty negotiated by the Texas Rangers in 1877, Lampasas County residents reflected that the two families had very similar backgrounds. They even settled in Lampasas County within months of each other in 1857. The town of Lampasas was founded four years before, some seventy miles from Austin on a river named after the prickly cocklebur plant. Moses Hughes was probably the earliest resident. He settled here in order to obtain a ready source of mineral waters for his ailing wife, from the seven creeks nearby. Soon the town had over six hundred residents, and eventually thousands of visiting Texans turned the small town into a seasonal resort filled with tents. Later, Lampasas boosters dubbed the place "The Saratoga of the South."

Benedict Horrell followed a long and arduous path to this land of abundant water, scrub brush, live oak, and rich grasses. Although the Horrell clan had originated centuries before in Devonshire, England, Benedict spent his early years in Kentucky. His first wife gave birth to Samuel about 1821, but little else is known of her. Father and son migrated to Hot Springs County, Arkansas, by about 1836, settling in newly established Fenter Township. There they operated adjoining farms, according to tax records reported about two years later.[2] Sam married Elizabeth Wells in 1838.

Evidently these farms did not produce the prosperity expected. About nine years later, the father-son partnership moved operations farther west to Caddo Township, which had been created only about five years earlier in Montgomery County. Now almost thirty, Sam acquired 142 acres adjoining his father's 66-acre tract by 1849. The 1850 federal census noted that Sam had five sons: William, John, Samuel, James Martin (Mart), and Thomas. Benedict now had another wife and two daughters. Then Benjamin was born about 1851 and Merritt two years later. Their next move west was to Texas, in 1857.

The journey took them about four hundred miles from their former homestead in relatively peaceful Arkansas to a place some ten miles northeast of Lampasas. Lampasas County had been formed from parts of Travis, Bell, and Coryell counties. The same year the Horrells arrived, their future nemesis, Pink Higgins, also took up residence in Lampasas County.

Soon the Horrells' new home was in the throes of a frontier conflict between settlers and two fierce Indian tribes. The

Lipan Apache and Comanche tribes had established a pattern of attack along the Texas frontier. Braves raided farms and ranches in groups of five to ten, usually targeting horses but sometimes killing settlers.[3] Such was the fate of the Jackson family living near the Horrells in 1857. The family was nearly wiped out by raiding Comanche who carried away and then uncharacteristically released two young survivors.[4] The raids continued, prompting Sam Horrell and his neighbors to join the Lampasas Guards, organized in July 1859. When six scout troops began a rotation of one-week patrols throughout the county, Indian raids quickly diminished—at least for the time being.

Sam Horrell, nearly forty, was now called "Old Sam." Two of his sons established family alliances that would become critical in the bloody feuds to come. John Horrell married Sarah Ann Grizell in 1860, and young Sam married into the Stanley clan the next year, taking Martha Ann as his bride.[5] These blissful events were soon overtaken by the conflagration that overwhelmed the United States following the presidential elections of 1860. Texas's preference for the Confederacy during the Civil War was a surprise to no one, since settlers in Texas had predominantly migrated from Southern and border states. Equally important, slavery powered the economy in many a Texas county. According to family tradition, William Horrell, now about twenty-three, joined a Confederate regiment and simply was never heard from again.[6] Such tragedies were an all-too-common occurrence.

Old Sam Horrell and his sons John and Sam Jr. served in a home guard unit stationed at Camp Colorado in Coleman County, a post commanded by Robert E. Lee before the Civil War. The trio never saw action.[7] Perhaps this was a disappointment because, as their mother once told neighbors, the Horrell brothers had been raised to be fighters.[8]

Even so, about three years after the war concluded,

when Lampasas County citizens were confronted with yet another series of Indian attacks, the Horrells elected to move farther west. The clan decided initially to drive their herd of some fifteen hundred cattle to California.[9] However, about six hundred miles into the move, at Las Cruces, New Mexico Territory, an opportunity for a quick sale at a good price presented itself.

Regrettably, this good fortune was followed by a series of tragedies. First, John Horrell was killed by disgruntled cowhand Early Hubbard at the end of the trail drive, in a dispute over wages.[10] Soon afterward, Old Sam and a Hispanic companion were ambushed and killed by Apaches while the large family party was going through San Augustin Pass about ten miles northeast of Las Cruces. Somehow, eighteen-year-old Tom Horrell survived. According to Horrell family tradition, his sister-in-law Sallie hid her small children in the wagon, then took up the fight, using Old Sam's pistol. The party fought a running gun battle along the way to Shedd's Ranch, some four miles away.[11] Later, Tom married Mattie Ann Ausment, an orphan who was traveling with the Horrells during the San Augustin attack.[12]

Discouraged by these tragedies, and with Benedict Horrell having died at a place and time unknown but before 1869, the surviving family members turned back toward Texas, traveling in two parties. Along the way, they encountered their old Lampasas County neighbor John Nichols on March 27, 1869, according to an interview Nichols gave late in life.[13]

Life was not any easier when the Horrells arrived back in Lampasas County. The Indian raids that prompted their departure had only worsened. Young Prince Ryan had been killed while searching the countryside for a cow, practically within sight of Lampasas, a mere prelude to more extensive attacks that began some two years later. Although unrecognized or perhaps ignored at the time, the root cause of such raids was apparently the failure of the federal government to honor the Treaty of Medicine Lodge. The Lampasas area and indeed the whole region were under attack by 1870. Raiding Indians stole horses and killed settlers with such frequency that some speculated the Texas frontier would have to be abandoned.[14] Circumstances were so dire that state authorities organized and armed militias called "Minute Men."[15]

Gen. William Tecumseh Sherman saw the seriousness of the situation personally during an investigation of allegations against Fort Sill Apaches and other Indians conducted in May 1871. Sherman led a detachment of some twenty soldiers from San Antonio on a tour of Texas forts, finally arriving at Fort Richardson on May 17 without sighting a single brave, although the Indians had certainly observed him. Unbeknownst to the general, a large war party of Kiowa, Comanche, Apache, Arapaho, and Cheyenne from Fort Sill had allowed the Sherman contingent to pass, then pounced on a wagon traveling the Butterfield mail route, killing wagon master Henry Warren and six of his drivers. Thomas Brazeal alone made his way to Fort Richardson, where he reported the massacre to Sherman. The tribal leadership at Fort Sill was arrested, marking the end of the relatively passive federal management of Indian agencies implemented by Quaker agents in the Texas-Indian Territory region. The Red River War and Battle of Palo Duro Canyon stopped Indian raids in Texas altogether by 1875.[16]

The Horrells had largely recovered from the ill-fated California expedition by 1872. Benjamin married that year, while two more children were born into his brothers' families.[17] Tom, Mart, Merritt, and Ben all joined the newly organized Minute Men. Although Tom was elected corporal, their twenty-man contingent soon disbanded without having seen action.[18]

A pecking order had emerged among the Horrell brothers. Twenty-two-year-old Tom was a natural leader and diplomat of sorts, according to the later recollections of their neighbor John Nichols. While Tom eclipsed his older brother Sam, Nichols described Mart as a round-shouldered troublemaker. Merritt was the youngest brother and apparently treated accordingly.

None of the brothers gambled, but all were somewhat serious drinkers, often described as fair headed with florid complexions, perhaps as a consequence of binge drinking.[19] Drunk or sober, they were always loaded for bear. Soon after the Horrells returned to the Lampasas area, rumors of their wide loop for stray cattle—that is to say, rustling—began to emerge. Perhaps this resulted from their friendship with the Short brothers.[20]

Marcus (Mark) Short and his brother George Washington (Wash) Short were born in Missouri and then migrated with their parents to Coffee County, Texas, in about 1850. They were no apparent relation to the notorious gunfighter Luke Short, but on Tuesday, January 14, 1873, they acted as if they might have been his brothers.

The Shorts created such a disturbance at Schoot's Saloon in Lampasas County that presiding judge W. A. Blackburn sent forty-year-old Sheriff Shadrach T. "Shade" Denson to arrest Mark. Denson, a Confederate veteran who served in Forney's Brigade, was elected sheriff in December 1869. As he headed to the saloon, he undoubtedly knew that he had trouble on his hands. His worst fears were realized when Mark began a scuffle that only ended when either Mark himself or his brother Wash shot Denson in the side, causing a wound that years later may have contributed to his death.[21]

Drunk or sober, Tom, Mart, and Ben Horrell then made two spur-of-the-moment decisions that changed their lives forever. When Thomas Sparks tried to help his brother-in-law the sheriff, the Horrells blocked his path. Worse still,

Shadrach T. Denson, sheriff of Lampasas County 1869-73. (*Courtesy of Jeff Jackson*)

after Sparks organized a posse, the brothers stopped and threatened the pursuers as the Shorts escaped to another county.[22]

Mark was arrested about three years later and returned to Lampasas, where he made bail. Sheriff Denson's son Sam soon found him. "You are my meat!" young Sam Denson exclaimed, just before he pumped three rounds into the suspect. The sheriff's son escaped to Montana, where he changed his name and lived peaceably for nineteen years. Finally in 1892, the year of his father's death, Sam returned to Lampasas and was acquitted of all charges.[23]

The 1873 Denson shooting did not please certain Lampasas city fathers, who promptly sought the assistance of Governor Davis and offered a $250 reward ($4,000 today).[24] Davis initially responded by extending the terms of an 1871 act forbidding the use of firearms by the citizens of certain counties, including Lampasas. The governor also sent State Police sergeant J. M. Redmon, who found the Lampasas citizenry less than cooperative.[25] Justice of the Peace Thomas Pratt, one of the individuals who petitioned the governor, later reported to Texas adjutant general F. L. Britton that no Lampasas citizen would make any complaint against the troublemakers, apparently for fear of their personal safety. Sergeant Redmon was left to do the heavy lifting alone.[26]

Although the citizenry complied with the firearms ban during the daytime, nights in old Lampasas were far less peaceful. Redmon suspected that once he left, a wave of lawlessness would return to Lampasas unless martial law was imposed.[27] He also reported that the Short brothers were not to be found, at least by the State Police. Worse still, other outlaws reportedly lurked in the area, notably including Wild Bill Longley, Richard "Dick" Dublin (Doublin), and Ace Langford, Jr.[28]

Britton turned next to State Police captain Thomas G.

Williams, who was sent to Lampasas with a detachment of only four men. Missouri-born Williams had arrived in Texas some twenty-five years earlier with his family and then served in the Unionist First Texas Cavalry under the direct command of Edmund J. Davis.

During the seventy-six-mile, two-day ride from Austin to Lampasas, the small detachment encountered a freighter, later identified as either Bill Means or Telford "Snap" Bean, both early Lampasas settlers.[29] Williams had been drinking and told the man he was on his way to "clean up those damn Horrell boys." Indeed.

Most probably, Williams and his small force arrived at Lampasas on Friday, March 14, 1873, just in time to observe Horrell associate Bill Bowen stride into Jerry Scott's Saloon on Third Street. Bowen was armed with a six-shooter.

Perhaps still in his cups, Williams strode into the unofficial Horrell headquarters with three unprepared men and a surly attitude. Local authorities had no idea Williams had arrived, but the Horrells were ready for him:

> Mart, Tom and Merritt Horrell, with some ten or fifteen cowmen, were in the saloon drinking, playing billiards, and having a good time generally. One man was picking a banjo and another playing a fiddle. Captain Williams, an exceedingly brave but unwise man, took in the situation at a glance as he walked up to the bar and called for drinks.
>
> He turned to Bill Bowen, a brother-in-law to Merritt Horrell, and said, "I believe you have a six-shooter. I arrest you."
>
> "Bill, you have done nothing and need not be arrested if you don't want to," interrupted Mart Horrell.
>
> Like a flash of lightning, Captain Williams pulled his pistol and fired on Mart Horrell, wounding him badly. The Horrell boys drew their guns and began to fight. Captain Williams and one of his men, Dr. Daniels, were shot down in the saloon. [Wesley] Cherry was killed just outside the

door, and Andrew Melville was fatally wounded as he was trying to escape. He reached the old Huling Hotel, where he died later.

Another account reported that Williams entered Lampasas with seven men and attempted to wrest a pistol away from Bowen, then was shot from behind by eight to ten men.[31] Irrespective of the exact details, Captain Williams and State Police privates Wesley Cherry and T. M. Daniels were riddled with bullets that day and died where they fell. Melville died on April 10. Tom, Mart, and Merritt Horrell, as well as feudists Ben Turner, Joe Bolden, Joe (Allen) Whitcraft, Jim Grizell, Jerry Scott, Billie Gray, and Bill Bowen, were identified as the killers the following day at an inquest. On March 25, 1873, the *San Antonio Daily Herald* reported that Adjutant General Britton expanded the suspect list to include Ben Horrell, Mark Short and his brother Wash, Jim Jenkins, Sam Sneed, and his brother Billy Sneed.

Once again aroused, however temporarily, the Lampasas citizenry organized three posses to scour four counties over a five-day period, only to find four suspects about March 20 back in Lampasas, where the posses started. Mart Horrell, Jerry Scott, Jim Grizell, and Allen Whitcraft were promptly quartered at Austin in the Travis County jail, then transferred to Georgetown, the county seat of Williamson County, about twenty-five miles north of Austin.[32]

The quartet languished there, comforted only by occasional visits from Mart's wife, who treated the injury her husband suffered during the battle of Scott's Saloon. Spring brought the usual stirrings of new life, as well as a howling mob of some thirty Horrellians who arrived at Georgetown near the witching hour on Friday, May 2. Their assurances that no one would be harmed were punctuated with intermittent gunfire aimed at the Williamson County jailers.

The turnkeys quickly ran out of ammunition, enabling Bill Bowen to free the prisoners. After a few hours of freedom, the Horrells and their closest associates realized that they faced a dilemma. Unable to show their faces back in Lampasas anytime soon, Tom, Mart, and their followers under indictment planned yet another trip west. They made arrangements to sell their surplus cattle to the cattle firm of Cooksey and Clayton, in Coleman County.

Sheriff Denson never fully recovered from his injuries at the hands of Horrell associate Mark Short, but he was back on duty. Though the Horrells were fugitives, they notified Sheriff Denson of their imminent departure, even giving him their probable route through Russell Gap. Denson made no effort to stop them, perhaps due to timidity.

Former Cooksey and Clayton employee and future Texas Ranger James B. Gillett was present when the Horrells delivered part of their herd to a cow camp on Horse Creek. Years later, he recalled that the brothers and their associates made no effort whatsoever to conceal their identity, and they carried Winchesters with them at all times.[33]

Curiously, John Nichols, the neighbor the Horrells met on the trail as they traveled east to Texas about four years earlier, now encountered them on the trail again. This time he met them at San Angelo, as they moved west toward Lincoln County, New Mexico, according to an interview Nichols gave in 1927.[34]

The Horrell party wasted no time moving bag and baggage up the Pecos River, pushing some one thousand cattle along the trail. Traveler's rest was found at Seven Rivers, a small community in present-day Eddy County, New Mexico, largely populated by Texans. The women and children recuperated from the trail drive as the men pushed ahead another 114 fourteen miles into Lincoln, the seat of the identically named county, arriving in May 1873.[35]

The Horrells soon found a favorable ranching prospect.

Texan Heiskell Jones and his Prussian-born, Irish-surnamed partner Frank Regan conveyed them a quitclaim deed to a claim at the mouth of Eagle Creek on the Ruidoso, according to one tradition. The Horrells bought necessary provisions from L. G. Murphy and Company in Lincoln on credit, and then settled in.

Troubles soon found them once again. The Lincoln County conflagration known to history as the Horrell War was not really started by that clan, but they certainly helped finish it. Many of the participants were the same individuals involved in the Lincoln County War, which propelled Billy the Kid to national notoriety only a few years later.

About two years before the Horrells arrived, a simmering conflict between Lincoln County Hispanics and Anglos boiled over into an August 1871 brawl at La Mesilla, in which several participants were killed. Several days later, an Anglo sawmill owner at South Fork notified Probate Judge Lawrence "Larry" Murphy that Alcalde (Mayor) Perfecto Armijo had gathered about him some fifty outsiders to vote illicitly in Tularosa on September 4.

Bloodletting was somehow avoided through negotiations, at least until February 1873, when two Hispanic cowboys left the John N. Copeland ranch near Fort Stanton, carrying away two horses and miscellaneous gear and household effects. A new saddle owned by Copeland's young Irish neighbor, John H. Riley, also disappeared.

Riley and Copeland quickly captured one thief. After some intense questioning, the bandit revealed that his accomplice was on the road to Tularosa. After Copeland found and killed the fleeing vaquero, all attention turned to the first prisoner. Since Lincoln was about fifty miles away, Copeland and Riley chose to deliver the surviving thief to Fort Stanton, about seven miles to the east. To nobody's surprise, the suspect darted into some scrub brush along the trail and was killed for his trouble, at least according to the participants.[36]

Riley and Copeland dutifully reported the incident to Riley's business partner, Lincoln County probate judge Larry Murphy. When Copeland and Riley refused to be arrested and simply left town, Juan Patron, Murphy's outraged probate clerk, promptly raised a Hispanic posse.[37]

Copeland was not available to greet these visitors the next morning, but Johnny Riley was caught unarmed. After some prompting, he led the posse to his ranch nearby for a hearty supper, with Riley himself no doubt scheduled to provide an evening's entertainment of a most deadly nature.

After Copeland finally returned to his ranch, the entire gang rode to the spot where the dead bandit basked in the sun, surrounded by predators, both animal and human.

"You shooty dat man?" hard-case Lucas Gallegos inquired, pointing his cocked pistol into Johnny Riley's ear for dramatic effect. While the crowd pondered that inarticulate yet critical question, a cavalry detachment from nearby Fort Stanton happened by, including the improbably named Lt. Argalus G. Hennessey. Posse leader Juan Patron now found himself under guard, as he and his minions were unceremoniously trundled off to Fort Stanton as prisoners.

Conveniently enough for Riley, fellow Hibernian William Brady, the past and future sheriff of Lincoln County, was temporarily ensconced there as the U.S. commissioner (modern term: U.S. magistrate). Brady's examination of the prisoners, such as it was, soon resulted in the release of Riley and Copeland.

The rest were not so lucky. The entire duly authorized posse was promptly reclassified as a mob of rioters and then jailed without bond, according to the February 19, 1873, edition of the *Santa Fe New Mexican*. Thus was the stage set for the Lincoln County water-rights conflict between Anglos and Hispanics, which erupted just as the Horrells arrived from Lampasas, Texas.

The Horrell War

On May 31, 1873, just after the Horrells arrived in Lincoln County, George W. Nesmith, a business partner of mill owner and former dentist J. H. Blazer, reported to the *Las Cruces Borderer* that about a week before, some thirty-five Hispanics had destroyed certain dams and ditches in Tularosa Canyon, then announced they would do so again if necessary.

The Anglos, often described generically by their opponents as "Texans," promptly attempted to repair one of the dams but were fired upon by a group of Hispanics. In a separate but related incident, a Lieutenant Wilkinson, who had been dispatched from Fort Stanton when the trouble began, exchanged gunfire with thirty-five to forty Hispanics, killing one about a mile from Tularosa. The next day, a delegation led by a local priest informed Wilkinson that he would not be permitted to enter Tularosa. Wilkinson did just that, leading his troops to the nearby Indian agency, where the soldiers spent the night.[38]

Given these ongoing difficulties, the indigenous population did not exactly welcome the Horrell family back to New Mexico Territory with a fiesta. Local Hispanics almost robbed the Horrells of their cattle-sale proceeds shortly after their arrival in May 1873, or so the Texans claimed. Local Hispanics later denied this, asserting with more credibility that the Horrells had enthusiastically joined the ongoing war over water rights by killing one of their number who was attempting to sabotage a gringo-created ditch, diverting water to which the earlier Hispanic settlers considered themselves entitled.[39]

Throughout the year, longstanding conflicts continued to simmer between the Texans and local Hispanics, who dominated governmental affairs with the assistance of several intermarried Anglo citizens. Ben Horrell discovered this the hard way on Monday, December 1, 1873, when he led four associates into Lincoln to pick up mail and raise a little hell. Ben was accompanied by former Lincoln County sheriff D. C. Warner, Texas Jack "Jackito" Gylam, Zacharias Crompton, and Jerry Scott, former proprietor of Scott's Saloon in Lampasas.[40]

First, the Horrell party made a boisterous and noisy entrance at the residence of John Bolten, who had been appointed Lincoln postmaster about a month earlier. Since his wife was lying ill in an adjoining room, he asked them to quiet down and they did so, but not for long. The revelers learned that a party was being held nearby and decided to attend, although their invitations had been lost or perhaps simply overlooked. Once again, the gang made a dramatic entrance, using gunfire with great effect. This drew the wary attention of town constable Juan Martin, who somehow managed to disarm them.

Less than an hour later, Ben Horrell and associates were rearmed and reinvigorated. The belligerents apparently believed that their original weaponry was at the residence of Probate Judge Jacinto Gonzales and started in that direction. Soon, D. C. Warner had a better idea. He suggested that the entire party go to a local bordello apparently operated by his sister-in-law. Then the real trouble began.

Constable Martin gathered a posse of four or five men, including William Warnick, a Missourian who acted as interpreter, at least until the pistols began to do the talking. Martin expressed his concerns to the Texans and was then dropped by a gunshot wound inflicted by D. C. Warner, or perhaps Ben Horrell himself. Martin was hardly conciliatory. He sent word to the mob surrounding the house of joy to "kill them all." And so they did, with two exceptions, although the manner and order in which the Horrell factionists were killed is a matter of dispute to this day. We only know for certain that Crompton and Scott were left alive.

According to a report submitted to the governor the next day, the posse opened fire on the Horrell party, killing three of the amigos immediately. A more dramatic and improbable version of events recounted in the December 20, 1873, edition of the *Silver City Mining Life* stated that Gylam and Horrell managed to escape from the bordello and almost crossed the Rio Bonito but could go no further due to their injuries. Gylam died then and there, with some assistance from the posse, which shot him ten more times for good measure after he surrendered. Ben Horrell was also finished off there, if yet another version is to be believed.[41] Particulars aside, yet another Horrell was dead in New Mexico, as were two family retainers.

Frank Coe saw conspiracy in this episode fifty-four years later, when he said that Ben Horrell and his associates were killed on orders of "the House," a mercantile establishment owned by wily Irishman Larry Murphy and his partner, Stuttgart, Germany, native Emil Fritz. Coe believed that Murphy's objective was to force the Horrells to abandon their herd, which could then be easily acquired, presumably to settle the Horrell debt to the House for provisions, a device Murphy had evidently used before.[42] Several years later, the House precipitated the Lincoln County War, in which William H. Bonney, known to history as Billy the Kid, became the most famous participant.

Still, the Horrells found plenty of trouble in Lincoln County without any help from Larry Murphy after their brother Ben Horrell was killed. Justice of the Peace Gutierrez had requested a detachment of troops from Fort Stanton immediately after the fatal conflict between Juan Martin and Ben Horrell, with good reason. On December 2,

Tom and Mart Horrell rode into Lincoln to retrieve Ben's body and demand the arrest of those who killed him. The authorities promptly told them that Ben and his gang were killed "resisting arrest."[43] The surviving brothers apparently had a different theory. Soon, two Hispanics were found shot to death in a pasture near the Horrell ranch, according to the December 27, 1873, edition of the *Tucson Citizen,* and a Horrell associate was observed riding near the death scene. The forces opposing the Horrells soon developed plans of their own.

On Friday, December 5, 1873, Alexander "Ham" Mills was appointed sheriff of Lincoln County by Probate Judge Larry Murphy. Mills was married to a Hispanic. Soon, the new sheriff formed a forty-man posse and rode toward the Horrell ranch at the mouth of the Ruidoso. The posse was well armed but somehow forgot to bring arrest warrants.

When confronted with this crew, the Horrells quickly noted that hard-case Juan Gonzalez appeared to be the real leader of the posse, and they declined to be arrested. A Fort Stanton contingent led by Capt. Chambers McKibbin watched these spirited discussions from a campsite at the mouth of Eagle Creek but did not intervene.

This stalemate was followed by about two weeks of peace, which proved to be only the calm before the storm. On Saturday, December 20, 1873, the surviving brothers crashed yet another party—this time a wedding *baile* in Lincoln.[44] Sam, Merritt, and Mart were accompanied by Zach Crompton, former saloonkeeper Jerry Scott, and new recruits Robert Honeycutt, C. W. King, James McLaine, and John Wilson, apparently a soldier stationed at Fort Stanton. The gang shot the lights out and then targeted anything that moved inside the building. Court clerk Juan Patron was apparently on a death list but not present. However, his father, Isidro, was among four Hispanic men killed and two Hispanic women injured.[45] After the melee, many of

Lincoln's citizens huddled together in the *torre* (tower) that had been built years before as "last stand" protection from area Indians.

Bereaved though he was, Juan Patron traveled to Santa Fe the next day and requested assistance from the territorial governor. A detachment of soldiers soon arrived in Lincoln, solely to serve as a deterrent. Active pursuit of the Horrells did not begin until January 1874, when $100 rewards were placed on the heads of Sam, Tom, Merritt, Zach Crompton, and Jerry Scott.[46] A super-posse of some sixty men led by Sheriff Ham Mills appeared at the Horrell ranch house on Tuesday, January 20, to arrest the brothers. Unable to do so, they shot or drove off all the horses they could find, prompting the Horrells to relocate their families that very evening.

The women and children were moved south to the Robert Casey ranch, according to the memoirs of Casey's daughter, Lily.[47] The Horrells then returned to their ranch and resumed operations, but soon decided that continuing was just too dangerous. After relocating their families even farther south, to Roswell, they determined to wreak revenge against the Lincoln population in general and Frank Regan in particular. Regan, it will be recalled, was the Prussian-born clerk who sold the Ruidoso ranch to the Horrells, apparently conveying a deed of questionable provenance. In early 1874, Regan simply disappeared under mysterious circumstances.[48]

After Regan was apparently dealt with, more invective was directed at local Hispanics, prompted in part by the gunpoint confiscation of Horrell household goods and hogs from Heiskell Jones and others between the Horrell ranch and the Missouri Bottom.[49]

The Horrells now began preparing in earnest for a return to Texas. Charles Miller bought the Horrell livestock, consisting of 1,098 cattle, four yoke of oxen, and 13 horses, on January 19 for about $10,000 ($163,000 today). Title to the livestock was soon transferred to Murphy associate Jimmy Dolan.[50] A day or two later, the Grim Reaper struck the Horrell faction again, when Ben C. Turner was ambushed while trying to collect on some corn he had previously bartered to a member of the Hispanic community at Picacho.[51]

Turner was shot out of the saddle, perhaps by local tough Martin Chavez, according to one source.[52] Another story tells that he had handled the recent cattle sale for the Horrells, and his life was threatened shortly thereafter.[53]

This was all reported to Major Price, who had arrived at Fort Stanton on Friday, January 23, 1874, in order to deter the violence that had overwhelmed Lincoln County. Two days later, according to Price, the Sheriff Ham Mills posse returned to Lincoln without any prisoners. Soon, Jimmy Dolan raised another posse to arrest the Horrells at their own ranch.[54]

The Dolan posse burned down the Horrell ranch house on January 25. They returned to Lincoln the next evening with the remaining Horrell crops and goods in hand, ready for a celebration, in which a few posse members were injured.[55]

Although reports of the time are confusing and contradictory, by January 30 the Horrells had apparently learned of the arson at their place on the Ruidoso and were returning for a clash with the Lincoln crowd. The Horrells sent a message ahead, calling out eight adherents of Murphy and Dolan, many of whom were Hispanics or intermarried with them.[56]

Three Horrell factionists, often identified as Edward "Little" Hart, Tom Keenan, and C. W. King, exacted revenge before they had even arrived back in Lincoln. The trio called Sheriff Ham Mills' brother-in-law Joe Haskins out of his ranch house adjoining the Robert Casey place and mortally ventilated him, perhaps suspecting him in the deaths of Ben Horrell, Texas Jack Gylam, or Ben C. Turner.[57] Now the Horrell gang divided into two forces. The first group killed five Hispanic freighters they did not even know about fifteen miles from Roswell, sparing only Anglo George Kimbrell.[58] Meanwhile, Horrell retainers Zach Crompton, Bill Applegate, Edward "Little" Hart, and a Mr. Still stole all of Sheriff Mills' stock, robbed Bob Beckwith of his horse and saddle, then took eight horses from Beckwith's Seven Rivers Ranch.[59] While the violence continued, Probate Judge Murphy offered the Horrells an acquittal if they would submit to civil authorities.[60] One military report also indicates that the Horrells recruited and led fifty to seventy Texans on an expedition to Lincoln, intent on killing everyone there. The Horrells had second thoughts and led the small army away from town to avoid a general massacre, or so the story goes. An even more dramatic version of events relates that the destruction of Lincoln was only averted when Larry Murphy sent the Horrells his Masonic ring with a message urging his fellow Masons to withdraw.[61]

Although the exact sequence of events is garbled, the Horrell gang clearly robbed one ranch too many before starting for Texas. Crompton, Applegate, Hart, and Still stole a racehorse from a ranch owned by Aaron O. Wilburn and Van C. Smith, near Roswell. A Wilburn-Smith posse tracked them all the way to a point near Hueco Tanks, about thirty miles east of El Paso, where hollows formed in rocks provided a natural watering place. When this quartet was surprised by the posse early one morning on or about February 18, Crompton and Still were killed, along with five Hispanic members of the posse.[62] Hart and Applegate were reportedly chased into Mexico.[63]

The main Horrell party was back in Lampasas by March 5, 1874, relating stories of their pursuit by the Lincoln County posse and even Indians.[64] However, their return to Texas had not been a surprise to the Lampasians. Arrest warrants for Tom, Merritt, and the other surviving participants of the Captain Williams shootout in Lampasas the prior year had been issued the week before the Horrell party even arrived.[65] The family clearly had trouble ahead, but they also left trouble behind them in Lincoln County, including indictments and warrants against the surviving Horrell brothers, Crompton (now dead), C. W. King, Jerry Scott, and many, many others.[66]

Four years later, their erstwhile Lincoln County opponent Juan Patron wrote that the pursuit of the Horrells had been instigated by Dolan and Murphy, who eventually acquired the stock, crops, and even the questionable land title formerly owned by the Horrell brothers.[67]

The Horrells had barely touched Lampasas County soil when they were confronted by a Texas posse led by newly elected sheriff Albertus Sweet, who captured Jerry Scott and Rufus Overstreet. Scott was shot through the lung. Although also wounded, Merritt escaped, at least for the time being.[68]

While the clan hid in the brush, they considered their options, particularly the possibility of surrendering to the authorities, now that the federally appointed Reconstruction governor had been replaced by popular election and the State Police had been disbanded. Local men of influence convinced them to surrender and face the murder charges stemming from the 1873 shootout with Captain Williams and his three State Police minions. When the preliminary hearing was concluded September 14, 1874, the Horrells were free as air on bonds of $10,000 each.[69] Mart, Merritt, and Tom were reportedly acquitted in October 1876, by a jury that did not even bother to use the deliberation room.[70]

The Horrells settled in and around Lampasas and then reentered the cattle business just as the depression known as the Panic of 1873 spread to Texas. The Panic had begun

with the September 14, 1873, collapse of the Jay Cooke and
Company bank in Philadelphia. The resulting 1874 slump
in the cattle market reduced the demand for beef by about
50 percent, causing hard times across the Lone Star State.
Tom, Mart, and Merritt survived these bad times, perhaps
supplementing their herd by swinging a "wide loop" to
retrieve lost cattle and strays.[71]

Birth of a Feud

According to some, the Horrells came into conflict with
Pink Higgins soon after their return from Lincoln County,
New Mexico Territory. Local stories tell that Pink killed two
Horrell employees caught rustling cattle. First, Zeke Terrell
had been caught butchering a Higgins steer. Higgins shot
Terrell, stuffed him inside the dead animal, then reported
the incident to the local sheriff as a birth miracle, or so the
story goes.[72] Higgins also supposedly killed Ike Lantier for
rustling at a watering hole. Some writers indicate that these
two incidents may indeed have taken place, but perhaps
later, when Higgins was working as a range detective.[73]

The next year, 1875, saw improved Texas cattle markets
and the establishment of a new trail north to Dodge City,
Kansas.[74] Although Lampasians were still without a bank,
they could at least drown their sorrows at any of the many
saloons that graced the town. Jerry Scott had recuperated
sufficiently from his wound to reestablish himself in the
saloon business. His place provided the backdrop for yet
another famous gunfight.

Although there is apparently no reliable record of
precisely when the Horrells first began to feud with Pink
Higgins over the ownership of cattle, on May 12, 1876,
Higgins found a yearling that he believed Merritt Horrell
had cut out from his herd on the Lampasas town square

with other cattle bound for the Jim Grizell meat market. Higgins swore out a warrant for Merritt's arrest, only to see the jury bring in a verdict of "not guilty" in the face of overwhelming evidence. Higgins then warned Merritt that the next time such a thing happened, he would resort to the Winchester rather than the courts.[75] Such a threat should not have been taken lightly by anyone who knew anything about Pink Higgins' ingrained hatred for cattle rustlers and horse thieves.

John Calhoun Pinckney "Pink" Higgins was the second child of the John Holcomb Higgins family, born Friday, March 28, 1851, in Macon, Georgia. He was named for South Carolina senator John C. Calhoun and the politically prominent Pinckney family of the same state.[76] His Higgins ancestors emigrated from Ireland to Maryland and at some point shed their Catholic identity, perhaps as an astute economic choice that was hardly unusual. Thomas Beer once commented on this tendency among some of the early Irish pioneers: "They melted easily into the westward movements . . . shedding their habits from prairie to prairie so that families named O'Donnell, Connor and Delehanty are now discovered drowsing in Protestant pews of Texas and Kansas."[77]

Pink's grandfather John migrated from Mississippi to northern Georgia as a missionary to the Cherokee Nation. He married a Cherokee chief's daughter, who took the name Mary Elizabeth, according to family stories. Pink's own father, John Holcomb Higgins, was born in 1823 and migrated with his wife, Hester West Higgins, from Georgia to Texas, probably by 1854, since two more children were born there. The Higginses had journeyed to Austin by wagon train, then acquired land in Travis County before moving on to northern Lampasas County in 1857. Two years later, they retreated with many others in the face of increasingly persistent Comanche raids, settling two counties to the east in Bell County, according to Nichols' interview.

The Higgins family returned to Lampasas County in early 1862, with the hope that the Comanche raids had subsided. They had not. The withdrawal of the United States Army and virtually wholesale transfer of the Texas Rangers into the Confederate army did not go unnoticed. The Comanche and other tribes were apparently quite aware that the Confederacy was unable to replace the Federal troops man for man, since the raids only intensified.[78]

Pink was too young to participate in the Civil War but joined informal pursuits of Comanche raiders, perhaps as early as 1868. He also joined the Ku Klux Klan, which was initially organized to resist Federal authorities and their local supporters. Later, Pink became part of the Law and Order League,[79] seen by some contemporaries as an "upscale" version of the Ku Klux Klan. His association with the League was the beginning of his lifelong campaign against rustlers. One unpublished manuscript relates that, in 1869, Pink joined a Law and Order League posse that pursued and captured a horse thief. As Higgins adjusted the noose that would send the rustler into the next world, the man supposedly acknowledged that he was going to hell and then kicked the horse out from underneath himself, since he said he wanted to be there in time to get a partner for the first dance.[80]

Higgins also found time for several cattle drives. As a seventeen-year-old, he participated in one such drive through New Mexico and Colorado into Wyoming. Later he worked on drives to Dodge City, Kansas City, and elsewhere. During these drives, he worked with several young men who would later become members of the Higgins faction after the 1876 quarrel over ownership of the calf tethered in the Lampasas town square morphed into the Horrell-Higgins feud. Bob Mitchell was a neighbor who rode with Pink on an 1868 trail drive to Montana. Through Mitchell, Higgins also met his ham-handed, six-foot-three-inch future ally, W. R. "Bill" Wren.[81]

After Merritt Horrell stole and slaughtered a Higgins calf in May 1876, without legal repercussions, he must have considered himself bullet proof, because he sold several head of Higgins cattle to Alex Northington on Saturday, January 20, 1877. When Northington discovered this, he prudently notified Higgins. Higgins promptly retrieved his cattle and tethered them elsewhere in Lampasas, leaving Merritt word as to where they could be found if Merritt believed he had better title.[82]

Higgins' temper apparently simmered over the weekend, because on Monday he rode into Lampasas with Sam Hess and Bob Mitchell and then strode into Jerry Scott's Saloon, where Captain Williams and his retainers were killed only four years before.[83] One apparent eyewitness later related that Higgins simply walked up to Merritt, said, "Mr. Horrell, this is to settle some cow business," and started shooting.[84] A report from the *Lampasas Dispatch,* reprinted in the *Galveston News,* January 30, 1877, indicated that Higgins shot Horrell four times with a Winchester. Merritt died on the spot without saying a word.

Tom was the second Horrell surprised by Pink Higgins that day. After killing Merritt, Higgins and his associates rode toward Tom's place on Mesquite Creek to conclude all family business, only to meet their unarmed victim on the road. One of the less reflective Higgins feudists suggested that Horrell should be killed right then and there. However, Bob Mitchell persuaded the others that killing an unarmed man would be a breach of feud etiquette. Thus, the leader of the Horrell faction was released unharmed to fight another day.[85]

Soon, the surviving Horrells convinced Deputy Sheriffs Doolittle and Walker to organize a posse. Although Higgins himself escaped, four alleged accomplices were jailed,[86] even as most of the Lampasas citizenry began to align itself with one faction or another. The initial Higgins recruits were hardly a surprise to anyone. Bill Wren, destined to become sheriff of Lampasas County sixteen years later, promptly joined, along with Bob Mitchell, now Pink's brother-in-law. The Horrells took a different approach. They established headquarters at Sulphur Springs, about six miles east of Lampasas, then gathered about them dependable neighbors and reputed outlaws, according to the recollections of one area resident interviewed late in life.[87]

Both sides remained quiet during the next couple of months, at least as far as the historical record is concerned. Sheriff Sweet immediately solicited the assistance of the Texas Rangers in the person of Capt. John C. Sparks, who, along with sixteen men of Company C, helped in an unsuccessful search for Higgins.

The Higgins faction was quiet for over sixty days but was ready to strike again on March 26, 1877, as Tom and Mart Horrell rode toward town to attend a court hearing. When the pair stopped to water their horses at a small creek about five miles east of Lampasas sometime before ten o'clock, the two Horrells were ambushed by Pink Higgins, Bill Wren, Bob Mitchell, and perhaps Bill Tinker, in an explosion of gunfire from nearby trees. The first volley injured both men and killed Mart's horse. Mart vigorously returned fire and then managed to mount Tom's horse—along with Tom himself—and escape.[88]

Ironically, Judge W. A. Blackburn had anticipated trouble and arranged for a complement of Texas Rangers to be on hand for the court hearing. Mart left Tom at a house near the creek, then rode into town for help. Captain Sparks raised a posse himself, after Sheriff Sweet insisted he had insufficient staff even to provide guides.

Tinker was arrested and Wren surrendered voluntarily, but only after Tinker was released on alibi.[89] After Bill Wren was also released, Bob Mitchell and even Pink himself surrendered on April 22, 1877, to answer charges in the

Merritt Horrell killing, posting a $10,000 bond ($163,000 today).[90] No one was ever tried, perhaps in part because the courthouse somehow caught fire on June 4 and all records within were burned. While the Higgins forces arguably had more reason to do so, given recent events, Horrell factionists John Dixon, Tom Bowen, and two Stanley brothers were the rumored arsonists.[91]

According to a newspaper account published twelve years later, a small number of men from each faction collided at School Creek, near the Higgins-Mitchell stronghold, on May 31, but no serious damage was done to any of the feudists, other than the loss of some personal effects by the Higgins crowd.[92]

On June 7, 1877, the feud spilled into Lampasas itself, during a two-hour running gun battle. That morning at about ten, a Higgins-faction quartet rode down Live Oak Street right into the three surviving Horrell brothers. Mart, Sam, and Tom were backed by at least five of their cadre.

North side of the town square in Lampasas, Texas, ca. 1880. The courtroom and district clerk's office were located on the second floor. The building caught fire on June 4, 1877. *(Courtesy of Jeff Jackson)*

"Over yonder comes the Higginses," yelled Tom, warning his crew in language that might have been spoken on the remotest Appalachian mountaintop, just before all hell broke loose. Higgins and his brother-in-law Ben Terry were riding behind Bob Mitchell and Bill Wren when the shooting began. Mitchell dismounted and promptly started a duel with Tom Horrell, whose life he had saved only a few months before. Tom had the practical advantage, using the corner of Mellon's store as cover. Neither duelist was injured, but future sheriff Bill Wren was not as lucky. He started toward Bob Mitchell's position to get in the fight, but was shot in the thigh (or buttocks) and put out of action. Wren climbed to the second floor of the Yates and Brown store, where he sporadically fired his Winchester at the Horrells from a window.[93]

Mitchell's thirty-four-year-old brother, Frank, had no earlier part in the feud and picked a bad time to join up. Seeing his brother under fire, Frank threw down some flour he had been loading in a wagon, borrowed a six-shooter from Bob, then mortally wounded hard-case Jim Buck Miller (alias Jim Buck Waldrup, alias Jim Buck Palmer) just before Miller or Mart Horrell mortally wounded him.[94]

While the battle roared, Higgins galloped away for reinforcements waiting for him about a mile outside of town. Within half an hour or less, he returned with twelve to thirty-five men.

The surviving Horrell factionists passed through Fulton and Townsen's Store and then ran down an alley to a seemingly impregnable building under construction.[95] The Higginses settled in for a half-hour sniping duel. However, at about noon, a delegation of Lampasas citizenry confronted both factions and asked them to kindly take their gunfight elsewhere.[96] Instead, the Higginses simply left town, even as the Horrell faction members were arrested, though promptly released.[97]

Maj. John B. Jones, commanding officer of the Texas Ranger Frontier Battalion, visited Lampasas on June 28, 1877. He advised the adjutant general that even though bonds had been posted by the principal feudists, Jones intended to try a new approach to resolving the conflict.[98] Further developments in late July only increased his determination. On July 24 or the next day, Higgins factionist Carson Graham was killed by persons unknown but presumed to be Horrellians.[99] Ranger chronicler James B. Gillett would relate that before dawn on July 27, Ranger sergeant N. O. Reynolds, known in later years as "the Intrepid," surrounded the Horrell stronghold at Sulphur Springs, then quietly moved his detachment inside the house as one or more Higginist guides rode away. Somehow all the Horrellians were arrested without a single injury. Reynolds accomplished this by assuring Mart Horrell that the prisoners would stay in the Ranger camp and not be turned over to the Lampasas County sheriff.[100]

Major Jones arranged for the prompt arrest of the leading Higgins factionists three days later and then negotiated a peace treaty of sorts between the two factions. He wrote elaborate, conciliatory letters confirming the deal, which the semi-literate leaders of each party dutifully signed.[101]

Sadly, the tranquility soon evaporated in the Texas sun. Sergeant Collins of Ranger Company C noted in correspondence dated April 9, 1878, that ill will between the Higgins and Horrell factionists had surfaced once again, prompted this time by court proceedings relating to the earlier killings.[102]

Worse still, the Horrells were soon accused of a new murder. On May 28, popular storekeeper James Theodore "Dorrie" Vaughn was shot down in cold blood about thirty miles west of Waco in Bosque County, by a gang that extracted $3,000 from his safe ($48,000 today). The incident had been observed by Vaughn's nephew and a store employee, who wounded one of the horses as the gang escaped. Waco detective W. H. Glenn trailed the wounded horse to the Mart Horrell ranch about sixty miles to the south, where he learned that the owner was Bill Crabtree, according to one report.[103] Another version of events related that Glenn found the dead horse about a mile from the robbery scene, removed a hoof, and then identified Crabtree by talking with area blacksmiths. More likely, Glenn simply focused on Crabtree based on his recent suspected criminal activities.[104]

On July 31, Glenn rode into Meridian, the seat of Bosque County, with Crabtree and an explanation of the Vaughn murder. Horrell riders Bill Crabtree, John Dixon, John Holt, and Tom Bowen had asked the old bachelor to open his store for a tobacco purchase, forced him to open the safe, and then killed him to eliminate a witness. This was reportedly at the direction of Tom Horrell, who had suggested that "dead men tell no tales." When Holt could not bring himself to kill the kindly old man, Tom Bowen did so without hesitation.[105]

The Crabtree arrest had been preceded by a false start with tragic consequences. Soon after the murder, a posse of some thirty to forty men was easily raised by Bosque County sheriff John C. Cureton, several Rangers, and Deputy U.S. Marshal John Stull of Coryell County. Stull already had a suspect in mind. Colorful, ill-tempered storekeeper Bill Babb of Babbsville, Texas, arrested on warrants sworn by Stull himself in mid-June, was hustled into Meridian with his son and three other suspects so quickly that Babb had to borrow meal money from the sheriff.[106] A sixty-day hitch without bond in the Bosque County jail apparently did nothing to improve Babb's disposition. He was released with the others on August 22, but later was unsuccessfully tried for the murder of his accuser, John Stull, who was shot down outside his own burning home on December 8,

1878. Babb later became a fast friend of Judge Roy Bean, "Law West of the Pecos,"[107] and died in 1911.

Tom and Mart Horrell were arrested on September 2, 1878, brought before Judge Blackburn in Lampasas, and then transported to Meridian, where they were held for trial without bail.[108] The gang members who carried out the Vaughn robbery with Crabtree reportedly fled the country, never to return.[109] Crabtree in the meantime completed his testimony against Tom and Mart Horrell on November 28 and was soon killed by persons unknown on the banks of the Bosque River. In the end, his reward for turning state's evidence was only the suit he was buried in.[110]

While the two Horrell brothers languished in the jail at Meridian, their enemies plotted. About five masked riders invaded the town on the evening of December 14, apparently to case the jail for a later visit. The next evening, when most of the town was at church services, Deputy Sheriff Whitworth was lured away from the jailhouse by a message falsely claiming that a member of his family was near death. Fifty or more masked men then gained admittance to the jail when one of them claimed to be Whitworth. Soon, the turnkeys faced armed men who were clearly not there for a social visit. Two brave jailers initially blocked the passage into the cell room, but the mob threatened to burn the entire building, and Tom and Mart awaited the inevitable.[111]

Apparently someone forgot the rope. While the brothers cringed in the darkness, a third prisoner was forced to hold up a lamp while the mob settled accounts then and there. Tom was game enough to dart about the cell, at least for a few seconds. Mart reportedly grasped and rattled the cell door, then defied the mob to the very end.[112] Afterward, the rabble fired a few shots into the night sky and galloped out of town.

An inquest report issued the next day revealed that Mart had been shot eleven times, while Tom died of five gunshot wounds.[113] The county purchased coffins for the Horrells and one Aran Jaba, another prisoner described in a separate but now unavailable inquest report as a vagrant, perhaps the prisoner who illuminated the death of the Horrells with a lamp.[114]

The authorities never identified the individuals who killed Tom and Mart Horrell. Perhaps they didn't even try. More Horrellians were killed within a few months. Mart Horrell's neighbor James Collier was hanged the evening of April 3, 1879, with a note pinned to his body warning that those who harbored thieves and murderers would end their days plagued with similar neck problems.[115] Three nights later, riders found Bill Van Winkle camped with three other men on Little Lucy Creek seven miles north of Lampasas and led him away to his death.[116] In late July, suspected rustlers and shirttail Horrell relatives Gus and Bill Kinchelo were found by unidentified riders at their stepfather's place near Higgins Gap, about seventeen miles from Lampasas. Their mother was a sister-in-law of Sam Horrell, but the brothers had apparently developed their own reputation for thievery. The brothers ran for their lives, but only Gus escaped.[117]

Young Sam Horrell now decided to seek opportunities elsewhere, in order to avoid a pending indictment for murder and other difficulties. He lived in Runnels County by 1880, but Rangers found him in July of that year at Camp Charlotte, about 115 miles southwest of Hackberry Springs. Initially, the Rangers jailed him at Austin for his own safety, but eventually he was returned to face the music at Lampasas. Sam made $3,000 bail and departed for points west.

Meanwhile, Pink Higgins continued to build his horse and cattle herds. While on the trail, he once saved a young cowhand from certain death at the hands of some crooked gamblers whose numbers the young man had reduced by one. Years later, Higgins encountered the grateful and now prosperous former desperado at a cattle sale in Muskogee, Oklahoma.[118]

Regrettably, life on the trail did little for Higgins' family life. He quietly divorced his first wife for infidelity, and then at age thirty-two married Lena Sweet, the fifteen-year-old daughter of the late Lampasas County sheriff. Albertus Sweet was first elected sheriff in November 1873.[119] Indicted with others for the Lampasas County courthouse burning, the sheriff was acquitted, only to be killed attempting to arrest a suspect in 1881.[120]

Higgins found himself on the wrong side of the law several times in the 1880s. In 1883 he was fined $100 ($2,000 today) for attempting to collect a $100 debt with too much enthusiasm. He also became involved in a border imbroglio concerning some questionably titled Mexican horses he bought with a $125 deposit. When his Mexican sellers refused to deliver the horses, Pink emphasized his unhappiness by killing one.

About seven years later, rustler-hating Pink Higgins found himself hoisted with his own petard. While trading cattle for horses, he sold a steer owned by Sam Jennings to a Lampasas meat market, inadvertently or otherwise. Following a twenty-two-month interlude at the Rusk Penitentiary, he returned to the cattle business, then moved his operations to Kent County in West Texas.[121]

The new Higgins place was between two acreages of the vast Spur Ranch, established by English interests in 1885. Pink signed on as a Spur Ranch range detective in 1899, joining Lampasas County native Bill Standifer on the trail chasing rustlers. Standifer had previously served as sheriff in both Crosby and Hartley counties. Their camaraderie was no doubt affected by Standifer's shirttail relationship with the Horrells. When Standifer lost his mother as a mere child, his father married a woman from the Horrell clan. Worse yet, Standifer's third wife hired Pink's son Cullen as her divorce attorney. These and other conflicts caused the Spur Ranch management to fire both men in August 1902, setting the stage for one of the last classic gunfights in West Texas.

Higgins was allowed one more month of employment than Standifer but was self-employed again by the first day of October. Although he suspected that Standifer was stalking him, Pink saddled his favorite horse that Wednesday morning for a trip into Clairemont. Soon he observed Standifer riding in the same direction and quickly looked for any sign that his foe wanted trouble. He did not have long to wait.

Standifer had only to lift his left foot from the stirrup to alert Higgins to danger. Pink jumped from his horse just in time to see it take a fatal rifle shot meant for him. Standifer shot several more times without effect, only to be dropped by Higgins' Winchester, not to rise again. According to Higgins, when he notified Sheriff Rodgers by telephone, the lawman urged him to go back and finish the job if necessary.[122]

Although Higgins was cleared by a grand jury, this was not the end of violence for the Higgins clan. Five years following Pink's own death from a heart attack in December 1913, Cullen was killed by assassins in Snyder, Texas. Hard-case Si Bostick confessed to the crime under harsh interrogation, naming two accomplices shortly before he was found hanged in his own cell under mysterious circumstances. One of them was accused murderer Will Luman, whom Higgins was prosecuting at the time he was killed in Snyder.[123]

Meanwhile, Sam Horrell had made an honest life for himself in Eureka, California. When he died of natural causes, the obituary published in the August 4, 1936, *Humboldt Standard* claimed erroneously that the old-timer knew Jesse James and Buffalo Bill Cody. The gangs of Lampasas were not mentioned at all.

CHAPTER FIVE

James B. Miller:
The Grim Reaper

"He always dressed well. He was intelligent, charming, and even somewhat handsome. He never drank, cursed, or chewed; he showed up at church on Sundays and was almost prudish in his contact with women."[1]

This description of James B. Miller is so accurate it is little wonder that one of Miller's nicknames was "Deacon" Jim. But the Deacon had a dark side and a moniker to match. He was just as often referred to as "Killin'" Jim.

Miller was born in Van Buren, Arkansas, on October 24, 1866.[2] His family moved to Texas when he was but one year old and settled in Franklin, a Robertson County community. When he was eight, his mother and father died. Young Jim was taken in by his grandparents living in Evant, Coryell County; the year was 1874.

Jim Miller was intelligent, charming, and handsome but had another characteristic that aroused curiosity. He possessed an egg-shaped knot behind each of his ears, called "murder bumps" by those who studied skull shapes in those times. Phrenologists of that day believed that the shape of the skull foretold mental tendencies. In his case, it did.

So when, in 1874, the eight-year-old boy was suspected of murdering his grandparents, a few in the community might not have been surprised.[3] Miller was arrested but never prosecuted, perhaps because of his age. Since his parents and grandparents were dead, the young Miller boy moved in with an older sister. She and her husband, John Coop, maintained a farm on Plumb Creek in Coryell County. Coop and young Jim had little affection for one other. Finally, after years of conflict, on July 30, 1884, seventeen-year-old Miller crept up beside John Coop while he was asleep and dispatched him to eternal rest with the deafening boom of his shotgun.[4]

This act established a pattern that would define Miller in his later career as a professional killer. His victims were usually surprised unarmed, and Miller would concoct nearly airtight alibis with corroborating witnesses. The murder of John Coop was no act of passion. Rather, the seventeen-year-old devised an alibi scheme that included young Georgia Large, who was supposedly with Miller at a religious camp meeting, as was Jeff Coop, the dead man's own brother.[5]

Despite this intricate plan, Miller was convicted and sentenced to life imprisonment. Yet Miller escaped punishment when his lawyer won a reversal through the Texas Court of Appeals.[6] By the time a second trial was put on the docket, no witnesses could be found and the case evaporated. Miller, it seemed, had gotten away with murder, perhaps for the second time. The pattern would be repeated many times over the next twenty-five years.

That same year in far southwestern Texas, two towns battled to become the seat of Reeves County. The election was won by Pecos, which took the honors previously held by Toyah to its south and west. During the years to come, the good citizens of Toyah rode into Pecos and shot the place up from time to time, perhaps just to show there were no hard feelings.

In November 1890, George A. "Bud" Frazer became the fourth sheriff of Reeves County. The next year, a courthouse, jail, and the town's first bank were established in Pecos.[7] The community was growing, and that meant added responsibility for Sheriff Frazer. A section of Pecos known as "dobie town" lay across the tracks from the "good" citizens. Dobie town harbored the more unpredictable and unconventional elements of Pecos society. Many dobie-town habitués were entrepreneurs given to less-than-honest ways of earning a living.

Frazer was looking for a good deputy when Jim Miller appeared in Pecos during the summer of 1891. Frazer was taken with the quiet, well-dressed man who seemed to know a great deal about cattle, guns, and business. Miller was introduced to the movers and shakers of the business and ranching communities and soon installed as the county's number-two lawman. Naturally, the position allowed him to move about the county with complete impunity, conversing with both the good and the bad elements of society without suspicion.

That fall, Miller married Sarah "Sallie" Clements, the sister of Emmanuel "Mannie" Clements, Jr. Since her deceased father, Emmanuel "Mannen" Clements, Sr., was a cousin of John Wesley Hardin, Miller and Hardin became related by marriage.[8]

Despite Miller's new social standing, he came under the scrutiny of some citizens who believed he was moonlighting as a cattle rustler. Miller initially brushed off the criticism, but then Barney Riggs, Sheriff Frazer's brother-in-law, bluntly accused Miller of withholding information regarding area cattle thieves. Barney Riggs then went one step farther. He somehow received information that a Hispanic prisoner Miller was instructed to transport to Fort Stockton was not killed while trying to escape, as Miller had claimed. Instead, Riggs told Frazer, the prisoner was killed because he knew where Miller had stashed two mules that were reported as stolen.[9]

Miller was fired from his deputy sheriff job, severing his once amicable relationship with Sheriff Frazer. Some Pecosians believed the "Deacon," while others did not.

Miller was charged with the mule theft but the case was dismissed for lack of evidence. Miller was not even charged in the case of the dead prisoner. Miller ran against Frazer for the sheriff's job in 1892 but lost. Nonetheless, Miller somehow managed to appoint himself city marshal. Jim established his office in his hotel room, where he and Sallie had maintained residence since they wedded. Soon his headquarters became a den for Miller confederates. John Denson, Sallie's cousin and a known gunman, became such a regular fixture that Miller appointed him night officer of Pecos. Another Miller associate of that time, Martin Quilla "Mart" Hardin of the old Dewitt County clan, was a hard case who would eventually figure in a plot to kill Sheriff Frazer.

Frazer was county sheriff, but he had no control over Miller. Frazer was initially forced to tolerate Miller and his growing faction, while keeping a watchful eye on them. Soon, however, Frazer had to take action.

While Frazer was transporting a prisoner to the state penitentiary, the denizens of the gambling parlors and saloons of Pecos became more and more brazen in their troublemaking. Soon drunks staggered through the streets, citizens were routinely accosted, and robberies occurred in broad daylight with few or no apparent consequences. City Marshal Miller did nothing to corral the hooligans. When word reached Frazer, he was furious and raced back to Pecos on the next train from Huntsville.[10]

Miller had plans for Frazer's return. Mart Hardin met with brothers John and Billy Ware in a dobie-town bar and plotted an ambush. The Ware brothers asked who would take the blame for the bullet that would end Frazer's term as sheriff. Hardin told them that Miller and Mannie Clements had arranged all that. The Wares were simply to distract Frazer with a pretended fight on the station platform as the sheriff stepped down from the train.

None of the conspirators paid much attention to a man downing drinks at a nearby table. Con Gibson quietly left by the back door and went straight to his brother James, the county clerk and a supporter of Frazer. James Gibson sent a telegram warning the sheriff of the plot. Frazer changed trains at El Paso and there informed Texas Ranger captain John R. Hughes of the ambush awaiting him back in Pecos. When Captain Hughes stepped from the train with Frazer, the scheme quickly dissolved into nothing more than a cordial greeting from Miller.

Frazer did not accept Miller's extended hand. Nor was he fooled by Miller's greeting. Frazer left the platform in silence with Hughes. Miller, Hardin, and Clements were all arrested and charged with conspiracy to commit murder. Hardin and Clements each made bail, but Miller had to languish in jail until his trial in El Paso. He was acquitted.[11]

Mart Hardin next stood trial in the conspiracy case but was also acquitted by an El Paso jury, as the prosecution was outdone by the host of attorneys Jim provided.

Now Miller went into the hotel business with Sallie, purchasing the very hotel where they had been living. For a time, the Miller-Frazer feud seemed to be over. Frazer knew, however, that Miller was marking time while waiting for another opportunity to kill him. Con Gibson, the informant who revealed the Miller plan to murder the sheriff, believed that Miller had plans for him too. Gibson left and headed west.

When he stopped in an Eddy (Carlsbad), New Mexico Territory saloon to wet his whistle, he found Miller associate John Denson standing at the bar. "Damn you, Denson, you've come to kill me!" Gibson yelled, as he went for a pistol. And with that, Denson did indeed kill him. The New Mexico Territory authorities declared that the killing was a simple case of self-defense, although Frazer believed that it was a premeditated revenge murder.[12]

On April 12, 1894, with the populace's faith in his abilities as sheriff waning and the memory of Gibson's death still fresh, Frazer took action. Miller stood in the street that day, with a foot hiked up on a wagon-wheel hub of a friend's rig. Frazer made several passes near him, but Miller did not notice. The friend with whom he conversed *did* notice and wondered out loud what Frazer was doing.

Miller soon found out. Frazer stuck the barrel of his revolver in Miller's chest and swore vengeance for the killing of Gibson. Miller hadn't a decent chance to go for his gun but stood there as Frazer fired into his chest. The sheriff was amazed to see that Miller did not recoil, fall, or die as planned but continued to stand and take lead. Miller finally reached for his own gun but Frazer shot his right shoulder, disabling his shooting hand. Miller then reached for a backup revolver with his left hand and fired at Frazer but hit a bystander in the hip instead. Frazer finally placed a round in Miller's lower torso and walked away, unscathed but baffled. Miller was carried off by friends, who tended to his wounds.

Only then did the long black coat that Miller wore even on the warmest of days make perfect sense to those in attendance. Beneath the garb was a heavy iron vest that had deflected the shots from Frazer's gun. Miller instructed his compatriots to deliver a message to his former boss. "Tell Frazer he can't convict me or kill me or run me out of the country. Next time, I'll get him."[13]

Still, George A. "Bud" Frazer was Texas through and through, a man not easily cowed. He was born at Fort Stockton on April 18, 1864, enlisted with the Texas Rangers when he was just sixteen years old, and served under Capt. G. W. Baylor. His father, G. M. Frazer,[14] had served as the Pecos County judge before there even was a Reeves County, and Bud had served as its sheriff.

So when, in the county election of July 1894, Bud lost

his bid for reelection, he was deflated. Frazer realized that anyone could be defeated in a reelection bid, but he was more distressed over how he lost. Many in the county, including Frazer's own friends, had lost confidence in his ability to quell the ongoing tension between himself and Miller. Daniel Murphy became the people's choice and Miller was only too happy to back him, realizing that by doing so he could help cause Frazer to lose not only his job but face as well. The loss hit Frazer hard. He put his property on the market and left for New Mexico Territory.[15]

By December 1894, Miller had almost recovered from the wounds he sustained in the Frazer gunfight. Before he left his bed, Miller declared, "I'm going to kill Bud Frazer. I'm going to kill him if I have to crawl all the way back to Pecos to do it."[16] The day after Christmas, Frazer returned from New Mexico Territory to conclude some personal business in Pecos. He left his horse corralled and was walking toward the bank when he was suddenly confronted by Miller.

Frazer had heard of Miller's threats against him while staying at the Toyah home of his brother-in-law, Barney Riggs. Suddenly Frazer was pouring lead at Miller before Jim even realized he was in a shootout. And again one of Frazer's rounds shot through Miller's right arm and disabled his gun hand. A second round slammed through Miller's left leg. Miller once again pulled out a concealed weapon with his still unpracticed left hand and returned fire. He was no more effective than he had been in the April shootout. Frazer kept shooting, probably with the uneasy sense that he had experienced all of this once before. Miller had inexplicably withstood his best marksmanship again, and so Frazer turned and ran.[17]

Frazer was arrested for attempted murder. The arresting officer was Daniel Murphy, who had replaced Frazer as sheriff. Miller was always one to be well represented, legally speaking. This time he hired his father-in-law's cousin, a lawyer who had recently been paroled after serving sixteen years of a twenty-five-year sentence for second-degree murder. This barrister had spent some of his prison time studying law and was admitted to the Texas state bar after his release. John Wesley Hardin practiced law in three Texas towns before he hung out his shingle in El Paso. This was the relative by marriage Miller recruited to assist in the Frazer prosecution.[18]

The jury was unable to reach a verdict, and Judge Buckler dismissed them from duty on April 14, 1895. A second trial was scheduled for May 1896, in Colorado City, Mitchell County, but on August 19, 1895, John Wesley Hardin was discharged from further legal service to Miller or anyone else, when he was shot from behind by former gunman turned El Paso constable, John Selman.[19] The killing allegedly had nothing to do with the Frazer case but was said to have been over a business deal that may have involved a murder. The jury listened to all the evidence at Frazer's second trial and acquitted him. This would be Frazer's last victory over Killin' Jim Miller.

A Double-Barreled Blast

Frazer made several trips back from New Mexico Territory to conclude his affairs in Texas. Each time, he made a routine stop in Toyah, to the southwest of Pecos. On September 14, 1896, while enjoying a game of seven-up in a Toyah saloon, Frazer's head was nearly torn from his body by a double-barreled blast from Jim Miller's shotgun. The blast caught Frazer at his Adam's apple, leaving a limp body sitting upright and dead in the chair. One of the men who was playing cards with Frazer later said, "I happened to be looking at Bud and like to have fainted when I saw his whole head disappear in a clot of splashing blood and bone."[20]

Frazer's sister was told of the killing and ran to the death scene, where she wailed at the sight. John Wesley Hardin had written in his posthumously published autobiography, "If there is any power to save a man, woman, or child from harm, save the power of the Living God, it is this thing called pluck."[21] Frazer's sister had pluck but failed to secure a pistol from any of the men at the scene. She ran home, told their mother what had just occurred, and grabbed a pistol, and the two of them chased after Miller.

When they arrived in Pecos, Frazer's sister boldly confronted Miller by pointing her pistol at his nose. Miller did not retreat but instead told her if she did not put the gun away he was going to shoot her in the face. The young woman put the gun down but gave Miller the tongue lashing of a lifetime. Miller later proclaimed that all the Frazers should leave Reeves County, with Barney Riggs in tow.

The news of Frazer's death had reached Riggs in Fort Stockton. When he returned home, a concerned wife told him of Miller's threats against him. The news did not send Riggs packing. Instead, he belted on a Colt .45 and rode to Pecos in search of Miller, who was easy enough to find, sitting in jail waiting for a hearing in the Frazer matter.

Riggs sauntered into the Orient Saloon, where he shared elbow space at the bar with Miller allies John Denson and Bill Earhart. Riggs knew both men and likely sensed that a violent exchange was imminent. Still, he remained calm.

"I hear your roommate said for me to leave the country," he taunted Earhart.

"You should have left," said Earhart, who then fired a shot at Riggs' head but only grazed him.

Riggs returned fire, shooting Earhart between the eyes. Denson attempted to wrest the gun out of Riggs' hand in the confusion. When that failed, he bolted through the saloon door and ran for his life. But he was not fast enough. Riggs stepped out from the saloon, took steady aim, and fired. The bullet sailed through the back of Denson's head, spilling a good portion of his underused brain matter out onto the dusty street.

After this, Miller posted bail and left town at the urging of his surviving friends. That steel plate would do him no good in a gunfight with Riggs, Mannie Clements warned. "He aimed at people's heads!"[22] Barney Riggs was probably the only man who ran off the notorious Killin' Jim Miller without ever having to face him. Miller took Sallie and the couple's two sons, a five-year-old and a two-year-old, to Eastland, a frontier town not far from Abilene whose population numbered less than one thousand. The Frazer murder trial was to be held there.

Undoubtedly, Miller hoped he would eventually muster a favorable jury. Thus he set about introducing himself and generally being congenial. He also accompanied a local preacher on his circuit. Together, the two men held preaching services throughout the county. Despite all this, Miller was nearly convicted of murdering Frazer by a jury vote of eleven to one at his June 1897 trial. The one holdout was long believed to have been a Miller plant. At an 1899 trial, Miller was finally acquitted of the Frazer slaying.[23]

Miller left Eastland and settled in Memphis, Hall County. Briefly serving as a Texas Ranger, he was involved in the investigation of a Collingsworth County man accused of murdering a prominent citizen in Eastland. Miller's interest in the case proved to be purely financial.

Joe Beasley was the accused, and although the evidence against him was thin, a $10,000 reward was enough to persuade Miller that eyewitness evidence of Beasley's guilt was needed. Luckily, Miller's associate Joe Earp was willing to provide just such testimony. However, when lawman Daniel R. "Dee" Harkey and the Forty-sixth Texas Judicial District Attorney Stanley conducted an impromptu deposition in a hotel room, Earp exposed Miller's plot. Miller lost any hope of collecting the reward and was indicted for subornation of perjury and convicted on the testimony of Joe Earp. When Miller's conviction and two-year sentence were reversed upon appeal, he boarded a train for Memphis and, in some rather unexpected company, promptly predicted the demise of Earp.

"Watch the papers, boys, and you will see where Joe Earp died," Miller advised, in a conversation with Judge Charles R. Brice and his brothers. Joe Earp was ambushed and killed about three weeks later.[24]

Even more curiously, Stanley soon died after dining at a Memphis hotel. An unidentified doctor ruled at the time that the cause was peritonitis. Many years after Miller's own death, the doctor revealed that District Attorney Stanley actually died of food poisoning. And, the good doctor added, the regular cook at the Memphis hotel had received an unexpected night off that evening. His replacement was allegedly a friend of Miller's.[25]

Miller was riding the plains of West Texas in and around Lubbock by 1900, working as a hired assassin who reputedly earned $150 for each killing. Business was good. West Texas cattlemen were fed up with sheepherders grazing open ranges to the nubbin, and Miller found plenty of work.

Soon, however, a different kind of warfare emerged when small farmers, derisively called "nesters," stood up to the threats and intimidations of the larger cattlemen. The nesters chose to wage war in an open courtroom. And they were successful, especially once they hired lawyer James Jarrott to plead their case. Sadly, the young lawyer would soon become just another paycheck for the Deacon.

Jarrott was killed on his way home as he stopped to water the horses pulling his buggy. The Deacon helped Jarrott find his way to an eternal home, but it was not easy. Later, he told an acquaintance that four close-range rifle shots were required to kill Jarrott. "He was the hardest damned man to kill I ever tackled," Miller marveled.[26] Incidentally, Jarrott was also the only man known to have been slain by Miller using a rifle instead of his preferred shotgun.

Miller spent the winter of 1904 in Fort Worth. While there, he dealt in land sales, many of which apparently involved lots to which Miller did not have title. The Deacon at least had the good sense to team with an honest local named Frank Fore, who enthusiastically promoted city lots in south Texas. But when Fore discovered that the lots he had been offering to law-abiding investors were nothing more than lines drawn on a map in the Gulf of Mexico, he threatened legal action.

Miller liquidated the partnership—and Mr. Fore himself in the washroom of a local hotel—and then surrendered himself to local authorities. Miller pleaded self-defense and had two witnesses to back up his claim. After he was acquitted, in the spring of 1905, he told an acquaintance that Fore squawked like a rooster when he saw Miller's pistol.[27]

The following year, Miller was recruited to even an old score between members of the Port Pruitt family and Ben Collins, an Indian policeman and former deputy United States marshal. All the participants lived near Emet, Oklahoma Territory. Collins had arrested Port Pruitt during a fine Fourth of July celebration in 1903, but only after a gun battle that left Pruitt partially paralyzed. When Pruitt sued Collins but lost, his relatives made revenge against Collins a family affair. The Pruitts hired a gunman to kill Collins, without realizing that the assassin and Collins were longtime friends. The unidentified gunman simply took his retainer, about half of the $500 promised for the job, and left the country.[28]

However, Ben Collins was shotgunned to death just outside his gate one evening in July or early August 1906. A load of buckshot cut into the policeman's stomach, throwing him from his saddle. Collins managed to fire some rounds into the surrounding bushes in a futile attempt to stop his attacker, just before a second round from the shotgun slammed into his face. Mrs. Collins now bolted down the lane with pistol in hand, but she could not help her husband. The policeman was already dead and the attacker had vanished into the night.

Miller and conspirators Dan Sie; Clint Pruitt, brother of the paralyzed Port; and Ahmed Washmood were eventually charged with Collins' murder. Miller was the only suspect held without bond. The ensuing months were unkind to the prosecution. Sie died of natural causes and Clint Pruitt was killed in Cornish during a fight with police officer Tom Gilstrap. Washmood was released on a writ of habeas corpus, and even Killin' Jim was granted bail in 1907 by Judge Townsend of Ardmore.

Miller departed for Fort Worth. There he learned that his brother-in-law Mannie Clements had become a constable in El Paso and needed his assistance in a matter involving a relative named Carl Adamson,[29] in Las Cruces, New Mexico Territory.

Patrick Floyd Garrett, the killer of Billy the Kid, was slain on the white sands of New Mexico Territory between Organ and Las Cruces on February 29, 1908, four months before his fifty-eighth birthday. Garrett was in the company of two men when he was murdered. One of the men confessed to the killing and the other man testified he had been a witness.

Garrett was born on June 5, 1850, in Chambers County, Alabama. The Garretts moved to a 3,000-acre cotton plantation in Louisiana in 1856. The six Garrett children were orphaned by the end of the Civil War. Pat Garrett moved west and took a job wrangling cattle, among other pursuits, in the Texas Panhandle before settling in Fort Sumner, New Mexico Territory. There Garrett eventually

Patrick Floyd Garrett posing while a candidate for sheriff of Dona Ana County, New Mexico Territory, 1907. *(Courtesy of The Haley Memorial Library and History Center, Midland, Texas)*

accepted a job as Lincoln County sheriff. During his tenure, he twice captured William H. Bonney (Billy the Kid) before gunning him down inside Pete Maxwell's house on the night of July 14, 1881.[30]

The death of Billy the Kid brought Garrett fame and easy access to investors for several ventures, both before and after he had retired from law enforcement. Although he tried other pursuits, including an irrigation venture, horse breeding and racing were high on Garrett's list of entrepreneurial endeavors. February 1908 found him in deep trouble with his investors and suppliers. Creditors were losing their patience and Garrett's reputation as a man hunter did little to keep the wolves from baying at his door. The former lawman looked for any kind of deal that would stay the loss of his standing in the community, not to mention his sizeable ranch.

On the morning of Saturday, February 29, 1908, Garrett dressed in a fine black suit and pressed white shirt to meet with Jim Miller, a man he believed would pump life into his sagging financial fortunes. Garrett bade his wife, Apolinaria,[31] goodbye and climbed into a buggy that would take him to his appointment.

Earlier that month, Garrett heard talk around Las Cruces that Carl Adamson was an agent looking for a grazing lease. His client was Jim Miller, a cattle trader who was bringing up a large herd of cattle from Mexico. Miller, it was explained, wanted to graze the herd until it could be moved to Miller's place in Oklahoma Territory. Garrett sought out Adamson, who told Garrett he and Miller would be interested in leasing his ranch.

There was one problem. Garrett's son had leased a portion of his ranch, known as Bear Canyon, to local cowboy Wayne Brazil (Brazel), whose father helped Garrett capture Billy the Kid. Wayne told Garrett he intended to place 1,200 head on the leased pasture. Regrettably for Garrett, the 1,200 head were attached to voracious, pasture-destroying goats rather than cattle.[32] Garrett had tried all sorts of tactics to break his lease with Brazil, even as the goats rapidly munched his grasses down to the nubbin. Brazil held Garrett's ground, as it were, successfully resisted court proceedings, and even refused to end the lease unless and until all his goats were sold.

Garrett was relieved to hear that Miller was willing to buy out Brazil's herd. But three days later, Brazil announced he had miscounted and there were in fact 1,800 goats. He would not budge unless every single animal was sold.

That pronouncement caused Garrett to slap Brazil across the face with an open hand. Tensions grew, but Brazil would not budge. Adamson told Garrett that Miller was ready to take the 1,200 goats but not the additional 600. After all, the price of $3.50 a head as originally agreed, together with the acreage cost, already made the deal quite expensive for Miller. One evening, Garrett met with Brazil and Adamson at Garrett's ranch, but the three men were unable to reach an accord. They hoped to resolve their differences the next morning in a meeting with Jim Miller.

Adamson and Garrett took turns at the reins as the two men drove toward Las Cruces, where they were to meet with Miller and discuss the lease. They planned to meet Brazil on the road from Organ. Approximately two miles east of Las Cruces on or near what today is Highway 70, Adamson reined the horses to a stop. Garrett climbed down from the rig and with an ungloved left hand unbuttoned his fly to urinate. He was still wearing the heavy driver's glove on his right hand when a bullet sailed through the back of his skull and exited at his right eyebrow. A second bullet, fired into Garrett's prone body, entered his stomach and lodged behind his shoulder.[33]

Wayne Brazil rode into Las Cruces and immediately reported the killing to Deputy Sheriff Felipe Lucero, claiming self-defense. Adamson was waiting in the buggy outside the sheriff's office and promptly corroborated Brazil's version of events.

Lucero immediately drove to the scene with a coroner's jury. Local physician W. C. Fields followed and made a careful examination of the scene, as he explained in later years. The following Monday, Garrett's son formally charged Brazil with murder. Two days later, a preliminary hearing was conducted in the presence of numerous New Mexico Territory notables, including Gov. George Curry and Atty. Gen. James M. Hervey, who asked Brazil and Adamson some probing questions. Hervey questioned how the shooting could have occurred as Brazil and Adamson claimed, since Garrett was shot from behind.

The mystery only deepened when Capt. Fred Fornoff of the Territorial Mounted Police examined the scene. Fornoff found what he believed were signs that Garrett had been shot from some nearby bushes. He also learned that the notorious Texas assassin Jim Miller was seen in Las Cruces on the very morning of the killing. Later, Governor Curry wrote that New Mexico Territory simply did not have the funds to pursue the lines of investigation suggested by Captain Fornoff's findings.

Brazil claimed self-defense in the preliminary hearing and again in his jury trial. Although Brazil was acquitted by a jury that deliberated only fifteen minutes on April 19, 1909,[34] the mysterious death of Pat Garrett had hardly been solved to the satisfaction of everyone.

Specifically, contemporaries who believed that Garrett was killed as part of an elaborate conspiracy were struck by both the fact that none of the official inquest or trial record was preserved and the hurried manner in which the jury trial had been conducted.[35] The only witnesses other than Brazil called to testify at the trial were those who arrived on the scene after the murder. Deputy Lucero, Dr. W. C. Fields, four members of the coroner's jury who accompanied Lucero to the scene, and Brazil all testified at trial.

However, the prosecution, led by District Attorney Mark B. Thompson, conducted only brief examinations of each witness, all of whom simply testified that Garrett had been slain. Neither the prosecution nor the defense asked the witnesses for any details. Brazil testified that he killed Garrett in self-defense but was not vigorously cross-examined at the trial. Adamson, the only witness to the shooting, was neither called to testify nor was his testimony before an earlier grand jury admitted as evidence.

Dr. Fields was particularly disappointed that his own testimony was cut short. Years later he told the *New Mexico Sentinel* that he made a thorough examination of the crime scene and "recorded everything." Just prior to the trial, Fields informed District Attorney Mark Thompson that he was prepared to give complete testimony. When asked about this during the newspaper interview, he responded: "Well, I never gave that testimony in detail, because I wasn't questioned!"[36]

Some of the facts Fields meticulously documented while at the scene could have turned aside Brazil's self-defense claim and supported a murder conviction against him. Most notably, Garrett was shot from behind, hardly an indication that Brazil was defending himself from an imminent attack. Fields said his autopsy revealed that long strands of Garrett's hair were "driven into the wound" at the back of his skull. He noted that Garrett had not removed the heavy driving glove from his right (gun) hand and that his fly was unbuttoned, indicating he was in the act of relieving himself and not preparing to shoot a man.

Fields also noted that the shotgun Garrett took along that day was a fold-down model, still in its scabbard when discovered next to his body. The shotgun appeared to have been placed there, not dropped, as no sand was disturbed, according to Dr. Fields: "When a man's shot in the back of the head, the way Pat was, he does one of two things with whatever he has in his hand. Either he clutches it convulsively tight or he throws it wide. There were no signs in the sand that the gun had been violently thrown."[37]

Fields said he removed a .45 slug from Garrett's body, lodged at the back of one of his shoulders. The bullet had entered at the abdomen, which indicated Garrett was on the ground at the time the second shot was fired. That single round convinced Fields that two .45 shells killed Garrett. The bullet that ripped through his head was, however, never recovered.[38] No one else was ever tried, indicted, or even charged even though other potential suspects were quite obvious. Garrett had made enemies through the years and some were prominent. Years before his death, Garrett investigated the murder of Albert J. Fountain and his young son Henry, a case that has not been solved to this day. His efforts to obtain the $10,000 reward offered for conviction of the Fountain killers only earned him the animosity of local ranchers Oliver Lee, Bill Carr, Bill McNew, and Jim Gilliland, who were charged with the murders but acquitted.

Further, A. P. "Print" Rhode, a silent goat-grazing partner and friend of Wayne Brazil, also had an old grudge against Garrett; it arose from the October 7, 1899, killing of his friend Norman Newman, alias Billy Reed, by Garrett's deputy Jose Espalin during an arrest attempt. Rhode even called Garrett out to fight after a December 1907 court hearing in which Garrett unsuccessfully attempted to oust Brazil and his goats from the Garrett ranch.

Even though such potential suspects loomed in the background, official interest in prosecuting the killer or killers of Pat Garrett after the Brazil acquittal disappeared as quickly as the impressions of his corpse on the windswept sands of the New Mexico Territory road where he died.

Still, over the last century, many writers, historians, and

others have pointed an accusing finger at Killin' Jim as the real assassin behind the death of Pat Garrett. Although not a single piece of solid evidence supporting this theory has been found, from the very beginning many marked Miller, not Brazil or any of the others, as Garrett's killer.

Garrett's personal friend, Gov. George Curry, attended the Brazil jury trial and believed it to be nothing more than a formality. Curry was aware of Garrett's negotiations with Adamson, Brazil, and Miller and was surprised these discussions were not mentioned at trial. This bothered him greatly and he wrote about it in his autobiography: "I knew of Jim Miller as a notorious bad man with a record of previous killings alleged to have been done for pay. Adamson also had a criminal record and it was difficult for me to understand why Garrett would enter into any kind of deal with such men, as he knew their records."[39]

That said, Curry later related details of a desperate letter he received from Garrett, saying he was broke and asking for a loan. "In one of his pockets the officers found a small uncashed check I had sent him shortly before his death, in response to a letter in which he had told me of his financial difficulties."[40]

Garrett's financial troubles were no secret and Miller's past dealings in real estate and cattle were widely known. Garrett had been out of law enforcement so long he may not have known about Jim Miller's man-killing reputation. Quite possibly, even if he did know, he might have brushed aside his concerns in a desperate attempt to rise from the ashes of insolvency.

On the other hand, Miller did not seem to have any personal animosity toward Garrett or any other incentive to kill him. No proof of his being contracted for such a task has ever come to light.

Even so, many of Miller's contemporaries identified him as Garrett's assassin. This included such men as Capt. John

R. Hughes, the Texas Ranger who once saved Sheriff Bud
Frazer from assassination by Miller. Hughes wrote that he
had obtained information from "unimpeachable sources"
that Miller was "close at hand when Garrett breathed his
last breath."[41]

Remarkably, many of Miller's assassinations are
documented in some way by witness statements, newspaper
accounts, court appearances, or even his own admissions.
He said things such as: "I'm going to kill Bud Frazer. I'm
going to kill him if I have to crawl all the way back to Pecos
to do it." "Watch the papers, boys, and you will see where
Joe Earp died." And regarding his assassination of lawyer
James Jarrott, Miller said, "He was the hardest damned
man to kill I ever tackled." Yet Miller had nothing at all to
say about the death of Pat Garrett, except two statements
attributed to Miller in a late-life autobiography written by
lawman Dee Harkey.

Harkey knew Miller personally and certainly knew of Pat
Garrett. Harkey claimed that Miller admitted the killing to
an unnamed acquaintance. Harkey's 1948 autobiography
also related that Harkey's ranch hand, Joe Beasley, lent
Miller one of Harkey's own horses, which Miller rode nearly
to death. Harkey asked Beasley about it and Beasley told
him Miller had borrowed the horse and "rode him over to
kill Pat Garrett."

According to Harkey, Miller told Beasley upon his return
with the nearly dead horse that Beasley should tell anyone
who inquired that Miller had spent the night on the Harkey
ranch.[42] However, this was the same Joe Beasley who nine
years before was arrested by Miller on a flimsy murder
charge and against whom Miller procured false testimony.
Beasley never testified under oath to this story but perhaps
saw a way to even the score by spreading the accusation
against Miller.

Still, the ride Miller allegedly made into Garrett country

and back from Harkey's place would have been impossible to make in just a few hours and with one horse. Even if Miller had managed the exhausting trip from Las Cruces, he still had fifty miles to go before he reached El Paso, where, according to one report, he was spotted the day Garrett was killed. Weighing that, Attorney General Hervey chose not to seek an arrest warrant for Miller.[43] The longer the case remained officially unsolved, the more people throughout parts of Texas and New Mexico Territory believed that Garrett died as a result of a conspiracy and that Killin' Jim was the assassin, although no hard evidence surfaced to support those claims.[44]

Governor Curry had his doubts about the outcome of the Garrett case, as previously noted. Curry described the murder charge against Brazil as one of concocted convenience. When Curry discussed the findings with Captain Fornoff of the Territorial Mounted Police, Curry said the report "differed materially from that of the local sheriff and medical examiner, and confirmed my impression . . . that Brazil was the victim of a conspiracy rather than the killer, an impression that later became a firm belief."[45]

Later historians and authors joined those decrying Miller. More and more it became evident that the invisible heads of some gigantic cattle ring had marked the territory's famed old sheriff for slaughter, according to Miller's biographer, Glenn Shirley.[46] And yet, four years after Miller's biography was published, Garrett's biographer concluded that more likely than not Brazil did kill Garrett, although he lied about *how* the deed was done.[47]

Meanwhile, Ramon Adams, the self-appointed scourge of careless Western writers, vacillated on the question of Garrett's killer or killers. Adams first implied that he was close to believing the conspiracy theory. "Many people think Jim Miller did the actual killing of Garrett although Brazil was tried for it. Of late years there seems to be some evidence that a member of the [William W.] Cox family might be implicated." Later, he wrote, "most historians now acknowledge he [Garrett] was ambushed by Jim Miller, a professional killer," and "it is now accepted that Jim Miller did the killing."[48]

Years after Garrett's death, Governor Curry wrote that Brazil claimed self-defense because he had no choice. "I believe he feared for his life if he told the facts."[49] Thus Curry added to later speculation that Miller was the triggerman.

On April 19, 1909, Brazil was acquitted in Las Cruces of murdering Garrett. In an odd twist of fate, Killin' Jim Miller was lynched in Ada, Oklahoma, a few hours earlier.

Miller had been accused of killing Augustus Bobbitt under contract. He and the three men who allegedly hired him were housed in the Ada jail, at least until a few local citizens broke them out and hanged them from the rafters of an abandoned livery stable nearby.[50]

One fanciful tale relates that just before he was hanged, Miller confessed to killing Pat Garrett. Ada resident Walter Gayne heard that story and begged to differ. He was the jailer guarding Miller and his three Oklahoma co-conspirators when the group was lynched. Gayne said years later that Miller did not mention Garrett or make any other confessions. "I ought to know," Gayne remarked, "because I hung him."[51]

CHAPTER SIX

Scott Cooley:
One Angry Man

Scott Cooley was full and content as he rode away from Fredericksburg toward a new life among friends. His mentor, Tim Williamson, was now fully avenged, and Scott himself would no longer hide from the authorities or fear for his life every waking minute. He carried a bottle of whiskey purchased just after dinner and probably drank some as he rode along. Soon, however, Cooley realized something was not quite right. He dismounted at the home of a family named Moore a few miles outside of Fredericksburg, lay on the ground, pronounced himself a very sick man, and within about five minutes was quite dead.[1] Another version of events told in late life by the descendants of a Mason County citizen indicated that Cooley ranted, raved, and then climbed a tree before he died on June 10, 1876, at the age of twenty-one, perhaps the victim of heavy-metal poisoning. The actual cause of his death is a mystery to this day.

Texas had been Scott's home since he was carried there as a baby from Missouri. He made a good start as a young man, serving in the Texas Rangers during the years when the fabled Rangers fought against the Comanche. Before Cooley and other Rangers were unwisely discharged in a penny-wise, pound-foolish effort to save money, he drove cattle to Kansas with his friend, adoptive father, and mentor Tim Williamson and others. Williamson and his wife had taken the young man in and even saved Scott Cooley from deadly typhoid fever by personally nursing him for days, according to some sources.[2] Now, Scott was farming on his own near Menardville.[3] Word of Williamson's murder on May 13, 1875, prompted Cooley to ride toward Mason, thirty-eight miles away, to determine just why his friend was dead. What he learned once he arrived there put Scott Cooley into a white-hot rage.

Tim had been riddled with bullets at the hands of a mob that claimed he was a cattle rustler. When Cooley learned the details of Williamson's death, he joined the conflict remembered to this day as the Mason County "Hoo Doo" War.

Traditionally, historians have described the Mason County "Hoo Doo" War (sometimes the "Hoodoo War") as a cattle feud between "German" Texans and "Anglo" or "American" Texans, aggravated by cattle rustlers who preyed on both sides.[4]

Contemporary newspaper accounts also referred to the German faction as the vigilance committee, the mob, and the law-and-order faction. One thing in this confusing historical record is certain. Generalizations about the ethnic origins and motivations of the participants must be viewed with caution.

German faction leader John E. Clark, for example, bore an "Anglo" name but may have been German on his mother's side,[5] while others with no obvious ethnic ties were associated with the German faction through marriage, blood ties, common economic interests, or simply friendship.

Finally, and perhaps most importantly, from time to time a number of known outlaws associated themselves with one faction or another for reasons of their own. The Dublin brothers and Caleb Hall, for example, had no apparent ethnic ties to the German faction but associated with them. Complicating matters further, cattle rustlers affiliated with *neither* side operated freely in Mason and adjoining counties throughout the Mason County War, sometimes even identifying themselves with one side or another to avoid detection and arrest. Moreover, one astute historian recently refined the traditional "German vs. American" theory by asserting that the Mason County War had much more to do with "German" opposition to the use of Mason County range lands by nonresident American cattlemen than with cattle rustling. A third faction was comprised of citizens who attempted to end the feud, while a fourth faction simply desired to be left in peace.[6]

Most mysterious of all to modern readers is the now-archaic term "hoodoo," said by many to be derived from an incident in which a Texas freedman inquired about a recent Mason County War killing by asking, "Who do it?" The word also carries a connotation of bad luck, suggesting that the term derives from "voodoo," which came to Texas with the slave population.[7]

The peaceful Hill Country of central Texas was hardly a predictable setting for a two-year feud that claimed so many lives and was the source of hard feelings well into the twentieth century. In the 1870s, much of Mason County was populated by hardworking first- and second-generation German-Americans who possessed a strong sense of order and valued stability above all other virtues.

This was prime cattle country, which had initially drawn much the same population that migrated to the rest of Texas from the South and the Border States. These "Anglo" pioneers were often, though not exclusively, Texas born or pioneers of Scots, Irish, or Scots-Irish stock from the highlands of Missouri or Arkansas, whose own ancestors had migrated from Tennessee, Alabama, or even Virginia and the Carolinas. Generally, they settled in the northern part of Mason County.

However, by the mid-1840s, the slow relaxed drawl of the "Anglos" was increasingly punctuated by accents from Prussia and elsewhere in present-day Germany. These Teutonic immigrants had often joined the Texas-bound

Adelsverein Immigration Company to avoid European turmoil and vigorously enforced military draft policies during a series of bloody European wars. Initially, they settled on the Texas coast around Indianola, a once-prosperous port that today is a ghost town. Eventually, they settled Fredericksburg, a still-prosperous burg named for the king of Prussia. New Braunfels was also settled by these immigrants. The pressure of more and more German immigration eventually moved some of this population north and west into the area that became Mason County. These immigrants were described by contemporary observers as being less fun loving and more pious than the Fredericksburg population.[8]

None of these ethnic distinctions mattered at all to the Lipan Apache and the Comanche, who rampaged from time to time through Mason County and even killed the first sheriff, Thomas S. Milligan, in August 1860, only two years after he was elected.[9] Mason County had been created in 1858 and named for a military post established within its confines seven years earlier to protect the local population from Indian attacks, which continued well into the 1870s. The Texas legislature had decreed that a county seat of the same name be established about two miles from the fort, just before the Civil War began.

The Mason County population hardly embraced the prospect of secession in 1860. Only 2 of the 770 eligible voters favored the Secession Ordinance, which was met so favorably in most parts of Texas. Still, most Mason County men of military age, German and non-German alike, who served at all joined the Confederate army or state militias under the control of the Confederacy.

This is not to say that there were no Civil War conflicts between the German immigrants and the Southern-oriented "Anglos" in Texas. Thirty-four German Unionists were killed by Confederate forces in an ambush on the Nueces

River about twenty miles from Fort Clark in August 1862, as they fled toward Mexico to avoid Confederate service. Nine of the men were reportedly executed after they surrendered.[10] Unionist sentiment was particularly strong in Mason County.

Once the Civil War concluded in 1865, cattle became big business in the Texas Hill Country. Herd populations there tripled between 1860 and 1870 in order to meet growing demand and appetites, particularly in the Eastern United States. Initial cattle drives from Mason County to markets in Louisiana were followed by even more lucrative journeys across Indian Territory to newly established Kansas railheads, such as Dodge City. Naturally, competition for good grazing land in Mason County grew with the increasing demand for beef. The invention of barbed wire and the subsequent enclosure of Mason County range land, which began in 1876, made good grasslands for the wandering longhorn even scarcer.

The Teutonic Texans, who then constituted about 75 percent of the Mason County population, closely managed their small, docile herds and expected their neighbors to do the same. This was a reasonable but impractical expectation, since range laws were originally written to accommodate the wild, wandering herds of longhorn cattle maintained by most Texas ranchers.

On the last day of 1873, John E. Clark was the fifteenth man to be elected sheriff of Mason County.[11] Little was known of his origins until quite recently. The seminal work, *The Mason County "Hoo Doo" War, 1874-1902,* revealed that this nominal leader of the Unionist German faction was a thirty-nine-year-old Kentucky-born former Confederate officer. Clark had previously served as a deputy sheriff in Ripley County, Missouri, and as a Mason County deputy sheriff in 1872.[12] Whatever his origins or experience, the source of Clark's political power was clear. First- and second-generation Germanic Texans expected Clark to control the Mason County range to the advantage of resident cattlemen and to suppress cattle rustling.

Sheriff Clark was not universally admired. Opponents claimed he used his office to pursue personal enemies.[13] Moreover, Texas Ranger Dan Roberts derisively described Clark as a "blue hen's chicken," that is to say, a former Confederate who served the Reconstructionist cause.[14]

Clark's first key appointment was Johann Anton Wohrle, a German-born Union veteran who most often is referred to in Mason County history as John Worley. Since Clark's mother's maiden name was Worley, an English surname sometimes used as an Anglicized version of the German surname Wohrle, John Clark and his deputy may have been related.[15]

Clark's conduct in 1874 and the following year clearly served the interests of the leading German ranchers or certain Anglos who were allies. He worked hand in glove with Dan Hoester, a scion of that locally prominent Germanic family.

Hoester assumed the most critical office in Mason County next to sheriff, that of brand inspector. Dan maintained friendships with many "Americans," notably Tim Williamson, who lived briefly in Mason County before he began farming near Menardville. Hoester's position gave him great influence just as range law and associated customs were changing in a manner advantageous to cattlemen who resided and maintained their herds in Mason County.

For many years, Texas law and custom had acknowledged that the wide-ranging longhorns could more easily blend into a new herd than be extracted from one. Thus, a rancher was entitled to sell another man's cattle, so long as he gave the proceeds to the rightful owner. Moreover, "mavericking," the practice of capturing unbranded cattle to grow one's own herd or on contract for an established cattleman, was once perfectly legal in Texas. All of this was about to change.

Pressure to revise and reform the Texas range laws grew as cattle ranching for the Eastern markets became big business. Effective March 23, 1874, "county branding" became the law in Texas. Each county was to have a brand inspector and, at least in theory, no steer or cow was to leave the county of its domicile without his permission.[16]

Resident stockmen attempted to use this new law as a means of reserving the lush green grasses and protective natural draws of Mason County for themselves. This was done by effectively preventing stockmen of adjoining counties from moving their herds over county lines without inspection, using the criminal enforcement provisions of the new law to discourage such herd movements.[17]

One of the first nonresident ranchers to run afoul of this law was Allen G. Roberts, an Illinois native who moved to Texas, then served in the Confederate-allied Texas Frontier Regiment. Roberts partnered with the Cavin brothers and John Baird (Beard) from time to time in cattle transactions. Mason County justice of the peace Wilson Hey charged in a letter to the governor of Texas, written June 24, 1874, that persons in the employ of Roberts had violated the new inspection laws by gathering and driving cattle from Mason County to adjoining Llano County without authorized brand inspections.[18] Hey erroneously charged that inspections performed by Inspector W. Z. Redding were unauthorized.[19]

Soon thereafter, on August 9, 1874, Mason County sheriff John Clark and a posse of eighteen men pursued cowhands employed by Roberts into Llano County, after an event known as the "Big Raid" in which Roberts' men took 200 head of his own cattle out of Mason County.[20] Clark arrested eleven cattlemen and jailed them in Mason on charges leveled under the new inspection statute. Eventually, five of the "Llano Eleven" were tried in Mason, found guilty, and fined $2,500 ($41,000 today) for unlawfully removing 100 head of cattle from Mason County.

Worse yet for Roberts, Clark drove the cattle in question back into Mason County and scattered them without inspection or branding. Roberts had contended that the fine should have been only $100 per head, totaling $200 ($3,250 today), if anything, since only two of the herd were improperly removed from Mason County. The leading modern expert on the Mason County War interprets this event as clear evidence that one leader of the so-called "German" faction was none other than Sheriff John Clark.[21]

Tensions Escalate

Traditional Mason County War accounts relate that about six months later, in early February 1875, a posse led by John Clark found cousins Lige and Pete Baccus (Backus); Charley Johnson, a cousin of Tim Williamson's wife; Abe Wiggins; and Tom Turley in possession of an entire herd of cattle, only two of which allegedly bore their brand.[22] The quintet was jailed at Mason on February 12, although according to one source, Clark first suggested that they be lynched rather than jailed.[23] A few days later, seventeen-year-old Allen Bolt was killed by persons unknown and dumped on the Mason-Menardville road. A card on his chest proclaimed that Bolt was killed because he would not stop stealing cattle.[24]

Six days after the Baccus party was imprisoned, a mob became impatient with judicial proceedings. That evening, ten or more disgruntled Germanic factionists gathered around the Mason County jail. Shortly thereafter, Sheriff Clark burst into Hunter's Hotel, just as Texas Ranger lieutenant Dan Roberts was preparing for bed, and begged for help. Roberts, Ranger James Trainer, and Clark arrived at the jail and Clark, armed with a pistol, took a position on the second floor, where he seemingly attempted to quell the disturbance. After the mob assured Clark that they would get the Baccus cousins one way or another, Clark gave up the prisoners.[25] The mob promptly hustled the accused rustlers to a draw just outside of town.

Clark, Roberts, and those few volunteers brave enough to face the danger arrived at the scene just after the Baccus boys and Abe Wiggins had been hoisted into the air. Clark's posse began shooting, prompting the mob to use their victims as targets for pistol practice. The sheriff's group did save young Tom Turley from certain death. In the confusion, Charley Johnson had managed to free himself while his feet were still on the ground, then escaped over a fence. However, the Baccus boys were already dead, and young Wiggins died shortly after the rescue effort.

While traditional accounts of the lynching itself have seldom been questioned in any serious way, the motivation for the pursuit of the Baccus party has recently been examined. Information provided in 1944 by Henry Doell, Jr., whose father was killed during the Mason County War, related the traditional story that the Baccus cousins owned hardly any cattle.[26] However, *The Mason County "Hoo Doo" War* states that the Baccus family was relatively well to do and maintained some six hundred head of cattle in Mason County at the time of the lynching,[27] although they resided elsewhere. This profile may have made Pete Baccus and his cousin Lige perfect targets for Sheriff Clark, who arrested them outside his own jurisdiction in adjoining McCulloch County.

That said, there is scant evidence that Sheriff Clark or Deputy Sheriff Worley were behind the lynching, which apparently was the action of an out-of-control mob that attempted to obtain the jail keys from Worley after invading his home but did not find them on his person. Moreover, his wife was so frightened she soon had a miscarriage, hardly evidence of a contrived occurrence. Thus, the direct involvement of either Worley or Clark in the lynching is doubtful. Clark simply gave up the prisoners under circumstances in which braver law officers might have resisted.

Later in February, persons unknown killed accused cattle thief William Wages in nearby Llano County. Perhaps motivated by this yet unsolved murder, Tom Turley, the sole surviving member of the Baccus crew other than fleet-footed Charley Johnson, promptly dug his way out of the Mason County jail on March 7, with another prisoner.[28]

That would be Caleb Hall, a known Mason County outlaw and an associate of the German faction. Curiously, Turley was never heard from again and therefore was unavailable to make any in-court identification of the vigilantes who lynched the Baccus crew. Whether Turley left for parts unknown to secure his own safety, or was killed by Caleb Hall as some speculate, remains a mystery.

Although the Mason County War is often described as a two-faction affair, a third organized group led by Tom Gamel has sometimes been overlooked. Gamel participated in a posse that attempted to arrest American "rustlers" during the early phases of the war but refused to join in the Baccus lynching or any other subsequent action by the German faction. This stance made Gamel a nuisance to the silence-prone German factionists who apparently tried to kill him. Gamel had turned down an invitation from the German factionists to participate in the Baccus lynching, delivered by none other than Caleb Hall.

Later, Gamel received a second invitation. This time he was asked to come into Mason for a heart-to-heart discussion with German factionists who Gamel suspected were plotting his death. Now Gamel assembled an anti-mob faction largely from adjoining Kimble and Menard counties, affiliated with neither the German mob nor the American "rustlers." He led 109 men into Mason, prompting Sheriff Clark to gather some 60 Teutonic factionists about him before returning there. Clark and Gamel met in Mason on March 19, 1875. After a few tense minutes, a peace treaty of sorts was declared, as the two factions mingled freely together.[29] Tranquility descended on Mason County, but only for six days.

On a spring day in 1875 lost to history, but perhaps during this lull in the fighting, Sheriff Clark rode to the house of Tim Williamson, a foreman for Karl "Charley" Lehmberg, hoping to collect some property taxes Clark contended were due on a lot Williamson owned in Loyal Valley, Mason County. Since Williamson was not at home, Clark emphasized that he would collect the taxes owing, in plain but insulting language heaped on the head and shoulders of Mrs. Williamson.[30] Tim was apparently not involved in the Mason County War at all.

Soon after Williamson complained directly to Sheriff Clark about his wife's treatment, Dan Hoester withdrew a bond he had posted on Williamson's behalf, stemming from an old charge that Williamson had stolen a single yearling.[31] Now Williamson faced possible jail time.[32] Mason County deputy sheriff John Worley arrested Williamson at Loyal Valley on May 13. Contrary to the custom of the time, Worley refused an offer from Williamson's employer, Karl Lehmberg, to post a bond for Williamson right then and there, insisting that Williamson return to Mason with him and post the bond personally. Even more curiously, Worley insisted that Williamson ride Worley's own, slower horse, while Worley rode Williamson's younger, faster steed.[33] The reason for these arrangements was soon apparent.

Soon after Lehmberg, Williamson, and Worley left

Lehmberg's ranch, about a dozen disguised men stopped the trio. Williamson begged Worley for a chance to outrun the mob, but Worley responded by shooting the horse Williamson was riding, according to several sources.[34] Williamson quickly recognized his predicament, as well as mob member Pete Bader. "Let's stop this right here." Williamson begged, after reminding Bader that they both had families. Bader's response was unique, if nothing else. "I've blowed my coffee and now I'm going to drink it," Bader rejoined, perhaps using a poorly translated German expression lost on those present.

Before anyone could ask what in hell Bader was talking about, the Teuton drew his pistol, killed the unarmed prisoner, and rode away.[35] This incident did not sit well with everyone in the German community. Henry Doell complained to several of the German "law and order" factionists about the Baccus lynching and Williamson murder. Those listening quickly changed the subject.[36] Little more than two months later, on July 21, Doell, Fritz Kothmann, and two others were hunting strays near West Bluff Creek in Mason County. Some two hours before sunrise, two shots rang out. Doell caught a bullet in the stomach and died four days later. Whether Doell was killed because of his critical comments about the Baccus and Williamson killings or, more likely, in a random Comanche attack is still unknown. However, one thing is certain. The Mason County War had not run its course.

Charley Johnson, the young Baccus crew cook who escaped death by hanging, was called in front of a Mason County grand jury in May 1875 but simply could not remember the identity of his assailants. More than one commentator has suggested that Johnson's memory was bad because members of the mob or their relatives were sitting on the grand jury itself.[37] John Worley had resigned shortly after Williamson was killed, then returned to his former job, carpentry. Perhaps he thought that his part in the feud was over. Williamson's best friend and champion, Scott Cooley, thought otherwise.

Cooley's family had moved from Missouri to Jack County, Texas, just in time to help defend that region from attacks by Comanche warriors. Some early writers suggested that Cooley's parents were killed by that tribe, an apparent myth. Recent evidence suggests that Cooley's father was killed by one Joseph Horton during a cattle dispute. Horton in turn was killed by Cooley's brother.[38]

Cooley served in Company D of the Texas Rangers during a seven-month period that began in early May 1874. He saw action in Lost Valley while serving as an escort for Ranger captain John B. Jones and fought in another action on July 12, 1874, in which two Rangers were killed and two wounded.[39] Before he was discharged by the financially strapped Texas Rangers, Cooley had earned a reputation as a fierce and brutal Indian fighter who took scalps from his dead enemies.[40] Coincidentally, Cooley once described himself as half-Cherokee on his mother's side.[41] When Scott Cooley learned while visiting a Ranger camp that his friend Tim Williamson had been murdered, he declared to all present that he would have revenge.[42] Traditional stories relate that he rode immediately to Mason County from Menardville and began to quietly ask a few questions.

Soon, he selected his first target, former deputy sheriff John Worley. On August 10, Cooley found the unarmed Worley working as a handyman and carpenter. Worley's odd job that day was repairing a water well, with Charles "Doc" Harcourt and a diminutive Northern man known to history only as "Doc's little Yankee."[43] The most reliable version of events suggests that Cooley simply asked Worley why he had killed Williamson, then shot Worley in the back of the head after Worley claimed "he had to." Naturally, Worley dropped the rope after he was shot, allowing Harcourt to fall downward into the well. After the "little Yankee" scurried off, according to another report, Cooley shot Worley six more times for good measure, took his scalp, and rode away.[44]

German factionist Karl "Carl" or "Charley" Bader, whose brother Pete Bader killed Tim Williamson, was next. Although the date of Karl Bader's death has long been a point of contention, church records revealed in *The Mason County "Hoo Doo" War* confirm that he was killed on August 19, 1875, on or near his own farm, soon after former deputy sheriff Worley was killed.[45]

The circumstances of his death and the identity of his murderers are both still in question. Scott Cooley and another man may well have killed him, as the only known contemporary account indicates, perhaps even mistaking him for his brother Pete Bader. Various sources identify John Ringo, George Gladden, Moses Baird, and even young Charley Johnson as suspects, without substantiation. However, Baird and Gladden were probably not involved, if their conduct after the killing is any indication.[46] Charley Johnson was also an unlikely participant, since he applied for service in the Texas Rangers a scant two months later and most certainly would not have invited Ranger scrutiny of his immediate past had he been involved in the Karl Bader killing.[47]

And still the killing continued. September 7 found Moses Baird and George Gladden in Loyal Valley, then referred to by some as Cold Springs.[48] Cooley and his associates were probably not expecting visitors that day, but gambler and ne'er-do-well Jim Cheyney (Cheney) arrived on horseback. Cheyney was paid $50 ($800 today) to deliver an important message to Moses Baird. Dan Hoester and Sheriff Clark needed to see him in Mason immediately. Baird and Gladden may have been suspicious when Cheyney quickly galloped away, but they mounted their own horses and began the trip. Knowing no better, they rode into a trap at Hedwig's Hill, a store on the eighteen-mile road between Loyal Valley and Mason where most travelers between those two towns stopped to rest.

When Gladden and Baird dismounted, Clark, Hoester, and others opened fire, wounding both men, who were scarcely twenty yards away. Thinking quickly, Gladden helped Baird onto his own horse and then attempted to escape. Gladden fell from the horse after being shot again, successfully begged for his life, and then watched helplessly as Baird rode down a nearby creek with Clark's posse in close pursuit. Pete Bader, the very man who had killed Tim Williamson, now finished off Moses Baird, then dismounted and cut off Baird's ring finger, taking a gold ring for himself.[49]

Gladden only survived the ambush because one of the German factionists insisted that he not be killed.[50] After this incident, Mason County observers and pundits inked their writing pens. Texas Ranger Dan Roberts described the incident as a fair fight, probably based on reports he received directly from Sheriff Clark.[51] Tom Gamel portrayed the incident as an ambush clear and simple.[52]

Calls to Resign

Soon thereafter, according to Henry M. Holmes, Mason County citizens asked the sheriff and certain other officials to resign. He did not initially do so and here, for the first time, we see John Clark as an outlaw protected by his office:

> The Sheriff has not done so [resign] but still is the leader of a band composed exclusively of Germans. He is a fugitive from justice there being five indictments against him in Llano County for Robbery and false

imprisonment—he cannot be arrested with the force at disposal of the justices and now holds the county in awe with some fifty men. The lives of all those who do not belong to the mob are in danger and quiet can hardly be restored until some steps are taken to bring the perpetrators of the late murders [ten] to justice and this cannot be done in this country by any grand or petit jury summoned from the victims.[53]

Reports of one Dreux in the *Austin Weekly Statesman* indicated that three factions existed: the Germans, the mostly American "outlaws," and the rest of the American population, who declined to oppose the outlaws for fear of becoming victims themselves.[54] Whatever the truth, Sheriff Clark soon produced two different reasons for his actions. First, he improbably claimed that Moses Baird and Gladden had attacked his posse of forty to sixty men. Later, he stated that the pair was shot "resisting arrest" for the death of Karl Bader. Now the hapless sheriff had made himself another notable enemy who would join Scott Cooley's private war against the "Hoo Doos."

John Baird recruited a contingent from Llano and Blanco counties, intent upon avenging the death of his brother Moses Baird. The thirty to fifty riders most certainly included Sam Tanner, Bill Faris, Joe Olney, and perhaps John Ringo, who was drawn into the conflict through his friendship with Olney and many others. Baird briefly returned to Llano, but he would not linger long. Scott Cooley apparently met with John Baird and others at Loyal Valley and now had the most effective ally he could have asked for.[55]

The Bairds (Beards) had come from Ireland to Missouri, and then, within perhaps three generations, some of the family had migrated to Burleson County, Texas. It appears that the next generation moved on to Burnet County, where brothers Moses Baird and John Baird fought frequently with their neighbors, placing themselves in legal difficulties.[56]

Their livelihood was apparently based on legitimate cattle ranching. Moses had once been accused of rustling but was acquitted about five months before he was killed.[57] Now John Baird sought revenge for his brother's death, even as the German faction in Mason began to dissolve in a wave of recrimination and bitterness, perhaps caused in part by Clark's failure to eliminate or even reduce Mason County cattle losses.

A storm began to rise in nearby Burnet and Llano counties. The first victim was Jim Cheyney, who had lured Moses Baird to his death at Hedwig's Hill, unwittingly or otherwise. Two men later identified as John Ringo and "Williams" found Cheyney on his front porch on Saturday morning, September 25, 1875. Cheyney invited the pair to breakfast and then was shot dead as he washed and dried his face, "Williams" may have been Jim Williams, a brother-in-law of American factionist Bill Redding.[58] Ringo and Williams then met Scott Cooley in Mason, enjoyed breakfast at the Bridges Hotel, and rode away, after commenting that some meat was available "up the creek."[59] Very soon thereafter, Pete Bader decided to pursue a new career in Florida and moved his family to Fredericksburg as a precaution.[60]

Now, for the first time, the Texas Rangers took the field to quell the Mason County War. On September 26, 1875, while on patrol in West Texas, Ranger captain John B. Jones learned of the Worley killing and was ordered to proceed into Mason. Lt. Dan Roberts had arrived in Mason thirteen days earlier. Jones was nearly ambushed on September 28 by none other than Sheriff John E. Clark, who was expecting to kill or capture George Gladden, John Baird, and Scott Cooley.

Clark was wrong again. Gladden, Baird, and Cooley were waiting in Mason that very minute—expecting to finish off Clark himself. Instead, they killed Dan Hoester, a former German factionist who had withdrawn a bond posted for Tim Williamson, leading intentionally or not to Williamson's death. Hoester had recently decided to pursue other interests unrelated to the ongoing feud.[61] Perhaps he was motivated by the recent untimely deaths of Worley, Karl Bader, and Jim Cheyney.

One controversial aspect of the Dan Hoester death was the fate of Bill Coke, who was with Cooley and John Baird shortly after Hoester was killed. Two posses, one consisting of Rangers, the other German factionists led by Sheriff Clark, searched for the killers. Among the suspects arrested by Sheriff John Clark was Bill Coke, who was never seen again. One German faction descendant insisted in a late-life interview that Coke had been killed.[62]

Responsible Mason County citizens were no doubt hopeful that fall that peace could be restored, but events on Sunday, October 3 reflected the complex nature of the dispute. Persons unknown, perhaps led by Sheriff Clark, rode into Loyal Valley that morning. This force of some forty men then proceeded to search every house for members of the American faction. One particular target was John O. Meusenbach, whose noble, Teutonic origins as Baron Ottfried Hans Von Meusenbach were no protection at all from the German faction, which ransacked his store and shot at him.[63] Baron Meusenbach and other Loyal Valley citizens promptly petitioned Captain Jones for assistance the next day, even as more violence occurred in the region on October 4 between Mathew Moss, Jr., an American faction supporter, and one Blue Foster, as was later reported in the October 11, 1875, *San Antonio Herald:*

> The cause of trouble was that Foster claimed a mark and brand belonging to Moss and had the same recorded in his own name. The same mark and brand had been recorded by Moss before the records were destroyed by fire last winter, but he had not re-recorded since the fire.

Foster went and recorded the same and claimed it was his own mark and brand. Moss sent word to him not to handle the cattle as they were his property, but Foster gathered the cattle, sold some of them and had others under herd. Moss came to the pen and talked to the cowboys a short time and then rode up to Foster and emptied both barrels of his shot gun at him, the shot taking effect in the left side, nearly under his arm, when Foster fell from his horse. Moss then drew his pistol, walked up to him and shot him in the chest and head, then waved the six shooter and asked the crowd if they wanted any of it, if so, he was the best man in the place, and then mounted and rode off.

Soon after Captain Jones took the lead in efforts to end the Mason County violence, he noticed that his Rangers were less effective than ever before while pursuing their former associate and friend, Scott Cooley. During a crucial confrontation with his men, Jones challenged those Rangers unwilling to vigorously pursue Cooley to step forward and resign from his company then and there. Despite a traditional story that over fifteen men stepped forward, records substantiate only the resignations of N. O. Reynolds and James P. Day on October 7, 1875, and Paul Durham four days later.[64]

A truce of sorts was arranged in Mason by October 23, facilitated by the election of James A. Baird as sheriff twenty-one days earlier. So far as anyone knows for certain, Sheriff Baird was not related to American faction leader John Baird or his deceased brother Moses.

Clark, nominal leader of the German faction, was still in hot water. In mid-October, he was bound over to a Mason County grand jury on false-imprisonment charges stemming from his raid into Llano County in August of the preceding year.

Although the grand jury voted a "no bill" (recommendation

of no prosecution) on November 12, Clark was not available
to celebrate his legal victory. He had fled the county, never
to be seen again. Clark apparently farmed the rest of his
life in a remote corner of Ripley County, Missouri, where
he died May 4, 1888.[65]

The acquittal of criminal defendants from both factions
and the patrols instituted by Ranger captain Jones may
have led many citizens to believe that hostilities were over,
but events proved otherwise.

Mason locksmith J. P. Miller was shot and nearly killed on
October 31. Suspected American factionist and fleet-footed
lynching survivor Charley Johnson had learned that Miller
found and kept an expensive, fancy pistol that Johnson left
behind as he fled for his life on February 12. When Miller
refused to return the pistol and later sold it to reimburse
himself for expenses incurred in burying the Baccus boys,
Johnson rode into Mason and shot Miller with a new
revolver. Although the reason for this attempted murder
seemed simple enough, some later speculated that Johnson
was actually seeking revenge for Bill Coke, his supposed
outlaw associate, who disappeared while in the custody of a
posse in which J. P. Miller participated.[66]

While the Rangers who patrolled Mason County made
some significant arrests and apparently even wounded
Scott Cooley himself on Saturday, November 20,[67] feudists
of both factions, as well as independent outlaws, still freely
roamed the region. A visitor to Loyal Valley named William
Cook was killed there by persons unknown the day after J.
P. Miller was shot. Although the German faction was quick
to blame John Baird and his associates,[68] the murder was
never solved.

Another cattle dispute unrelated to the Mason County
War was settled with the gun less than a month later at
the ranch of Rance Moore, whom some German factionists
suspected in the still unsolved Henry Doell killing five

months before. Moore and drover James Polk Mason had agreed that Mason and another rancher would keep some of Moore's cattle on shares. Despite a seemingly minor quarrel over the disposition of some camping equipment associated with the venture, the men were able to reach a financial settlement. Mason, however, was still embittered. He rode to the Moore ranch on December 12, proposed to settle the camping-equipment dispute with pistols, and did just that, killing Moore as Moore walked out of his house with his own shooting iron.[69]

Two days later, Cooley and about ten of his associates appeared in Mason, to the consternation of G. W. Todd and other citizens who played no part in the feud. Todd immediately wrote Texas Ranger captain Jones, indicating where Cooley might be found on his occasional trips to Austin.[70] On December 27, 1875, Cooley and John Ringo were arrested and jailed in Burnet following an altercation with Sheriff John Clymer and Deputy Sheriff J. J. Strickland, over matters that are still unclear. Clymer soon found that arresting this pair was an expensive proposition. When armed men vigorously demanded the release of Cooley and Ringo, Clymer had to arrange for the jail to be guarded by some fifty men at county expense before the pair was transported to Austin. There, prisoners and guards alike enjoyed an undoubtedly fine meal at Salge's Snack House before Ringo and Cooley were confined in the Travis County jail on January 2, 1876.

Not long afterward, Pete Bader began a trip from Fredericksburg to Llano, where he planned to settle some business before moving to Florida. Undoubtedly, he hoped to begin a new life with all worries about Scott Cooley left behind in Texas. Cooley was not the problem after all, as events proved on January 13 near San Fernando Creek. As Bader and others rode on the thirty-nine-mile journey to Llano, John Baird stepped from behind some rocks in front of the travelers. "Hello, Bader," Baird said, just before he pulled the trigger of his shotgun. Bader managed to ride some fifty yards before he fell dead from the saddle. Legend has it that Baird retrieved the ring that Bader took from Moses Baird"s body about four months earlier—by cutting the ring finger off the corpse, just as Pete Bader had.

The death of Pete Bader was probably very cold comfort indeed to Ringo and Cooley, who languished still in the jailhouse in Austin. They journeyed to Burnet accompanied by a posse of ten in late January without incident.[71] There they were indicted for the confrontation with Sheriff Clymer, then transported in mid-March to Lampasas, epicenter of the notorious Horrell-Higgins feud.

Forty-five days later, threats to bodily remove Ringo and Cooley from jail materialized when riders apparently led by a quartet of Baird partisans made a futile breakout attempt. A larger contingent returned three days later, obtained the keys from Sheriff Sweet at his home, then removed Ringo and Cooley without freeing the other prisoners. John Baird was probably among the liberators.[72] In a brief but tense chance encounter with Llano County sheriff William P. Hoskins at the Joe Olney place, John Ringo shook hands with the sheriff then moved on, arriving in Mason on May 8 for a reunion with Tom Gamel. Noted outlaw Jeff Ake commented in his late-life memoirs of uncertain veracity that the German and American factions met with the sheriff and the Rangers, then agreed to a peace treaty of sorts whereby the American faction would move west.[73] Cooley's whereabouts during the next thirty days are not known, although by June 10, he was traveling from Fredericksburg toward Blanco County.

He dined at Fredericksburg's Nimitz Hotel, founded, owned, and operated by the grandfather of World War II naval hero Chester Nimitz. Although Cooley's friend Tom Gamel speculated late in life that Cooley may have been poisoned, contemporary newspaper reports only reference "congestion of the brain,"[74] a diagnosis that, in those days of medical uncertainty, could be most anything. Yet another late-life recollection relates that a "Wid Felps" found Cooley raving in a tree before his death.[75] Whatever the precise medical cause, Scott Cooley's war was over.

Yet the Mason County War had taken on a life of its own and continued throughout 1876, even after the death of those instrumental in beginning or sustaining the conflict. Jim Williams, who may have assassinated Jim Cheyney with John Ringo, was himself killed by persons unknown near Cat Mountain in Llano County on September 10, 1876.[76] His associate Ed Cavin escaped the same fate.

Little more than two weeks later, two young men, probably misidentified as members of the American faction, were lynched on the Upper Llano River, according to the September 27, 1876, edition of the *San Saba News*.

Ben Erwin, who was affiliated with the American faction solely by kinship with his cousins the Olney brothers, was murdered by Teutonic mob affiliate and thug Jiles Mackey, who fled to Indian Territory.[77] Soon, the American faction was just as much in decline as their enemies. M. B. Thomas, who worked for Allen G. Roberts during the "Big Raid" of 1874, moved west and was killed by William Austin on December 11, 1888, over a card game in Alzada, Montana.[78]

George Gladden was eventually tried and convicted of the murder of Pete Bader. He began his sentence at Huntsville prison in December 1877 but was released years later on the petition and recommendation of leading Llano County citizens. Gladden moved to Arizona, where he was associated with the Llano County Blevins clan involved in the bloody Pleasant Valley War. Eventually Gladden returned to Texas and was known to be living in El Paso as late as 1895.[79]

John Baird's fate after the Mason County War is also something of a question mark. The late-life memoirs of Tom

Gamel indicate that Baird became a lawman and was killed near Santa Fe in 1877 or the next year, while Jeff Ake later claimed simply that Baird was killed in Socorro.[80]

John Ringo's finale was the most mysterious of all. After several trials and some significant jail time, he was released in late 1878 or 1879 and briefly served as a constable in Loyal Valley. He eventually moved on to Tombstone, Arizona, where he concentrated on drinking and making new enemies, perhaps in part as a result of the battle fatigue that plagued several other Mason County War veterans.[81] Ringo became a partisan of Sheriff John H. Behan and a foe of the Earp faction. This choice earned him a place on the short list of suspects in the attempted assassination of Virgil Earp in December 1881.

Ringo died in Turkey Creek (or Morse's Mill) Canyon near Tombstone on July 14, 1882, probably by his own hand or perhaps otherwise, as suggested by the unusual arrangement of his clothing and other oddities at the scene. The suspects in his death are legion, notably including gambling-house denizen Johnny O'Rourke, Lewis W. Cooley (no apparent relation to Scott Cooley), and Wyatt Earp himself.

Although the Mason County troubles that began in 1874 caused ill feelings among the local citizenry for years, many writers have considered the conflict effectively concluded with Scott Cooley's death in June 1876 or even more definitively with the suspicious fire that engulfed the Mason County Courthouse and all feud-related records in January 1877.

Still, in a sense, the conflict may have not really concluded until retired German faction adherent Robert F. Rountree (Rowntree) became the last Mason County War feudist killed, on July 20, 1893, possibly as revenge for his part in the feud. Charges against his accused murderer, an opponent whom Rountree attempted to shoot back in 1874, were finally dismissed in 1902.[82] Rountree's murder was never solved.

CHAPTER SEVEN

Sam Bass: Saloons, Horses, Stagecoaches, and Trains

He was quite as poor a prospect for a hero as ever blossomed into notoriety. He was about five feet eight inches in height, dark sallow complexion, dark hair and brown or hazel colored eyes. He had a thinly scattered black beard, which habitually appeared about a week old. He was stooped in his shoulders, and wore a downcast look, more of embarrassment than of villainy. He rarely spoke, except when under the influence of whiskey, and when he did, his words were drawled out with a shrill, nasal twang that was devoid of melody and exhibited a total absence of refinement. He was dull in all but trickery, but it is said to his credit he was a faithful and trustworthy servant.[1]

Sam Bass was hardly the latter-day Robin Hood portrayed in myth. He was born on July 21, 1851, near Mitchell, Indiana, and orphaned twelve years later. He lived five years with an uncle, David L. Sheeks, before leaving the family farm in 1869. After a short and disenchanting stop in St. Louis and another in Rosedale, Mississippi, Bass traveled to Denton County, Texas, with merchant Robert Mayes and his wife, Elizabeth.[2] Once there, illiterate young Sam was employed as a cowboy and teamster. Denton County sheriff William Franklin Egan took an early interest in young Bass and hired him to work around his ranch. Eventually, Sam began calling the sheriff "Dad" Egan, along with most others in the county.

Despite Dad Egan's influence, young Sam had a wild streak that soon led him to join the horseracing circuit. Sam and Sheriff Egan's younger brother, Armstrong "Army" Egan,[3] took a gray mare named Jennie and searched for high times and adventure. Throughout north Texas, the horse and its handlers challenged many, mostly winning. Jennie was known throughout north Texas as the "Denton Mare."

This horseracing partnership was viewed unfavorably by Sheriff Egan, who knew only too well the bad habits of many in the racing crowd. The sheriff bought out his younger brother's interest and ended the partnership. Soon afterward, Bass was involved in a fight over whether the Denton Mare had prevailed in a particular race.

Sheriff Egan told Bass to choose the mare or his employment with the Egan family. Bass chose the mare and apparently found a new partner. Young Sam and Indiana ruffian Henry Underwood chose to debut their alliance by racing Jennie near Fort Sill, Indian Territory. The story goes that Jennie won one contest hands down, but the losing Indians refused to relinquish their wagered ponies. Bass and Underwood had to steal the string of ponies, according to one author.[4] Yet another account states that Bass and Underwood refused to surrender the horses to federal marshals acting on behalf of angry tribesmen. The marshals threatened legal action as they rode away emptyhanded.[5]

Although he began acting like his lowlife companions, at times Bass seemed a little confused. Bass once rescued Denton County deputy sheriff Tom Gerren from a surly crowd that threatened Gerren at a country dance, according to one source.[6]

Still, his continued association with Henry Underwood and his brother Nathan guaranteed trouble. Henry Underwood was probably born between 1846 and 1848. His older brother Nathan was born on January 26, 1844, also in Indiana. Both men served in Indiana infantry regiments during the Civil War.[7] Young Henry married British-born Mary Ann Emery in 1872.[8]

After the war, the brothers turned to cattle rustling and thievery instead of honest work. Henry even briefly associated in 1875 with the notorious rustler and bank robber Joe Horner. Later, Horner reinvented himself as Frank Canton and became a respected lawman of Wyoming and Oklahoma.[9]

The firm of Bass and Underwood was involuntarily dissolved when Henry was incarcerated for allegedly setting fire to the Denton County courthouse and later a Presbyterian church where the court records had been transferred. Underwood stewed in the Denton County jail and in late 1876 was moved to the Gainesville jail. He remained there for part of the next year.[10]

Meanwhile, Bass and the Denton Mare sought greener pastures in San Antonio. Eventually Bass met and partnered with Joel Collins, a saloonkeeper with other interests, such as crooked horseracing schemes.

Texas drovers of that era often bought cattle on credit, added other animals belonging to their neighbors, and drove the herd to market, later returning to pay the owners what they expected and retaining a profit for themselves. Bass and Collins entered into such an arrangement once Collins sold his interest in the saloon. Bass may have sold the Denton Mare to invest in the cattle herd.[11] Joel Collins' brother Joe may have owned some of the cattle Bass and Joel pushed north. Joel and Sam may have been joined by Jack Davis and Bill Potts.

Davis was born about 1846 and may have been from Fort Smith, Arkansas. He sometimes called himself Jack Reed. Potts, known also as Billy Heffridge (Helfridge), apparently began his criminal career in or near Collin County, Texas, where he was indicted in May 1872 for stealing a gelding the previous month.[12] In October 1875, Potts and two black men allegedly stole two wagons and eight oxen at Fort Sill, Indian Territory, then proceeded to Wichita, where they were arrested November 5 by lawmen Wyatt Earp and Mike Meagher, according to the November 10, 1875, *Wichita Beacon.*

The newly assembled group pushed the herd north through Dallas into Indian Territory and on to Kansas, where it may have been sold. Collins pushed this herd or other cattle acquired later through Dodge City and then on to Ogallala, Nebraska, in 1876. Since Bass sold his interest for $8,000[13] ($141,788 today), he had some money to invest when he and some other drovers moved on to Deadwood, Dakota Territory.

Deadwood started inauspiciously enough in 1876, named as it was for the dead trees that littered the original town site. Deadwood founders Charles and Steve Utter had hauled in a supply of commodities for the miners who labored in the nearby Black Hills that year. A fame-seeking nobody named Jack McCall became somebody on August 2 at the No. 10 Saloon in Deadwood by killing James Butler Hickok, known to history as "Wild Bill," apparently for no reason at all.

That very year, Bass and Collins arrived in Deadwood and then invested in a failed whorehouse, a dried-up quartz mine, an unprofitable freighting business, good times, and fast women, although not necessarily in that order. Then the financially strapped young men considered their options.

On March 25, 1877, Bass, gang leader Joel Collins, and a few other handpicked toughs made their debut as stage robbers. Robert "Reddy" McKemmie (McKimie), sometimes inexplicably called "Little Reddy from Texas," James F. Berry, Tom Nixon, Potts, and James F. "Frank" Towle rounded out the crew.[14]

McKemmie was a redheaded bastard son of Hamilton County, Ohio. After joining and deserting the army, he moved on to Kansas, where he may have been a rustler before going on to Utah in search of loose cattle. After serving time for a Utah murder, he escaped from prison and then pushed on to Denver, Cheyenne, and finally Deadwood.

James F. Berry supposedly served with Bloody Bill Anderson during the Civil War. We know with more certainty that he married Mary E. Craighead and then left Callaway County, Missouri, to seek gold in the Black Hills of Dakota Territory. He drifted on to North Platte, Nebraska, where he established a grocery store in partnership with a Mr. Garrison (Garretson), then bilked a prominent citizen out of some money deposited for the purchase of goods before returning to the greater Deadwood area.

Tom Nixon was born about 1852 according to the Pinkerton Detective Agency, which described him as about five feet eight inches, weighing 150 pounds, with light hair and a long, neat mustache. He had supposedly worked as a blacksmith before joining the Collins gang. Nothing is known about Frank Towle's early life.[15]

The stage running between Cheyenne and Deadwood was chosen for their first robbery, but things did not go as planned. When the stagecoach horses panicked during the robbery attempt, Reddy shot and killed stage driver Johnny Slaughter, without any reason at all or perhaps even accidentally. Afterward, brewery salesman Walter Iler somehow untangled the frightened horses from their harness and then drove the stage into Deadwood in spite of two wounds.[16]

Bass and the others were angered by the lost opportunity to rob the stage and the needless killing, which was sure to bring more trouble than they bargained for. Before the robbery, all had agreed there would be no gunplay except in self-defense. Since Reddy had violated their agreement, Collins considered killing him on the spot. Instead, McKemmie was simply abandoned, while the gang rode away with nothing to show from the holdup except the possible prospect of early graves. The concern about payback was realistic. Johnny Slaughter was so popular that two funerals were held in his honor, one in Deadwood and one in Cheyenne.[17]

The Collins gang may have committed other stagecoach robberies early that spring. However, their immediate prospects dried up when bad weather caused the temporary suspension of most stagecoach runs.

The robberies began again on the first day of June 1877, north of Hat Creek Station about one hundred miles south of Deadwood, when three unidentified men stopped a stagecoach but were sent packing by well-armed citizenry in the cool of the evening. Twenty-four days later, in a robbery between Deadwood and the Cheyenne River, bandits were temporarily hampered by the strength of the rivets that anchored the stagecoach strongbox. Even so, they took about $1,400 ($27,000 today) from passengers. Among the victims was a Potato Gulch mining magnate named Irwin. The same stage was robbed near the same place on the Cheyenne River the next evening. This time, the gang brought a hatchet to deal with the strongbox and carried away about forty pounds of gold, then worth about $13,000. These three robberies were later ascribed to the Blackburn and Pelton gang, which now included Reddy McKemmie, who soon returned to Ohio. He eventually was captured, pled guilty to burglaries in two counties, returned to Utah, served time there, and finally escaped from a California prison into obscurity.[18]

Bass later claimed that during this period he joined Jack Davis and Tom Nixon in a series of Deadwood-area holdups directed at the Cheyenne and Black Hills Stage Company, with little to show for their efforts. Several such unsuccessful robberies did occur in July and August of 1877, although the identity of the bandits is uncertain. The

Deadwood-to-Sidney stage was robbed at about midnight on July 10, yielding the bandits virtually nothing. This was followed by a robbery about seventy miles south of Deadwood three days later, in which the bandits recovered an unreported amount of cash and some dentist tools. One exasperated bandit quipped that the gang might soon go into the "tooth pulling" business. A robbery on July 17, another the following day, and two others in August netted the culprits a grand total of ninety-four dollars.[19]

Frank Towle apparently left the Collins gang at about this time. He was later shot and killed on September 13, 1877, while robbing a stage on his own. The stage driver who killed him tendered Towle's severed head to substantiate his claim for reward money.[20]

Five days after Towle's death, the Collins gang committed the seventh train robbery in American history. Some say Potts, Berry, Collins, and Nixon hatched the plot in the back room of the grocery and saloon that Potts supposedly operated with Anse Tippie. Others believe the scheme was born at Collins' home near Deadwood.[21] The target was a Union Pacific train near Big Springs, a remote Nebraska watering station.

Joel Collins purchased several grain sacks and twine about twenty-two miles away in Ogallala, Nebraska, on the previous day, as James Berry attempted to purchase some boots on credit from merchant M. F. Leach, a storekeeper with some prior experience as a detective. Since Berry had cheated someone in the area the previous year, Leach refused to extend credit and Collins paid for Berry's new boots.

On Tuesday, September 18, 1877, the Collins gang struck gold at Big Springs, but not with picks. The train express car contained $60,000 ($1.2 million today) in gold coins, which the gang quickly gathered up, even as they tripped over 100-pound silver bars inexplicably scattered on the floor. Fortunately for the Union Pacific, the silver was just too heavy to haul off. Among the passengers delayed was Central Pacific Railroad president Leland Stanford, who later founded Stanford University.[22]

The next day M. F. Leach approached a railroad superintendent and was hired on the spot to track the Collins gang. The *Mexico (MO) Ledger* described Leach's appearance the next month in its October 18, 1877, edition:

> He was a short, wiry-looking fellow dressed in a very outlandish manner. He had on an old pair of shoes, almost worn out pants, a new hat and a loose coat with the tails cut off. The only thing in his appearance that would strike a casual observer was the brilliancy of his eye. He had an eagle eye surely; under his coat he carried a long "45" pistol with two belts full of cartridges. He was evidently "fixed" for anybody.

And so he was. Although Leach would pursue the Collins gang for the next three months, the railroad had other means of tracking down the stolen money and the bandits. The Union Pacific offered a $10,000 reward or a prorated part thereof for the capture of the Collins gang and return of the money. Railroad officials also asked the Third Cavalry at Camp Robinson in northeast Nebraska for assistance.[23]

Still, Leach was determined to bring the bandits in himself and collect the reward. He promptly began trailing the gang, according to his later claims, and discovered their camp on Saturday, September 22, shortly before midnight. As Collins and company slept early the next morning, Leach examined their possessions. He said later that he sent a message to the railroad and then watched the gang split the money, exchange future contact information, and take an oath of silence in a new camp near Beaver Creek on Monday, September 24. Then he stumbled into the gang at Sappa Creek, Kansas, the next day. Jack Davis evidently recognized him or otherwise suspected Leach was a pursuer. The bandito attempted to bring Leach down with a pistol, then gathered other members of the gang and chased the detective into the brush. Leach avoided capture, even though the gang came within 100 yards of his hiding place.[24]

Realizing by now that authorities expected them to run for Texas, the gang devised countermeasures. They scattered, with Collins and Potts proceeding toward Texas through Buffalo Station, Kansas (now called Gove), seventy-eight miles west of Hays, while Bass and Davis traveled south over a slightly different route. Berry and Nixon rode east toward Callaway County, Missouri, where Berry lived with his wife and children when he was not robbing people.[25]

Law and Order

In the meantime, the forces of law and order were gathering. Nine soldiers including one musician were sent to assist Ellis County, Kansas, sheriff George W. Bardsley and two others in the pursuit, riding in a "special" car that was nothing more than a cattle carrier where the posse stabled their horses on the trip. Understandably, the posse chose to ride on top of their special car rather than in it, discussing the potential division of reward money as they sped toward Buffalo Station, which would serve as their headquarters. They arrived on the evening of Tuesday, September 25, and established their camp.

Collins and Potts found themselves riding through heavy fog into Buffalo Station at about 8:30 the next morning. When they spotted the posse, it was too late to turn around without further arousing suspicion. They casually went into a makeshift general store in the basement of the railroad section house. When Collins pulled his wallet out to pay for some fruit and a coffeepot, he exposed a letter addressed to himself, drawing the attention of station agent William A. Sternberg. When the agent asked if he was Joel Collins, the bandit readily admitted his identity. Although Collins and Potts were allowed to ride out, the posse soon realized that their chance for reward money was drifting away in the fog. Sheriff Bardsley and four soldiers galloped after them, leaving the musician and the others behind. Once Collins and Potts were located, the sheriff casually asked them to return to the station. They agreed to do so, but after exchanging glances, they each drew a pistol and were promptly shot down by the posse. Potts died instantly, while Collins lived long enough to fall on his knees, then roll to the ground dead. Among Collins' possessions was a popular poem of the time, copied in the handwriting of a young girl, entitled "Will You Love Me When I'm Old?" The bandit's sweetheart, whoever she was, would never know.

Berry returned to Mexico, Missouri, on Friday, October 5, by railroad. His associate, Tom Nixon, stayed on the Chicago-bound train and perhaps traveled on to Canada. In any event, Nixon was heard from no more. The same could not be said for Berry.

The ne'er-do-well made a dramatic entrance into the little Callaway County town that fine October day. Berry promptly exchanged some nine thousand dollars in gold coins for bills, then deposited about sixteen hundred dollars in a local bank. Jim told someone he had struck it rich in the Black Hills, and then he started a spending spree. Naturally, more than a few people in Mexico knew that Berry had never been lucky before. Soon local law enforcement learned about the Big Springs robbery and tracked Berry to a friend's home in a remote corner of Callaway County, where on October 14 he was shotgunned resisting arrest. He was returned to Mexico for medical treatment, and although the wounds were not initially believed to be life threatening, gangrene developed and he died on October 16.[26]

Bass and Davis returned to Texas, arriving in Denton County about November 1, 1877. Sam recruited prospects for his own gang during the next few months, with little difficulty. Seaborn Barnes, Arkansas Johnson, Francis M. "Frank" Jackson, and his old partner Henry Underwood became the first Bass gang.

Seaborn Barnes was an illiterate Texas cowboy with a huge Adam's apple, who worked for a potter before starting his criminal career. One researcher concluded that Arkansas Johnson may have been a John McKean from the Knob Noster area of Johnson County, Missouri. Another writer identified him as an Irishman named Huckston. Frank Jackson was an orphan, born about 1856, who lived with his sister and brother-in-law Benizett F. Key, a Denton tinsmith.[27]

The Sam Bass gang committed at least two stage robberies and four train robberies in the Dallas area during a crime spree that began in late December 1877 and continued into April of the next year. They began on Mary's Creek, about ten miles west of Fort Worth in Tarrant County, early in the morning of December 22. Bass, Underwood, and Jackson stopped the Concho Stage making the run from Cleburne to Fort Worth, then relieved the passengers and crew of a paltry forty dollars. Several days later, Henry Underwood was surrounded while enjoying Christmas with his family in Wise County and extradited to Kearney, Nebraska, to stand trial for the Big Springs holdup, along with his old pal Arkansas Johnson.

The Bass gang was undeterred by this development, if they even knew about Underwood's misfortune. Bass and Jackson returned to Mary's Creek on the morning of Saturday, January 26, to rob the Weatherford and Fort Worth stage of $400.[28]

Bass now took the gang in a new direction. When the Houston & Texas Central No. 4 train arrived in Allen, about twenty-five miles north of Dallas, on the evening of Friday, February 22, Bass, Barnes, Jackson, and their new recruit Tom Spotswood were ready to commit the first successful train robbery in Texas history. Spotswood was a Denton County widower with a glass eye who reputedly had killed men in Texas and Missouri. He was described by one observer as about thirty-five, blue eyed, with long fair hair. Tom was said to own a gray pacing pony.

The gang relieved the Houston & Texas Central express car of about $1,400, but not before express messenger James L. A. Thomas exchanged shots with the robbers and noticed Spotswood's affliction. Tom was arrested four days later, but on March 12, or the next day, Henry Underwood and Arkansas Johnson escaped from the Kearney, Nebraska jail and began the trip back to reinforce the Bass gang in Texas.[29]

The firm of Bass, Jackson, and Barnes struck again in Hutchins, nine miles south of downtown Dallas, at ten o'clock on the evening of Monday, March 18. There they robbed the Houston & Texas Central train of $617, leaving behind about $4,000 hidden by Henry "Heck" Thomas, a cousin of the express messenger robbed the previous month. Heck Thomas later became a deputy U.S. marshal in Indian Territory and one of the most authentically heroic lawmen in American history.

About two weeks later, Bass and company began to patronize a different railroad line. Sam Bass, Arkansas Johnson, and two recruits who may have been Matthew Gray and James Tyler robbed a Texas and Pacific train on April 4 at Eagle Ford,[30] west of Dallas, stealing $234 ($3,800 today).[31] Gray was the nephew and namesake of former Denton County sheriff Matthew Gray. The two new recruits were indicted for the crime but provided alibis and were never prosecuted.

One of the railroad detectives asked to track down the outlaws was hardly a pillar of the community himself. Jim Curry (Currie) was a reputed killer who had worked as a locomotive engineer for the Kansas Pacific Company, which later assigned him to work as a railroad detective. The day after the Eagle Ford robbery, Curry was one of many detectives from many different railroads asked to assist in the pursuit of the Bass gang. Working with Texas Express detective Tom Finley and a posse, he tracked gang members Henry Underwood and Frank Jackson to a farmhouse where a gun battle ensued. When Curry and Finley determined that neither of the two men was Bass himself, they inexplicably abandoned the fight and lost an opportunity for heroism that might have been useful in Curry's later sentencing hearings.[32] Less than a year later, while in his cups in Marshall, Texas, Curry shot actor Maurice Barrymore, a remote kinsman of modern actor Drew Barrymore, then mortally wounded another actor. Curry escaped punishment by pleading temporary insanity, killed another man in Lincoln County, New Mexico, and rode into obscurity after serving six years in prison.[33]

When he attacked the Texas and Pacific again on April 10, Bass had the men he wanted. More desired to go along, but Bass evidently was afraid that too many crooks might spoil the plot. Bass prepared himself more carefully for this robbery. The gang was picked, the plan was set, and the target was the train station in Mesquite, a scant ten or so miles east of Dallas. Mesquite was a town of modest proportions in 1878, consisting of one store, a blacksmith shop, two saloons, a few houses, and the railroad station.

That evening six men rode with Bass. He ordered Underwood, Jackson, Johnson, Barnes, and new recruits Albert G. Herndon and Samuel J. Pipes to pull their bandannas over their faces as the Texas and Pacific No. 1 train approached the station around eleven o'clock on the evening of Wednesday, April 10, 1878.[34] Herndon was born about 1858 and was once arrested with Belle Starr's brother on a minor weapons charge. Pipes was an associate of Joel Collins' brothers Henry and Billy Collins, with whom he had been arrested for assault in January 1878. He was also reportedly wanted for theft in Llano County.[35]

Station agent Jake Zurn was accosted first and then told to stand where he was on the platform. The train chugged to a slow stop and Bass called to his comrades to board her. Jackson covered the engineer and fireman and ordered them to take a place beside the station agent.

Zurn's wife, Agnes, came out to the platform but quickly retreated inside the station, despite orders to stop and gunfire that struck the door.[36] When train conductor Julius Alvord was accosted by one of the bandits, he pulled a double derringer and shot at the man. The outlaws fired back, and the Illinois Union veteran returned to the sleeper car to retrieve his six-shooter. Alvord was later shot through the wrist, giving him a lifetime of stories back in Marshall, Texas. Express messenger Spofford Curley (Kerley) fired five shots in the direction of the attackers but missed. Baggage master Benjamin Franklin Caperton was also blasting away at the robbers with his shotgun, even as train guards Jack Allen and J. G. Lynch fired their own pistols and a shared shotgun. The guards hit Barnes in each leg, just before the bandits sent a hail of gunfire toward them, ending the exchange.[37]

Even the candy and peanut vendor tried to join the melee. When he stepped to the platform with pistol in hand, one of the bandits told him no one wanted to buy peanuts just now and ordered him back to the train.[38]

When the shooting stopped, Bass directed the men inside the express car to surrender. Soon, the aroma of engine oil being poured over the car for a fire prompted the express messengers to open the door.

The gang rode away with a mere $162.50 and a gold ring. Today, the take would be worth $3,100, hardly commensurate with the injuries sustained by the outlaws. Barnes had bullet holes in each of his legs and Pipes was shot in his left side. Even so, the robbers managed to reach the town of Duck Creek as the train continued on to Dallas. The bandits were not the only ones suffering. Wounded conductor Alvord was treated at the Windsor Hotel by Dr. L. E. Locke.[39]

The Mesquite robbery marked the fourth such incident in just two months near Dallas. Merchants and leaders in the upstart town knew what to do. They called for the Texas Rangers. Maj. John B. Jones, commander of the Frontier Battalion, led law-enforcement efforts to capture the Bass gang.[40] While Major Jones prowled about Dallas for clues as to the gang's whereabouts, other law officers joined him. William Pinkerton, of the famed Pinkerton Agency, headquartered at the La Grand Hotel in Dallas with a contingent of detectives from the company's Chicago office.[41] U.S. District Attorney Andrew J. Evans came from Tyler, bringing U.S. Marshal Stilwell H. Russell.[42] The Bass gang undoubtedly observed these developments and went into hiding.

Denton alderman Henderson Murphy owned numerous large land tracts and several herds of cattle in Denton County. He also had an interest in the Parlor Saloon. His partner was William Riley Wetsel, who later became a Denton County deputy sheriff. Murphy had two sons.[43] Sam Bass became fast friends with young Jim Murphy and relied on this relationship as his troubles deepened. The gang hid at a place called Cove Hollow, confident that if a posse came too close, the Murphy family would warn them in time for an escape.

Meanwhile, on the morning of April 22, 1878, Sam Pipes was located and captured while recuperating from his leg

Maj. John B. Jones, commander of the Frontier Battalion, Texas Rangers. *(Courtesy of the Texas Ranger Hall of Fame and Museum, Waco, Texas)*

wounds at the Duck Creek home of Albert G. Collins. The Rangers also arrested Albert Herndon just one mile away at the home of Tom Jackson.[44] Herndon and Pipes were incarcerated in the Dallas County jail, released, rearrested, released and rearrested again, then transported to Tyler and jailed on federal charges of robbing a mail carrier. Eventually, they even spent time in jail in Austin with John Wesley Hardin.

Although Herndon and Pipes were convicted of the Mesquite robbery, they were ultimately released from prison in late February 1886, for their bravery treating fellow prisoners in a typhoid epidemic so bad that some doctors abandoned their patients. Herndon became a Dallas grocery-store clerk and disappeared from the pages of history. Ironically, Pipes was wounded in a gun accident and died on Sunday, February 16, 1889. He had married Sallie Collins after her first husband, Bass associate Billy Collins, died. Sallie lived on until 1929.[45]

Soon, members of Bass's gang were supposedly seen in various Dallas locations. Frank Jackson, for example, was reported to be in town, but when the woman making the claim searched barrooms and brothels with the town marshal, he was nowhere to be found. Events turned comedic when a few amateur detectives donned false black beards and top coats to disguise themselves, but captured no one.[46]

The search also continued in Denton County, the home of the bandits. Ranger forces, sheriff's posses, and private citizens combed the region. Although the numerous posses began inadvertently chasing one another, events took a serious turn on the twenty-ninth of April, when Sam Bass and his gang fired on members of Capt. Lee Hall's company of Texas Rangers as they neared the Cove Hollow hideout on the Denton County-Cooke County line.

This was not a banner day for Sam Bass. Although he

was separated from his pursuers by a canyon, an incoming round tore several cartridges from the outlaw's gun belt. A second round shattered his gun, causing Bass to alert his comrades that it was time to "git."[47] They cut a path to the south, stopped long enough to leave $100 with Henry Underwood's wife, Mary, and then doubled back to avoid posses.

The posses under the leadership of the Texas Rangers and Sheriff Egan soon began to tighten a net around the Bass gang. One of the other professional lawmen was Junius Peak, a Dallas resident and city recorder. Earlier on April 16, Peak was appointed second lieutenant commanding a detachment of the Frontier Battalion Company B of the Texas Rangers.[48]

Dallas and Denton counties now prepared for war with the outlaws, yet Bass and company eluded even the best of their pursuers, riding the narrow trails of the briar-laden thickets of the swamps and adjacent timberlands. Sometimes, posses even passed by the concealed bandits. When Denton County judge Thomas E. Hogg[49] joined the hunt, at least five detachments of riled citizens, lawmen, and company detectives were searching for the elusive Bass gang. Hogg eventually wrote a book about the Bass gang. Curiously, he noted that Bass would not look into the eyes of any person addressing him but instead would gaze no higher than "the central button on the second party's shirt front."[50]

Peak, Egan, and Hogg conducted wide-ranging searches of both counties while Major Jones continued sleuthing around Denton. Stephens County sheriff Berry Meaders was prowling around that county, Palo Pinto County, and points beyond with a small posse. Yet another man who respected no boundaries was Grayson County sheriff William C. Everheart. He joined the hunt with a few Texas Rangers borrowed from Captain Lee Hall's company. In the meantime, mere acquaintances of the gang were routinely rounded up and jailed. This widely spread net even snared a deputy sheriff and one town marshal. In the midst of all this, Bass and his gang left the swamps for the drier open grounds to the southwest.

Although the gang was continuously on the move, they were never able to avoid the posses for very long. One skirmish after another forced them out of their hideouts. Proceeding to the northwest, Bass and his men rode into Young County. The gang came upon McIntosh's store in Dillingham's Prairie on Sunday, June 2, 1878,[51] and purchased provisions, using some of the double-eagle gold pieces stolen during the Big Springs train robbery.

Three days later, the gang was spotted riding along Denton Creek. Deputy Sheriff Clay Withers took up the hunt but quit at nightfall, then sent a messenger to inform Sheriff Egan of his efforts. The messenger became lost in a rainstorm but eventually found Egan.

On Sunday morning, June 9, Egan and his posse raided a campsite used by the bandits but found only empty fruit cans. Continuing on, they picked up the trail and at once saw tracks showing that the outlaws had separated. Egan decided to follow just one set of tracks rather than splitting the group into separate posses. His choice proved a sound one, since the tracks soon converged.

At about eleven o'clock that morning, eight miles south of Denton, Bass and the others settled in for breakfast in a clearing behind the farm of Frank's brother, David Warner Jackson. Gunfire shattered the morning serenity as Sheriff Egan led a charge into the outlaw camp. The bandits got away but not before wounding posse man John Work and killing his horse.

They also killed the horse of posse man Alex Cockrell[52] but took a few rounds themselves. Henry Underwood was shot in the arm, recent recruit Charley Carter sustained a leg wound, and Arkansas Johnson's neck was creased by a bullet. The foxes somehow scurried away hungry but still alive.

Although Sheriff Egan was still in the hunt, Grayson County sheriff Everheart soon overtook the bad men, interrupting yet another meal the next day. Lunch ended in a flurry of outlaw boot heels and britches as they made for their saddled horses while dodging Everheart's incoming gunfire. Amazingly, the entire gang escaped without injury into the low cliffs along Clear Creek.

One story relates that even Fort Worth city marshal "Long Haired" Jim Courtright got into the chase. On June 9, while on patrol in Denton County with two other lawmen, Courtright thought he recognized a Denton carpenter in the distance and hailed him. Instead, he had only alerted Frank Jackson, who rode away to warn the Bass crew.[53]

Bass and his cohorts emerged on Tuesday, June 11, at a Bolivar store, where they purchased provisions from a reluctant shopkeeper. Bass directed the merchant to deliver a message asking his stalkers to let up on the chase, since he hadn't slept in three days. His frustration was understandable. When one posse gave up, another was always ready to continue the pursuit. Although they were bone tired, Bass and company outran the posses and escaped into Wise County. They concealed themselves along the bank of Salt Creek about ten miles southwest of Decatur.

The sound of gunfire broke the tranquility of a warm Thursday afternoon on June 13 as the combined posses of Ranger Junius Peak and Wise County sheriff George W. Stevens took Bass completely by surprise. The outlaws made a run for the woods without their horses, breaking through the underbrush and into a cave where they concealed themselves. Soon they noticed that Arkansas Johnson was missing. He had sustained a bullet wound to the chest; he was buried where he fell.[54]

Once it was safe to do so, some of the gang members began to drift away from Sam Bass, each with his own excuse. The first to go was Henry Underwood. Soon, Charley Carter rode off. Now Bass, Seaborn Barnes, and Frank Jackson were all that remained of the once dreaded desperado gang.

On Saturday, June 15, tired and saddle worn, Bass and Barnes rode to Jim Murphy's place near the small town of Rosston.[55] Jim met them outside his home, and Bass invited him to join the gang. Murphy hesitated and then agreed to go with them, but only after his wheat crop was threshed. Satisfied, Bass handed Murphy fifty dollars to exchange for smaller bills in Rosston before rejoining the gang on Monday.

Murphy developed his own plans. Apparently, he telegraphed U.S. Deputy Marshal Walter Johnson from Rosston, informing the lawman of Bass's whereabouts. Johnson and Sheriff Everheart led a posse to Murphy's place. After a short skirmish, the outlaws escaped again, this time with informant Murphy riding along. He sent word to Denton County deputy Clay Withers that the gang planned to camp near Bolivar that Monday night, yet much to his surprise, nothing happened.

On Wednesday, June 19, Bass, Jackson, and Murphy were on the road to Bolivar, seemingly free as air. One afternoon, Bass separated from Murphy and Jackson near Franklin, to find Henry Collins. Soon Bass and Collins returned with two strangers. Much to Murphy's surprise, one of the horseback strangers, "Jake," urged Bass to kill Murphy then and there.[56] Bass seemed calm enough, but Murphy probably realized his days as an informant or perhaps even as a living human being were numbered.

Soon, the gang approached a lone church, where a whistle was heard. Bass whistled in return. Seaborn Barnes revealed himself and related some news. The authorities in Fort Worth had received a telegraph identifying Jim Murphy as an informant. Murphy was to lead them into a robbery at Fort Worth with the connivance of the Rangers, who would be waiting in ambush.

Bass and Barnes drew down on Jim Murphy and prepared to settle his hash. Murphy must have inherited more than his share of blarney from his Irish ancestors. He excitedly explained that the entire scheme was one he concocted as a means of *getting rid* of the Rangers. He had no intention of following through.

Fortunately for Murphy, he had a strong ally in Frank Jackson, whom Bass respected and liked. Even though Barnes was eager to kill Murphy, Bass took Jackson's advice and declined.[57] Soon Henry Collins and "Jake" departed, hardly an unusual occurrence among outlaw gangs of that era. Now Jackson, Barnes, Bass, and Murphy were all that remained. Murphy was only alive because Frank Jackson had saved him.

On Sunday afternoon, June 23, the quartet reached Rockwall, a town established in 1854 on the site of a geological formation then assumed to be a rock wall constructed in ancient times. The gang arrived around four o'clock and camped about fifty yards from a very curious spot. A gallows had been constructed earlier to hang a murderer. George Garner had cheated the executioner, but at a price. His wife had smuggled in poison for them both, but when the concoction proved ineffective, Garner managed to hang his better half with a bucket bail and then suffocate himself with strips of clothing.

While Murphy slept on the morning of June 24, Barnes and Bass agreed to kill him, but Jackson intervened. Bass and Barnes put away their pistols, but each kept a wary eye on Jim Murphy.[58]

The men continued south to the town of Kaufman, in the county of the same name, in search of a bank whose funds would support lives of leisure in Mexico. Small Kaufman was not even prosperous enough to warrant a bank, and the only store in town did not appear to be worth a holdup effort.

The bandits rode on to the Trinity River, turned north, and continued to Ennis. There they found the prosperous bank they were looking for, but it was heavily guarded. Cutting a trail back to the south, the gang turned toward Waco, seventy-four miles away.

They probably did not know that on July 2, Tom Spotswood, easily identified because of his glass eye, was found guilty of the Allen train robbery. Upon his conviction, he lunged toward young express messenger Heck Thomas, was subdued, and was then shipped off to Huntsville prison on a ten-year sentence. Spotswood was granted a new trial later that month, was acquitted two years later, married his sweetheart in Collin County, and apparently started a new life in places yet unknown.[59]

The gang camped about two miles north of town on Sunday, July 6.[60] Waco had three banks to choose from. Bass sent Murphy and Jackson ahead to scout out their best bet. Jackson was favorably impressed by the first bank they entered. A large cache of gold coins and currency was visible, just out of their reach. Murphy knew that when Bass heard this, he would be only too eager to rush the bank before Murphy could warn the Texas Rangers. Murphy began telling Jackson about the potential pitfalls of robbing that particular bank, but Jackson was not to be dissuaded.

Gold and greenbacks whirled in Bass's and Barnes' heads like leaves in a summer dust devil when they heard about the treasure just waiting for them. Bass vowed that they would all be richer and happier in the next few days, but Murphy was unenthusiastic. Bass tried to raise Murphy's spirits, but nothing seemed to work.

Bass surprised the whole lot at breakfast the next morning when he gave in to Murphy's worries. The outlaw leader announced that maybe Murphy had a good point after all.

Bass now made a decision that would shorten his life. The gang would bypass Waco and Murphy would choose the next holdup. Murphy selected Round Rock.[61] The men headed south once again. Barnes left the group long enough to steal a fresh horse and then rode back, leading his old horse. When the outlaws reached Belton, Murphy sold the animal to a blacksmith and signed his name to a bill of sale, hoping to alert local law enforcement as to the gang's whereabouts.[62] Apparently Murphy was not as well known as he hoped, because his plan did not work.

Now Murphy had to inform the Rangers, even as he was being closely watched by the suspicious Bass and Barnes and his protector Frank Jackson. Any opportunity to escape would be fleeting at best. Then, on Sunday, July 13, Bass sent Murphy into Belton alone on an errand. While in town, Murphy hastily penned a note to Sheriff Everheart in Sherman, Texas, and also to U.S. Deputy Marshal Walter Johnson. "For God's sake, come at once," Murphy implored, telling the sheriff and Johnson that the gang was headed to Round Rock to rob a bank.[63]

Round Rock

Situated in south-central Williamson County, Round Rock, first known as Brushy Creek for its proximity to a creek of the same name, was established in 1848. An Austin blacksmith, Jacob M. Harrell, packed up shop and traveled the sixteen miles north to Brushy Creek, where he established a new shop and the new town. Three years later, Brushy Creek postmaster Thomas C. Oats was asked by post office officials to designate a new name for the town. Oats and Harrell submitted Round Rock.[64] The name was derived from a large rounded limestone rock in the nearby creek where they fished. Round Rock was soon a stopping place for herdsmen traveling north to Kansas. The Chisholm Trail then became a prime source of income for Round Rock's growing population. The International-Great Northern Railway almost came to town in 1876. When tracks were laid some distance south and east of Round Rock, the citizenry quickly grasped that the town had to be moved to the railroad if it were to survive. Many townspeople now abandoned "old" Round Rock and established "new" Round Rock near the train station. When Jim Murphy nominated new Round Rock as the Bass gang's next holdup site, it boasted numerous buildings housing all manner of professional men, hotels, the William Walsh lime plant, a broom factory, and, of course, a bank. It is little wonder then that Sam Bass readily agreed that Round Rock should be their next target.

They reached Georgetown on the San Gabriel River about ten miles north and east of Round Rock and camped outside the town limits. When two gang members went into town for supplies, Williamson County deputy sheriff Milt Tucker and Town Marshal Chamberlain eyed them suspiciously. Neither man recognized the outlaws, so nothing was done.[65]

On Wednesday, July 16, Murphy managed to write a third letter, this time to Major Jones in Austin, warning again that the gang was headed to Round Rock to commit a robbery. Just as Murphy handed the letter to the shopkeeper/postmaster at the town store, Bass walked in and wanted to know what was keeping him. Murphy claimed that he and the shopkeeper were haggling over the price of a newspaper. The merchant was savvy enough to hand Murphy a paper to look at but not keep. Since Bass was illiterate, Murphy read him the latest news, returned the paper, and both men exited the store.

After breaking camp, the gang left for Round Rock.

Arriving later that night, the bandits made camp on the San Saba road just outside of town. The following day, Barnes and Murphy rode into town to scout the bank. Barnes liked what he saw.

Now Murphy had to buy time for the Rangers to close in. He convinced Barnes that they should let their horses rest in preparation for their upcoming hell-bent-for-leather getaway. Barnes in turn convinced Bass, and all agreed that for the next few days the outlaws would lie low. While the men and the horses rested, plans were made to take the bank. Major Jones in the meantime directed Ranger corporal Vernon Wilson to make haste for Lampasas, about seventy-five miles northwest of Austin. Wilson was to instruct Lt. N. O. Reynolds of Company E[66] to hurry to Round Rock, where Jones would meet him. Wilson rushed to Lampasas but learned the Ranger company had moved fifty miles west to San Saba. Although the corporal had ridden his horse to death during the hard ride to Lampasas, he was undaunted. Wilson boarded a stagecoach and eventually found Reynolds' company camped on the San Saba River. Reynolds rode toward Round Rock without delay.

Meanwhile in Austin, Major Jones ordered Rangers Richard C. Ware, Chris Conner, and George Herold (Harold, Harrell) to Round Rock. These were the only Rangers available in Austin that day. Jones also summoned Capt. Lee Hall and later Lt. John B. Armstrong, who had gained fame about a year earlier for arresting the notorious John Wesley Hardin. Along the way, Jones recruited Travis County deputy sheriff Maurice B. Moore, on the assurance of plentiful reward money. Unbeknownst to Bass, a small army was assembling, and his gang was nearing extinction.

Lieutenant Reynolds had an entire company of Rangers at his disposal, so recruiting a squad for the Round Rock assault was no problem. Although Reynolds was too sick to ride with the squad, he and Corporal Wilson followed in

Lt. N. O. Reynolds, Company E Frontier Battalion, Texas Rangers.
(Courtesy of Chuck Parsons)

a mule-drawn wagon. Those who rode on ahead included Sgt. Charles L. Nevill, Sgt. Henry W. McGhee, Cpl. James B. Gillett, Abe Anglin, David L. Lygon, William Derrick, John R. Bannister, and William L. Bannister.[67]

Although Reynolds and his men were not going to arrive at Round Rock when Jones had expected, his plan was coming together. Meanwhile, Bass now had some suspicions. He noticed some men in Round Rock who sure looked like Texas Rangers. He sent Murphy and Jackson to scout the town, but they reported that there were no Texas Rangers. With that, Bass led his gang into town for supplies and one last look at the bank before the planned robbery.

On Saturday, July 19, 1878, at about four o'clock, the boys casually rode into "old" Round Rock. Murphy suggested that he should stay there and watch for Rangers. Murphy

N. O. Reynolds (left) and his brother-in-law, Charles L. Nevill. *(Courtesy of Chuck Parsons)*

hitched his horse at the store operated by Livingston M. Mays and J. M. Black.[68] Then he joined the men already sharing the cool shade of the awning.

Bass, Barnes, and Jackson coolly rode on to "new" Round Rock and tied their mounts in an alley at the edge of town. They proceeded directly to Henry Koppel's general store, where they planned to purchase tobacco. Deputy Moore was outside near the livery stable when the men walked by. The stable's owner, Henry Albert Highsmith, was standing with Moore as the three ambled past.

Highsmith pointed the men out to Moore, saying they were strangers to him. Moore then scrutinized the trio more closely. He thought it odd that two of them carried their saddle bags. More disturbingly, he observed the bulge of a concealed pistol beneath one man's coat. Rather than confront the men alone, Moore walked nonchalantly up to Williamson County deputy sheriff Ahijah W. "Caige" Grimes[69] and voiced his suspicions. The two lawmen followed the strangers into Henry Koppel's store.

As the trio completed their transaction and made light talk with the clerk, Simon Juda, Grimes placed one hand on Bass's shoulder and asked if any of them were carrying a pistol. The store was instantly filled with muzzle flashes, gun smoke, and chaos. All three bandits had spun around at Grimes' question and answered in simultaneous gunfire. Grimes was knocked off his feet by the lead balls that shot him to pieces, and he was dead within seconds. His pistol never left its holster.[70]

Moore managed to draw his weapon and fire through the blinding, choking smoke inside the store. One of his rounds ripped through Bass's right hand, separating his middle and ring fingers. Deputy Moore was also seriously wounded but staggered from the store, fired once more at the fleeing outlaws, and then reloaded and chased them on foot. Soon the injury began to sap his strength. Seeing his condition, Dr. A. F. Morris cautioned the tenacious lawman not to continue his pursuit unless he wished to die. Rangers Conner, Ware, and Herold took up the chase, exchanging bullets with the gang. Even one-armed J. F. Tubbs blasted away at the outlaws with Grimes' pistol.[71]

The bandits ran for their horses, turning back to shoot at their pursuers from time to time. Bass was bleeding badly, but Jackson and Barnes were still unscathed and provided covering fire for their leader. The lawbreakers failed to notice Ranger Ware as he stopped, took careful aim, and squeezed off a round in the direction of Seaborn Barnes. It sped straight to the bandit's head, ending his criminal career and his life.[72]

Even now, the battle intensified. Jackson fought the encircling citizens and lawmen with badgerlike ferocity, while somehow keeping the physically sinking Bass on his feet. Jackson was even able to load the injured Bass onto his mount while firing back at the town defenders.

"Oh, Lord!" Bass cried out as a round fired by Ranger George Herold struck his spine and ripped upward, exiting to the left of his navel.[73] Jackson untied his own horse and then, holding the reins of Sam's horse, galloped toward "old" Round Rock.

Jim Murphy shared small talk with the locals even as Bass and Jackson raced past the store. Murphy was still standing there when Major Jones and a few citizens galloped by after the bandits. He yelled to Jones, who was so focused on catching Bass that he failed to notice Murphy.[74] After Jones lost the trail, he turned back with several citizens in tow. He planned to resume the hunt for Bass the next day with professional lawmen.

In the meantime, Jackson returned briefly to the outlaw camp, then found a concealed, wooded area. Since Bass could hardly sit his saddle any longer, Jackson stopped, helped the once formidable desperado from his horse, and bound his wounds as best he could. Then Jackson rode away, leaving Bass alone to face a grim future. Thus, Jackson disappeared from sight and from history—perhaps.[75]

The next morning, Sunday, July 20, Lieutenant Reynolds and his contingent of Rangers camped on Brushy Creek without realizing that Bass was barely clinging to life nearby. Soon, Lt. John B. Armstrong and his men arrived and were joined by Constable Olander C. Lane of Georgetown and Deputy Sheriff Tucker of Williamson County, none of whom knew the extent to which the outlaw gang had been decimated.

Major Jones acted on the assumption that he was chasing a band of seven or eight extremely dangerous and cunning men. He divided the lawmen and citizens into posses, one of which included Jim Murphy.

Thirst eventually got the best of Bass, but no one would help the bloodied brigand. First he was refused assistance by a black wagon driver. Next, Bass appeared at the home of John Sherman, whose wife, Semantha, may have slammed a door in his face,[76] although one account relates she gave Bass a cup of water.[77] Desperate, wracked with pain, and losing blood, Bass pressed on. He eventually came upon a camp of railroad men, who gave him some water. Bass claimed he was a cattleman who had simply run into a little trouble at Round Rock and got himself shot up. Exhausted from staggering the few hundred yards from where Jackson left him, Bass slumped beneath a live oak tree.

Sergeant Nevill and his Rangers rode past Dudley Snyder's pasture and noticed Bass from a distance but assumed he was part of the railroad crew. Then, one of the workers pointed toward Bass and mentioned that he had attempted to hire someone to carry him away. Nevill and his men approached and then ordered the stranger to identify himself. Bass weakly raised one hand and managed to say, "Don't shoot. . . . I am the man you are looking for. I am Sam Bass."

N. O. Reynolds reminiscing from his front porch many years after his Texas Ranger service. *(Courtesy of Chuck Parsons)*

Nevill approached Bass warily with pistol drawn and cocked, then holstered his weapon when it became obvious that Bass would offer no resistance.

"Your gun is cocked; you will shoot your foot," Bass warned. Nevill sheepishly uncocked his pistol.[78]

Back in Round Rock, Bass languished on a bare cot in August Gloeber's tin shop. Richard C. Hart, manager of the hotel next door, refused to lodge Bass but furnished the dying prisoner a sheet and pillow.[79] Dr. C. P. Cochran treated the seriously wounded man amid the din of coffeepots, tools, and other merchandise being produced in a tin shop much like that in which gang member Frank Jackson grew up.[80] Major Jones persistently asked Bass for the names of his accomplices and information about the Texas robberies he had committed, but Bass refused to cooperate. Most of Bass's confederates were dead, imprisoned, or long gone as he lay nearly penniless, alone, and dying as locals treated his presence with the reverence of a carnival display, all because a deputy had inquired about a concealed pistol.

Deputy Moore's wounds were not life threatening but serious enough that he was accompanied by Dr. Morris to Austin, where he would recuperate at the home of Mr. Petmecky,[81] a close friend. Moore's mother was notified and left her Galveston home to be with her son.

Bass too had those who worried about him. A few concerned citizens even thought the dying outlaw should have an opportunity to cleanse his soul. Round Rock Christian Church pastor Austin Cunningham Aten was asked to offer spiritual consolation to Bass, but initially refused because he did not believe in deathbed conversions. The reverend was eventually convinced to approach Bass, but only inquired if the bandito wanted to be prayed for. Bass was not religious, and perhaps more out of politeness than anything, he told the preacher to go ahead, "if you think it will do any good."[82] The preacher's second eldest

Sgt. Charles Nevill, Company E Frontier Battalion, sometime after Reynolds' retirement. *(Courtesy of Chuck Parsons)*

son, Austin Ira Aten, would later serve with distinction in the Texas Rangers.

"The world is bobbing around," Sam Bass supposedly remarked, just before he died with a slight jerk of his head at 3:55 on Monday afternoon July 21, 1878, on his twenty-seventh birthday.[83] The following morning Bass's coffin was loaded in a small wagon, with two African-American men charged with burial detail at the cemetery in "old" Round Rock. Methodist minister John W. Ledbetter[84] was appalled at the sight of the two men riding astride the coffin as it passed his home. He stopped the wagon, made the men climb down, and then accompanied them to the cemetery. After the reverend prayed over the outlaw, Bass was interred next to Seaborn Barnes. Deputy Grimes, the first man slain in the Round Rock gunfight, was buried a mere eighty yards from his murderers.[85]

The fate of Bass lieutenant Frank Jackson, who rescued the gang leader during the gunfight at Round Rock, remains a mystery. Once he bound the frail Sam Bass's wounds, he rode away for good. Or did he?

The informant, Jim Murphy, claimed to have periodic contact with Jackson, according to Murphy's correspondence with Maj. John B. Jones. Murphy himself did not return to Denton County until August 1, when he ingratiated himself into Peak's camp.[86] Murphy informed Jones that Jackson still trusted him but that the Collins family was ready to kill Murphy, according to Frank Jackson, indicating Jackson's possible presence in the area.

The *Galveston Daily News*[87] reported that Jackson had been seen in Denton twice following the Round Rock shootout. Murphy again wrote Jones that he had been in contact with Jackson. This time, he said, Jackson met with him on August 27 to tell him that Jackson was not seeking vengeance in the death of Sam Bass, as some had imagined, but was very much interested in receiving a form of amnesty for his crimes. Murphy wrote that Jackson even offered to help Henry Underwood and other members of the gang "if it will have him turned loose."[88]

Murphy no doubt remembered that Jackson had saved him from death at the hands of Bass and Barnes more than once, because they correctly suspected Murphy of being a Ranger informant. Jackson was indicted for the murder of Deputy Grimes on September 20, 1878.[89] Jackson may have believed that his association with Murphy could somehow bring him closer to appeasing the Texas Rangers, but if so, his hopes were dashed.

Murphy suffered from an eye condition that was being treated by Dr. Ed McMath.[90] The doctor was using an antiseptic that, if swallowed in any amount, was lethal. On Thursday, June 5, 1879, Murphy arrived at the doctor's drugstore for his routine but precarious treatment. The doctor carefully had Murphy lie on his back during the treatment, to keep the poisonous liquid away from his mouth. After being treated, Murphy sat up to light a pipe, allowing a small remnant of the medicine to enter a corner of his mouth. He was immediately wracked with convulsions and died later that night.

From then on, Jackson was as elusive as a ghost, although sightings were reported across the country. He supposedly occupied prison cells in Texas and Arizona at various times during 1881. One acquaintance claimed that Jackson was working a silver mine somewhere in Colorado.[91] Or perhaps he turned his life around completely to become a lawman in California, a traveling salesman in Houston, or a rancher in Big Spring, Texas.[92] Adding to the confusion, lawman M. F. Leach suggested that Jack Davis and Frank Jackson may have been the same person.[93]

In the meantime, Henry Underwood returned to Indiana to be with his wife and family, who had left Texas in September 1878. He was indicted in the federal court in

Indianapolis in 1881 for counterfeiting, sent to prison, and then released in April 1885, under the name Henry Jones. Underwood was in and out of Indiana prisons until 1906 and died a free man the next year in Jamestown, Indiana.[94] His brother Nathan reinvented himself and fared much better after his outlaw days. He married, fathered six children, and became a civic leader in San Antonio. He even ran once for sheriff before he died peacefully in 1931.[95]

Jackson was said to have been in the custody of lawmen in Oklahoma in the early 1900s. Authorities there supposedly ransomed him for a $500 reward. Williamson County sheriff Samson Connell allegedly attempted to extradite Jackson from Oklahoma but returned to Texas alone.

Texas Ranger Frank Hamer tried to locate Frank Jackson in 1927.[96] He had better luck finding Bonnie and Clyde seven years later. The last official attempt to contact Jackson came in 1932, when Jackson would have been seventy-six years old. Former Ranger William Warren Sterling,[97] then Texas adjutant general, recruited his former associate James B. Gillett to find Frank Jackson, but the effort failed.

Four years later, on December 21, 1936, a motion was filed in Williamson County to dismiss the murder indictment against Jackson in the Grimes killing. It was granted that same day by Judge H. A. Dolan.[98] Jackson was either a very grateful eighty-year-old or a dead man.

Marshall Ratliff. *(Courtesy of Conrad Hilton Center and Museum, Cisco, Texas)*

CHAPTER EIGHT

Marshall Ratliff:
Season's Greetings!

On Friday, December 23, 1927, Marshall Ratliff moved down East Fifth Street in the homemade Santa suit that was supposed to keep the good citizens of Cisco from recognizing him. Perhaps he wondered if the disguise was worth it, as more and more children began to follow him and became a nuisance. "How about some candy?" asked one little tyke, even as the older children began to realize that this was no ordinary department-store Santa. One even asked suspiciously where he worked.

Ratliff had to keep them all happy or at least quiet as he walked toward his destination, so he talked briefly to a small child in the high-pitched voice he imagined should belong to Santa. Then he told her young mother that he was going to lunch. When the twenty-something mom asked whom he "represented," his response was one she long remembered. "You'll find out pretty quick," Ratliff replied, with more than a hint of sarcasm.[1]

The First National Bank Building was just a converted storefront whose most prominent architectural detail was a set of old-fashioned teller cages dating from the last century. On this day, only one was occupied, by cashier Jewell Poe, who was busy taking a deposit from a wholesale grocery company manager.[2]

Two other customers were waiting in line. Twelve-year-old Laverne Comer and her friend Emma were there to withdraw some savings for Christmas presents. They had

Downtown Cisco, Texas, ca. 1927. *(Courtesy of Conrad Hilton Center and Museum, Cisco, Texas)*

opened the account with money earned from the sale of some calves.

Alex Spears sat nearby, greeting customers. Spears had become a banker in a time-honored way. He married the daughter of bank president Charlie Fee, who was home enjoying a good lunch. When Ratliff appeared, Spears was talking with young Marion Olson, a student home from Harvard Law School destined to become a successful San Antonio attorney.

Harvard seemed a world away from Cisco, Texas, once called Red Gap, a town of about fifteen thousand that had only existed for fifty-two years but was now experiencing its share of prosperity in the Eastland County oil boom. One of the town's hotels was the first such place owned by Conrad Hilton, great-grandfather of the famous twenty-first-century bad girl Paris Hilton.

Nearby, in the drab bank bookkeeping room, Vance Littleton and Freda Stroebel were doing their best to catch up with the morning's transactions, a very tall order two days before Christmas.

Santa seemed hardly out of place as he strode through the door. Spears wondered for a moment why the old guy had not responded to his greeting. Then he saw three men holding guns as they walked in the front door, right behind the white-bearded one.[3]

Only when one of the bandits said, "I mean business, big boy," did Poe realize that a robbery was in progress. Strangely enough, the thieves seemed to know the bank layout, and Santa even directed his helpers as if the whole thing was well planned.

Six-year-old Frances Blasengame and her mother changed all that when they burst through the bank door, trailing Santa Claus and drawing the immediate attention of holdup man Louis Davis, who should not have even been there.

Employees of the First National Bank in Cisco robbed by Ratliff and gang: Jewell Poe, Vance Littleton, Freda Stroebel, George P. Fee, Ethel McCann. *(Courtesy of Conrad Hilton Center and Museum, Cisco, Texas)*

Times were hard for more than a few Texans, even in the midst of an oil boom, and the mouths to feed in the Davis home were many. And so when ex-convict Henry Helms recruited him to substitute for Ratliff's brother, he agreed to come along. This was Davis's first bank robbery, and perhaps he had told himself it would be his last. Helms and the other ex-convicts had told him repeatedly that there would be no need to use their weapons. Yet, before he knew it, Helms himself was screaming, "Shoot!"—all because of an inquisitive little girl and her mother.[4]

Young Mrs. Blasengame was a quick study who recognized as soon as she cleared the front door that a robbery was in progress. She guided little Frances toward the back of the building, despite gruff orders from the bandits to stand still. She pushed the little girl past them and through the bookkeeping room. Finally, mother and child forced their way through a door and screen door into the alley.

Within seconds, Mrs. Blasengame alerted Police Chief G. E. "Bit" Bedford, who twenty-five years before had been elected sheriff of Eastland County.[5] Bedford sounded the alarm and had no problem finding men and even boys willing to help.

The robbers and their hostages were oblivious to all this. Robert Hill and Henry Helms were guarding the bank staff and customers, while Santa removed a small pistol from the teller cage and then shoved Jewell Poe toward the vault.

Henry Helms was a morose and unfriendly preacher's kid, the son of Rev. J. C. Helms of Oklahoma City. Robert Hill had been orphaned at a young age, something he was always quick to mention. Soon, he would find that sympathy for orphaned bank robbers was in very short supply.

Under Santa's watchful eye, Poe began to throw checks, cash, and coins into the *Idaho Potatoes* sack that Ratliff had stuffed underneath his belt for extra girth as part of his disguise, before he became a mean-spirited bank robber.

Poe was aware that two sacks of currency he pretended to overlook were worth almost as much as the $5,000 in his cashier's drawer back in the teller cage.[6]

Santa now had what the gang came for and signaled his accomplices that it was time to leave, just before someone outside peeked through the front window into the bank, setting in motion events that would claim the lives of two good men, not to mention three of the four bank robbers.

One of the three bandits fired at the face in the window, and Robert Hill fired more shots into the ceiling, strictly as a warning. Surely, no one in the bank expected what happened next. The little bank was suddenly transformed into a shooting gallery, as gunfire poured in from all sides. The Cisco citizenry either did not realize that bank customers and staff were trapped inside or were too panicked to think about it.

Although the robbers had intended to be long gone by now, events had thrust a new and improbable role upon them. Bullets whistled throughout the bank lobby as Santa moved his charges toward the one possible refuge the building offered. Ratliff pulled his tacky white beard down long enough to comment that the entire town must be firing into the building, as he herded the hostages under the counting table.[7]

Chief Bedford had two sworn officers available that day. George Carmichael and R. T. Redies waited for the robbers from positions viewing the door that accessed the alley behind the bank. Other citizens were ready to join in, encouraged by hardware-store clerks who promptly handed loaded rifles and shotguns to anyone who would take them. Then too, some of the volunteers may have had visions of winning the $5,000 Dead Bank Robber reward recently offered by the Texas Bankers Association.

This should not have surprised the Ratliff gang. About fifteen months before, Texas Ranger captain Tom Hickman accepted an Association gift of $1,000 after killing two bank thieves exiting the Red River National Bank in Clarksville, following a daylight robbery that netted A. M. Slayton and T. L. Smallwood $33,125 for about five seconds.[8] Hickman, two other law officers, and a volunteer learned of a possible robbery, established a stakeout, demanded surrender, and then promptly liquidated the firm of Slayton and Smallwood when surrender was refused. An article in the October 26, 1926, issue of *The Texas Bankers Record* announced the creation of a $500 standing award for future dead bank robbers, but not a penny for those captured.

Just the month before Ratliff and the others walked into the First National Bank in Cisco, the reward was increased from $500 to $5,000, which today would be worth about $55,000. The month after the Cisco robbery, *The Texas Bankers Record* would boast about the sharp reduction in successful bank robberies over the last few weeks.[9] In fact, the program would continue for many years, even after famed Texas Ranger Frank Hamer made a strong case that certain law officers used it as a lucrative "murder machine" in an isolated incident in Stanton, Texas, the very day of the Santa Claus robbery.[10] Hamer may have been wrong about the details of other alleged abuses, but he prompted reforms that kept the Dead Bank Robber reward program in existence until it outlived its usefulness in 1964. This was all in the future, but now the Cisco boys were about to become a 1927 statistic.

Soon, the usually quiet burg began to take on the appearance of Coffeyville, another small town 438 miles away in Kansas, whose citizens had confronted the Dalton gang on a beautiful fall day thirty-five years before and killed them all save one.[11]

Likewise, the James-Younger gang met disaster 576 miles north of that small Kansas town in Northfield, Minnesota, sixteen years before the Coffeyville defenders destroyed the Dalton gang.[12]

Had these ex-convicts spent any time studying such things in the prison library, or even listened to prison lore, they might have offered to surrender and saved themselves more serious trouble than they already had. Instead, they instinctively returned fire, even as they wondered where all the shooters had come from. Ratliff paused long enough from reloading to complain that the citizens were all after the reward money.

Then, Santa pulled the customers and bank employees from beneath the counting table and moved them toward the back door. Alex Spears was the first hostage forced out the door and into the alley. He was shot in the jaw almost immediately and ordered to get into the Buick the gang had stolen and positioned in the alley, but he hurried past it. Marion Olson was forced into the car, despite a bullet wound. Soon, however, Olson jumped out of the car and ran through the gunfire to safety.

Now Spears and all of the hostages escaped from the bandits, except the little girls who were just too young to get away by themselves. Both girls were forced to briefly stand on the running boards of the Buick. When they began to cry, the bandits relented and pulled Laverne and Emma into the car as the bullets flew around them.[13]

When Santa came out of the bank, Officers Bedford and Carmichael both shot at the red target, but Ratliff returned fire and knocked Bedford right on his back. Next, Davis came through the door but was immediately met by a shotgun blast. Somehow, he staggered into the backseat of the Buick. Soon, Officer George Carmichael sustained a mortal wound as he charged the bandits.[14]

Café owner R. L. Day now ran up to the Buick, aimed his shotgun at the driver, but heard only a harmless "click" as he pulled the trigger. His second effort was no more successful than the first. Only when he pulled the trigger the third time in exasperation did the shotgun fire, blasting

First National Bank in Cisco, after the robbery by Ratliff and gang. *(Courtesy of Conrad Hilton Center and Museum, Cisco, Texas)*

a hole in the rear wall of a nearby department store but injuring no one.[15]

Now the Buick rolled past a blind beggar playing for tips on the sidewalk. He was fiddling away at "Soldier's Joy," an old song that entertained American soldiers during the Revolution, perhaps accompanied a time or two by the same sound of bullets that now followed the bandits.

Several men pursued the sedan on foot, firing their weapons as they ran. Postman Coldwell was prominent among these stalwarts, and he or perhaps another town defender shot out one of the rear tires, causing the getaway car to career wildly from side to side.

Men in other automobiles soon took up the chase. Cisco policeman R. T. Redies was picked up by a civic-minded motorist even as bank officer Guy Dabney and his nephew

Carl Mauldin joined the pursuit. The bandits were hardly difficult to identify through the gunfire: their stolen Buick was something of a novelty in 1927 due to its blue exterior. The simple bank robbery planned by Marshall Ratliff had become a fight for survival, one that Louis Davis was losing. There were other reasons no one inside the getaway car was celebrating. The fancy gas gauge that the Buick sported revealed a disturbing message to the bandits: e-m-p-t-y. The gang astutely decided to trade up.

Rising Star resident Ellis Harris was resting comfortably in the backseat of his brand-new Oldsmobile while his fourteen-year-old son Woodrow finished the twenty-one-mile drive into Cisco. No doubt Ellis had great confidence in his son's driving skills, what with Ellis's eighty-something mother-in-law watching young Woodrow's every move, when she was awake.

"Get out of the car!" screamed one of the bandits, at the intersection of Fourteenth Street and Avenue D.[16] Young Woodrow did not have to be asked twice, but his grandmother was another matter. After yelling at her twice and seeing not the slightest hint of understanding in her eyes, Robert Hill lifted Sarah Graves out of the car and gently put her down on her feet, just before the entire Harris family was ordered to run away. Other cars, many with shotguns and rifles sticking out of the windows, began to approach the scene. Everyone in the gang except Santa and Davis started shifting cargo from the Buick to the Oldsmobile. The unconscious Davis was eventually placed with the valuable *Idaho Potatoes* sack in the backseat of the new car.

Potatoes indeed. The sack contained $12,200 ($134,000 today) in cash, as well as $150,000 in securities, which today would have a face value of $1.65 million.

While the young girls were placed in the front seat, gunfire from about a block away began to pour into the brand-spanking-new Oldsmobile. Suddenly, the bandits realized that fourteen-year-old Woodrow had carried the ignition key away in his pocket and was now safely hidden behind one of the many nearby structures. Now the bandits were forced to return to the Buick and just hope that it still had enough gasoline to carry them out of Cisco under the increasingly heavy gunfire. Naturally, they left a few things behind as they sped away. Louis Davis was one of them.

Hours later, he was roused to consciousness just long enough to give his name, have his picture taken, and briefly explain how he became a bank robber. Louis was a family man from Wichita Falls who most recently had worked in a Bristow, Oklahoma glass factory. He had been desperate for money and was lured into the crime by ex-convicts, none of whom he identified. One of his hopes, at least, was fulfilled. Louis Davis would never rob a bank again.

Robert Hill, Henry Helms, and Marshall Ratliff had all been criminals long enough to realize they were now in much more serious trouble than they had bargained for. Chief Bedford was probably dead, meaning that they now faced the death penalty in a state that kept an electric chair at Huntsville humming.

Worse still, the surviving trio now realized that something else had been left behind with Louis Davis—the small fortune in cash and securities they had stolen. Each bandit had about two dollars on his person, hardly enough to finance a trip to Fort Worth, much less South America. Furthermore, twenty-four-year-old Marshall Ratliff had sustained a bullet wound that had saturated his chin with blood.

Ratliff, Helms, and Hill drove south out of Cisco that Friday afternoon and soon found themselves near a farm established by Congressman Robert Quincy Lee.[17] Nearby, they forced the young captives to close their eyes and cover them with their fingers as the bandits scampered away into the mesquite and underbrush. Unfortunately for the

Quick-thinking fourteen-year-old Woody Harris, who, when accosted by the gang for his family auto, grabbed the keys and took off on foot, leaving the bandits with their original getaway vehicle that was about to run out of gas. *(Courtesy of Conrad Hilton Center and Museum, Cisco, Texas)*

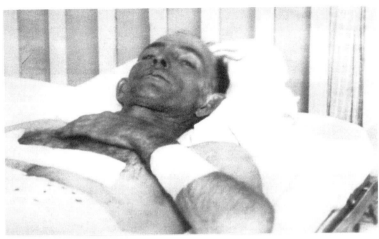

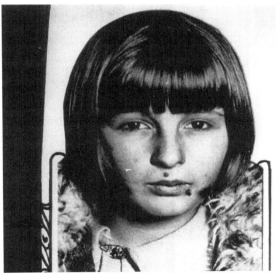

Top: Louis Davis lies in a hospital mortally wounded after the bank heist. *Bottom:* Twelve-year-old Laverne Comer lives to tell about being kidnapped by the Ratliff gang during the bank robbery. (*Courtesy of Conrad Hilton Center and Museum, Cisco, Texas*)

fugitives, they were traveling a tad too lightly. Their meager food, water, and other supplies had also been abandoned in the Oldsmobile.[18]

The posse led by Eastland County sheriff John S. Hart now had much better luck when they stumbled upon the blood-soaked Santa suit Ratliff had discarded in some bushes.[19] The bandits could not be far away, some posse members undoubtedly told themselves as visions of the $15,000 in reward money for the trio ($165,000 today) danced in their heads. A big payday was surely within reach.

The bandits had other ideas and doubled back toward town on foot. Meanwhile, the posse gathered at the abandoned Buick and came within a hair's-breadth of shooting the young hostages, whom they briefly mistook for the outlaws. When the posse began to ask questions, Laverne revealed something she kept to herself during the entire episode. She recognized Santa Claus. He was Marshall Ratliff, the son of the woman from whom her mother had recently purchased a small café.[20]

One thing was now obvious to Ratliff and associates. Someone needed to steal a car, and quick. Since Bedford was all but certainly dead, the posse members had an additional reason to kill the trio on the spot.

Ratliff, Hill, and Helms walked in the increasingly chilly wind toward the edge of Cisco, hoping to find a sedan that could carry them all away from the posse. Instead they found an open Ford touring car,[21] which offered a swift but breezy trip away from town on those few deserted highways, dirt roads, and cattle trails the posses had missed. Once the car was secured, the trio parked in seclusion and slept through most of the next day, even as the posses doggedly pursued them without success. Late that Christmas Eve, Helms began to drive south, skirting the hamlet of Putnam and moving toward a small frame house on an oil lease occupied by Doris and Rob Englin. Stopping here was a risk, but one

Marshall Ratliff with his children: Annie, Leroy, Uellan, Lee, Ella.
(Courtesy of Conrad Hilton Center and Museum, Cisco, Texas)

that could not be avoided. Doris was Louis Davis's older sister, who by this time may have known that Louis was in serious condition if not dead. Helms was also Rob Englin's least favorite brother-in-law. The pair had quarreled more times than anyone could remember. Worse still, the gang had visited here before the robbery and allowed Louis to assure his older sister that they were headed south for nothing more serious than a moonshine purchase. They wondered if the Englins had learned about the disaster at Cisco.

When the cheap, unadorned door opened early that Christmas morning, Doris looked every one of her forty-five years and more. She knew about Louis and was planning to go into Wichita Falls later that day, hopefully to see his body. Trouble had been her constant companion, and now her husband's archenemy, Henry Helms, had brought death itself to her family. She offered some coffee, leftover chicken, and a cake, then mentioned without really complaining that not much more food remained in the house. The bandits departed quietly, grateful that they had something to eat after two days on the run and thankful that Rob Englin had not confronted them.

Daybreak that Christmas found them hiding in some trees near a pasture, still within an ever-tightening circle that law enforcement had established around the Cisco area. Later that day and three more times in the days that followed, the fugitives returned to the Englin house for food. Ratliff had hoped that Helms' father, the Oklahoma City preacher, could make arrangements to meet a doctor through the preacher's landlady, Midge Tellet, who was periodically in touch with Doris Englin. Instead, everyone in Texas involved in the medical treatment effort, including the doctor himself, was eventually arrested.

While Helms drove the stolen Ford in yet another wide circle designed to break out of the roadblocks the posse had established, the trio was spotted by a car whose every move indicated that the gang had been discovered. When Helms maneuvered off the road to avoid further detection, he struck a gatepost, which took the Ford out of action. Marshall Ratliff had caught his second wind in spite of his wounds and now led the other two to a nearby farmhouse, just after midnight on Monday, December 26. The farmer, R. C. Wylie, was fortunate enough to own a farm with the richest Texas crop of all. Three producing oil wells on the property made life for the Wylie clan quite tolerable.

The gang knocked on the farmhouse door and R. C. cautiously opened it, expecting to find his twenty-two-year-old son, Carl, who was at a Christmas party with his younger cousin Riley and due home any time. Instead, he was confronted by three bedraggled men who claimed they wrecked their car while transporting one of their wives to the hospital. The farmer was suspicious of their story but revealed that Carl would be returning in the family car from a Christmas party soon and could help them then. The strangers declined to bring the "wife" inside but waited outside for the young man.

When Carl turned the nearly new Dodge into the driveway, he was accosted by the three bandits, who demanded the car. In the confusion, young Riley jumped from the car and ran to the house unmolested, just before the gang ordered Carl to drive them away as fast as possible.

Mr. Wylie evidently saw the strangers stealing his car but did not notice that the driver was his own son. The farmer aimed and fired his shotgun into the dark, injuring Carl but missing all the bandits.

Ratliff and the other robbers were hardly sympathetic. Wounded though he was, the hostage now found himself chauffeuring the Ratliff gang through the Cisco area, as they continued the search for a breakout point. The young kidnapping victim drove the gang back to the Englin place twice for food and even avoided a search plane. Finally, Ratliff released him in the early morning hours of Tuesday, December 27, but only after they had stolen yet another Ford.[22] Somehow, Helms managed to drive the newly stolen car around the roadblocks surrounding Cisco. Only then did the three fugitives realize that law enforcement was waiting for them at the Brazos River, the main obstacle between them and their homes in Wichita Falls. Once Ratliff, Helms, and Hill understood they either had to get across the Brazos or surrender, they quietly approached the hamlet of South Bend, whose chief attribute was a large bridge crossing the river beyond the north end of town.

J. B. "Jim" Foster was the twenty-third sheriff of Young County and eventually served five consecutive terms. Among the men he succeeded was Marion D. Wallace, who had been killed in the line of duty thirty-nine years previously while attempting to arrest Boone Marlow, a once famous outlaw who roamed Texas and Indian Territory, glamorized later in a movie entitled *The Sons of Katie Elder*.[23]

Foster had a real problem on his hands this morning. He half-expected the Cisco bank robbers to roar through South Bend toward the bridge north of town at any minute, yet the lawmen and citizens in his posse were tired, hungry, and increasingly impatient. The free hot coffee no longer placated the posse as they sat near the bridge in the cold.

Any worries the sheriff had about keeping his posse in place evaporated a few minutes after nine o'clock that Tuesday morning when a Ford meeting the description of the one reported stolen earlier that day hove into view at the south end of town. The bandits soon realized they were spotted and quickly reversed direction. No doubt, many in the posse had one word on their minds when the bank robbers showed themselves: "reward!"[24]

Helms sped south, away from South Bend. He made a sharp left turn at the first opportunity, only to learn that they were blocked by a dead end. Now the only chance the bandits had was to escape by foot into some nearby trees. Helms and the others were out of the car, running as best they could, when the posse found them.

Ratliff heard gunfire from a short distance away and turned to fire a few shots of his own. His weapon was barely raised when Deputy Sheriff Cy Bradford knocked Ratliff to the ground with a single shot. Santa Claus would run no more. Bradford also shot Henry Helms before he and Hill dashed into the nearby trees, even as Ratliff was being hauled off to a refuge of a different sort.

Wednesday, December 28, found Santa confined in the small, stark Eastland County jail. The squabbles about who would get the $5,000 in reward money from the Bankers Association had begun in earnest the day before. Posse members vied with civic leaders, who brashly suggested that the survivors of the deceased law officers should get the money. Even Mrs. Blasengame, the young mother who ran through the bank with her daughter, made a play for the reward, contending that Bedford and Carmichael were just doing their job, while she had made the capture possible by sounding the alarm.

While Ratliff slumbered in the lockup, a crowd of over 150 men searched for Hill and Helms, even as the fugitives tried to find a remote place to cross the quicksand-infested Brazos in a cold drizzly rain. Finally, they were able to cross and sleep for a few hours before they heard the search plane, on the morning of Wednesday, December 28.

Manuel T. "Lone Wolf" Gonzaullas of the Texas Rangers was leading the search from this high vantage point. The fugitives dodged him throughout Wednesday and even managed to cook some corn they foraged from a barn.[25]

Two mornings later, the search ended with a whimper rather than a bang in Graham, Texas. Helms and Hill had wandered into town early in the morning and then asked a bright young boy for directions to a particular boardinghouse, where they hoped to find refuge. Instead, they soon faced three lawmen with weapons pointed in their direction, even as they attempted to run for cover. Helms and Hill were so exhausted, they simply collapsed on the ground, surprised they had not been killed for the reward money.[26] No one ever collected reward money for the death of Louis Davis either.

The Eastland County authorities were quick to act, indicting all three survivors for armed robbery and murder. Although the prosecuting attorney declined to pursue Hill's murder charge, Hill pled guilty to robbery only a week after he was captured, then served part of a life sentence before being granted a pardon. Reportedly, Hill moved to West Texas and an anonymous, honest life.[27]

On the other hand, Ratliff and Helms were sentenced to death for the murders of Bit Bedford and George Carmichael and sent to death row at Huntsville prison. Helms soon became a talented mimic on death row, following the example of fellow inmate Harry Leahy. Somehow Leahy's attorney discovered an obscure Texas law that prevented the state from executing a prisoner who became insane after sentencing. Although the Supreme Court of Texas granted Leahy an opportunity to prove his insanity at a hearing, in the end he was executed, after supposedly telling Helms that he just couldn't act the part well enough. Helms vowed that he would do better, although by that time his own execution was only about a month away.[28]

Helms suddenly became a virtual songbird who warbled morning, noon, and night, only interrupting his routine long enough to shout "aye, aye, captain" to a chain gang boss no one else could see.[29] None of this was any help when the prosecutor produced five insane-asylum superintendents who testified that poor Henry showed no signs of madness whatsoever. The jury deliberated only twenty minutes before deciding Helms should ride Old Sparky within a week. Ratliff observed all this but was not discouraged. He, too, thought he would do better.

The execution of Henry Helms sent poor Marshall over the edge, or so he wanted everyone to believe. The very evening Helms was electrocuted, Ratliff began to refuse his food, twitch, moan, and babble frantically, occasionally throwing scripture quotations around for good measure. All of this fooled his poor mother, who spent her meager savings having lawyers petition for a sanity hearing in Walker County, where Huntsville prison is located. Judge Davenport of Eastland County, where the robbery and murders occurred, promptly issued a bench warrant requiring poor Marshall to appear on armed-robbery charges associated with the attempted theft of the Oldsmobile from the Harris family. The Walker County judge commented that Eastland County was determined to prevent Ratliff from getting his sanity hearing.[30] The judge was dead right.

Soon, Ratliff found himself in the Eastland County jail, waiting to be tried on the new charge, even as he continued to rave day after day. E. P. "Pack" Kilburn had been elected sheriff of Eastland County twenty years beforehand and had served two terms.[31] Now he was county jailer. Sheriff Foster asked him to watch Ratliff's every move for any sign of insanity. Kilburn did so enthusiastically and even occasionally tested Ratliff's feigned stupor by pretending to poke the prisoner in the eye, which never drew a reaction.[32]

Eventually Kilburn was convinced that Ratliff was demented. That was one reason he asked temporary assistant jailer Tom Jones to stay an extra week beyond his original appointment. Now Ratliff was so helpless that Jones fed him and even helped with his toilet visits.

Even though Jones had eight kids, he did not really need to work, thanks to the oil that had been discovered on his hardscrabble farm outside of town. Serving as assistant jailer gave him something to do, now that the family lived in Eastland. Besides, it was something of a favor for his nephew Jim Jones, the county attorney.

The evening of Monday, November 18, 1929, started routinely enough at the jail, almost two years since the Santa Claus robbers killed two good officers after knocking over the First National Bank. Ratliff was handfed his supper, as usual, just before Jones was asked to help with two other prisoners elsewhere in the cell block. Since he was hurried, he left Ratliff's cell unlocked. This was all Ratliff needed to miraculously recover from the insanity that he had shown the world these past few months. He searched Kilburn's desk drawer for keys but found a revolver and picked it up, hoping to force his way out of the locked cell block.[33]

Soon, Kilburn was looking at the working end of his own pistol with Ratliff's finger, on the trigger. Ratliff shot assistant jailer Jones at point-blank range. Kilburn himself was nearly killed getting the revolver away from him and still was not entirely in control. He pointed the pistol at Ratliff's head and pulled the trigger, but the hammer fell on an empty chamber.

In the jailer's residence elsewhere in the building, Kilburn's grown daughter heard the commotion. She appeared from nowhere, prepared to kill Ratliff herself with Kilburn's spare pistol. Her father convinced her not to shoot.[34]

The next day, citizens began to gather around the Eastland County jail, slowly at first. Within hours, a substantial crowd lingered about with no apparent purpose. Most were citizens of Eastland, who were concerned even though the hospital bulletins assured the crowd that Jones would recover. Sheriff Foster left with a deputy in the morning to deliver one of the condemned prisoners back to Huntsville, 260 miles away.[35] Pack Kilburn was on his own.

Later in the afternoon, the familiar faces of Eastland citizens were joined by total strangers, who might have come from Cisco, only ten miles away. The crowd was larger at dusk, and by the time darkness had descended, an unruly mob confronted the lightly armed and undermanned jail staff. "We want Santa Claus!" they cried, even as the curious young kids among them were shoved aside by menacing adults. Kilburn's best efforts could not stop what happened next. He tried to convince them that Ratliff's appeals would probably be denied and he would be dead within sixty days.[36] The crowd wanted the killer dead that evening and did not find this theoretical argument the least bit compelling. Soon, Kilburn was mobbed himself and watched helplessly as his jail keys were forcibly removed from his pocket.

Ratliff heard the crowd surging upstairs and moved quickly to the back of the jail cell, only to be confronted by angry mobbists who offered to emasculate him with a long knife right then and there. Soon, the prisoner felt his head bouncing down the stairs. Now, he was in the air, hanged from a utility pole and choking to death. When the rope broke and he fell to the ground, Ratliff thought that the crowd was satisfied. However, the mob obtained another rope from a hardware store whose owner opened just for this after-hours occasion.

Soon he was hanged again, from the same utility pole that is carefully preserved to this day, with a monument describing the event inside a white picket fence behind the old Connellee (now Majestic) Theater in Eastland. This time, the crowd used a rope that the hardware clerk guaranteed was made from the best manila hemp in Texas.[37] This time, the rope did not break.

Most of the mob was too excited and too hurried to hear what Ratliff mumbled just loud enough for a few of the bystanders to hear. Perhaps he somehow realized that he had mortally wounded Tom Jones, who was still alive but soon would be dead. Jones was a man who had shown him nothing but kindness. Ratliff's last words were said in a whisper.[38]

"Forgive me."

CHAPTER NINE

Clyde Barrow:
Trigger Happy

It was not thunder, backfire, or someone dynamiting tree stumps. There was just too much of it. Even at distances far across those vast northwest Louisiana swamps and among pines and stubborn underbrush competing for space and sunlight, it just did not sound right. The plinking was something shooters know as the sound bullets make when striking a metal target. This told some people what they would find on the scene before they even arrived. What they found then is still very much a topic of conversation today. It was Wednesday morning just after 9:15, May 23, 1934.[1]

The well-dressed young couple had been seen by the people of Bienville Parish at area restaurants and grocery stores. Some had marveled at how skillfully the young man zipped along in his tan Ford over back roads that were nothing more than gravel logging trails.

Now, Bonnie and Clyde were bloody corpses inside that tan Ford, riddled by forty-six large-caliber bullets, including five head shots between them.[2] They had been acquaintances—no—friends of Ivy T. Methvin,[3] his wife, Avie (Ava), and their son, an ex-con named Henry.

Clyde Chestnut Barrow was born near Telico, Texas, on March 24, 1909,[4] but raised in the streets of west Dallas. He committed his first murder on October 29, 1931, while he was serving two years at Eastham Prison Farm in the Texas state penitentiary system for burglary and auto theft.[5]

His first victim was Ed Crowder,[6] a building tender

Bonnie and Clyde on a blanket at the once-popular Dexfield Park in Iowa. Clyde was said to be meticulous about the condition of his firearms. *(Courtesy of the Texas Ranger Hall of Fame and Museum, Waco, Texas)*

(prison trusty) for Eastham Camp 1 whom Clyde whacked across the forehead with an iron pipe for tormenting him. Although tenders were supposed to keep peace among the other inmates, Crowder was a large man who preyed upon the smaller inmates—especially the young ones like Clyde Barrow. On more than one occasion, Crowder raped and beat Clyde.[7]

Barrow struck a deal with building tender Aubrey Skelly[8] (Scalley), who agreed to assist with an attack on Crowder. Barrow let Crowder see him go alone to the stalls of the latrine. Crowder made his way to where Barrow pretended to be urinating. When he was within striking distance, Barrow whipped out a piece of pipe hidden in his trousers and cracked Crowder's skull wide open. Skelly appeared and, using his own knife, superficially cut himself across the stomach, all the while screaming obscenities at Crowder. Then he plunged the blade into Crowder's lifeless chest. Skelly took the rap for Crowder's murder, but the death of Ed Crowder meant nothing to the prison guards.

Crowder was only the first of at least fourteen people eventually killed by the murderous Barrow gang or their associates. Eight were active-duty law-enforcement officers. One was a prison guard killed during the January 16, 1934,[9] prison raid conducted by Barrow and others. The remaining four victims included two merchants, a temporarily paroled convict, and a family man they killed while stealing a car on Christmas Day. There may have been more.

Clyde was one of seven children born to Henry B. and Cumie T. Walker Barrow. Unlike Bonnie, Clyde never cared much for school, except for the endless parade of girls it offered. Clyde worked steadily in his teenaged years, hoping to earn enough money to attract one or more of those girls with fancy clothes. He first worked for the Brown Cracker and Candy Company in Dallas for one dollar a day. He later was employed by Bama Pie Company and even Procter & Gamble Company, earning thirty cents an hour, before he was hired by United Glass Company.[10] Clyde worked there as a glazier for two years, using his earnings to buy clothes and rent cars, all in an effort to impress the girls. The gangly teen fresh from the boonies apparently believed he needed something other than his looks to keep the girls interested. His transition from country boy to city dweller was a common one at that time.

Following World War I, the demand for wartime cotton came to an end. Soon the crop sat in the fields or the gin silos, slowly rotting. Clyde's father, Henry Barrow, had depended on raising cotton for his living. Now he could not keep up with farm rent or other expenses even with his second and third jobs, one at the Telico Cotton Gin, the other at a brickyard in Ennis. By 1922, Henry packed up what was left of his family—the older children left long ago for the bright lights and busy nights—and moved to Dallas—west Dallas precisely.[11]

The Barrows joined other former tenant farmers who sought better times in the big city. There were few wood-frame houses in the area of west Dallas where the Barrows and many others camped, which was informally named Cement City, after the plant that could be seen across the Trinity River. There were no paved roads here. Most of the inhabitants erected tents, lean-tos, and other makeshift housing. The few homes that were heated featured a single room with a wood-, coal-, or oil-burning stove.

Several years after the Barrows arrived, Henry had amassed enough money and materials to construct a combination service station and dwelling, which he moved to 1620 Eagle Ford Road (now 1221 Singleton Road). He purchased two gasoline pumps and built a storefront to serve motorists. Along with gasoline, Henry sold an assortment of snacks, sodas, and groceries. He called the place Star Service Station.[12] This supported the family while the nation experienced an unemployment rate reaching 25 percent. Before that, Henry earned his living by selling anything he could load on the back of his horse-drawn wagon. The old family horse used to pull the wagon was hit and killed while crossing a Dallas bridge, but Henry never faltered in providing for the family. Despite the hard times, only two of the Barrows—Buck and Clyde—took the bandit road to a dead-end future, although three others spent time in prison.[13]

Marvin Ivan "Buck" Barrow was born on March 14, 1903. He was Clyde's older brother and role model—an unfortunate choice.[14] Even as a boy, Buck had an eye for shady schemes such as rooster fights, dogfights, and selling stolen goods. No one was surprised when the police caught Buck with a carload of stolen brass and arrested him.

Soon, Clyde was also arrested for failing to notify a car-rental business that he was going to drive to another town. Doing so would have cost Clyde more money, but he did not think the rental company would ever discover his intentions. When he failed to return the automobile on time, the police traced his whereabouts to a house in East Texas occupied by relatives of his girlfriend, Eleanor Bee Williams. This incident instantly ended Clyde's engagement to Eleanor and forced him to hitchhike into Dallas, on December 3, 1926.[15]

Buck and Clyde then attempted to unload a truck full of rustled poultry. Clyde only escaped conviction because Buck convinced the authorities that his little brother was innocent. When Buck was arrested in San Antonio for attempted car theft in 1928, his parents traveled the 270 miles to his hearing by horse and wagon, since they had no car.

The next year, Clyde, Buck, and Frank Clause were implicated in burglaries from Dallas to Waco. Sidney Moore accompanied the Barrow brothers to a Denton service station known as the Motor Mark Garage, on November 29.[16] Instead of dynamiting the safe there, the thieves loaded it in the getaway car and drove out of town. Suspicious officers gave chase until Clyde lost control of the car. Buck was shot through both legs and captured with Moore, but Clyde avoided arrest by hiding beneath a vacant house.

In February 1930, the police came knocking at the door of Clyde's new girlfriend, Bonnie Parker Thornton, usually called Bonnie Parker. Her husband, Roy Glenn Thornton, was doing time in the Texas state penitentiary at Huntsville, and she was living with her parents.[17]

Bonnie Elizabeth Parker was born to Emma and Charles Parker in Rowena, Texas, on October 1, 1910.[18] Bonnie had a normal childhood, occupied with family, home, and school, where she did rather well. Her early teenaged crush on Thornton led to a marriage while the two were high-school sophomores.

Perhaps Clyde met Bonnie in early January 1930, while visiting the sister of his friend Clarence Clay. Another source says they met while he was visiting in the home of her older brother, Hubert Nicholas Parker, called Buster.[19] Soon Bonnie and Clyde were inseparable. It is small wonder then that Clyde was discovered in the Parker house some two months after the Denton, Texas, robbery and returned there for trial.

Buck was already installed at the Texas state pen at Huntsville, serving a four-year sentence for burglarizing the Motor Mark Garage.[20] Although the authorities did not convict Clyde on a similar charge, he was convicted on seven counts of burglary and auto theft in Waco. He was sentenced to two years in prison and transferred to Huntsville, but only after briefly escaping from jail.

Curiously, the brothers escaped separate jails in March 1930. Buck simply walked away from a prison farm along the Trinity River north of Huntsville and found his way to Dallas. There he resumed his romance with Blanche Caldwell Callaway, who was estranged from her husband, John.[21] Buck and Blanche hid briefly at the farm of his uncle, near Martinsville, Texas, and he managed to elude any pursuers for the next twenty-one months.

Clyde escaped from the McClendon County jail on March 11, 1930, with more flair than his older brother, brandishing a pistol smuggled in by innocent-looking and petite Bonnie, who had just committed her first crime.

Inmates William Turner and Emory Abernathy helped Clyde escape. They ducked the hot lead chasing them down a darkened street, then stole a green Ford coup that belonged to Mrs. J. M. Byrd. Clyde was the likely getaway

Bonnie Parker's high-school portrait. *(From the collections of the Texas/Dallas History and Archives Division, Dallas Public Library)*

driver as the trio sped into the night and stole another car from Dr. W. L. Souther,[22] at 2005 North Seventh Street in Waco. This one was borrowed from a friend earlier in the day, when Souther's own car broke down. The doctor later reported that he noticed around eight o'clock that night that the car was gone but believed that the owner had retrieved it. He did not realize until 7:30 the following morning that the car was stolen. Clyde eventually made his way to Middletown, Ohio.[23]

Lawmen throughout the country were soon looking for the three fugitives, who were considered armed and dangerous, since Abernathy faced a ninety-nine-year sentence for a Waco murder.[24] A rash of overnight Middletown, Ohio, burglaries caused the police there to wonder whether the Texas fugitives were in their town. Clyde answered the question himself on the morning of Tuesday, March 18, 1930, through ineptitude.

The prior evening, unidentified burglars stole about $58 ($700 today) from a B& O Railroad train depot. Ticket agent Bernard J. Krebs gave police the description and Indiana license-plate number of a car containing three suspicious men who had asked for a train schedule.[25]

Middletown police officers Harry Richardson and George Woody had just interviewed Krebs when they observed three men in the very car Krebs described, driving toward them. Clyde and company had lost their way, spent the night in the countryside, then drove right back into town and the arms of the police.

The trio realized their mistake only when they saw the very train depot they burglarized the night before. By that time, officers Richardson and Woody had piled into their squad car and were giving chase. Later, papers wrote derisively about the "the dumbbell bandits,"[26] who were unceremoniously cuffed for extradition back to Texas.

Back in prison, Barrow undoubtedly commiserated with

fellow inmate Ralph Fults, who had escaped in early 1930 from Eastham Prison Farm and wandered far and wide from Illinois to California, avoiding Texas altogether. He was nineteen years old and already had more "in" time than some convicts two or three years his senior. Fults committed a rookie mistake while burglarizing a St. Louis, Missouri, hardware store. Working alone, Fults made his way to the store's upstairs safe. Crouched before the inner door of the safe on a comfortable rug, he reached around for a burglary tool. Fults' searching fingers instead found the smooth, rounded leather of a detective's shoe. When Fults asked how this happened while being handcuffed, the detective bent low and lifted the small rug on which Fults had been kneeling. Beneath it was a button. The button was connected to a buzzer.[27] The buzzer sounded a silent alarm at police headquarters. Fults had done himself in.

Clyde received a provisional parole on February 2, 1932. He celebrated by holding up the payroll office of Simms Oil Refinery at 2435 Eagle Ford Road in Dallas on March 25, with Fults and Raymond Hamilton. The job was supposedly conducted to finance a raid on Eastham Prison Farm in order to free as many prisoners as possible. The midnight refinery raid netted nothing, since their inside man, known only as Scotty, apparently got the facts wrong and the men came away emptyhanded.[28]

Raymond Hamilton was born in a tent on the banks of the Deep Fork River near Schulter, Oklahoma, forty-seven miles south of Tulsa, on May 21, 1913. His father abandoned the family in 1918. When he reappeared in west Dallas in 1920, he summoned the family. By 1922, however, Papa Hamilton had disappeared again and never returned.[29] Clyde and Raymond first met and became friends in west Dallas.

Hamilton was jailed in September 1931, on an auto-theft charge. He pled guilty and received a three-year suspended sentence. A few months later, he was again arrested for stealing a car in McKinney.

While in jail there awaiting trial, a chance encounter with Ralph Fults allowed Hamilton to cut his way to freedom. Fults regularly walked down an alley between Tennessee and Kentucky streets on his way home from a morning of gulping coffee at City Café. One morning an inmate called to him. Another man inside, the inmate said, knew Clyde. After a brief visitation inside the main jail, Fults furnished Hamilton with hacksaw blades slipped into the spine of a detective magazine and delivered by a young woman recruited by Fults. The very next morning, January 27, 1932, the town was abuzz with the news that Hamilton had escaped.[30]

Nearly two months later, Fults and Barrow rolled up in an alley behind Hamilton's house and recruited him to participate in the ill-fated Simms Oil robbery, although Hamilton really preferred car theft.

Barrow, Hamilton, and Fults conducted several small safecracking jobs in and around Dallas before deciding to target banks. Again, Hamilton balked, but he was soon convinced to stay in the gang. They drove out of Texas and wound up in Okabena, Minnesota.[31] The bank there looked like a good enough place to rob, but the rough country roads still covered in ice and snow were a deterrent. None of the hooligans believed that escape would be possible in such treacherous conditions. They turned the Ford around and headed south.

Fults would claim that the gang cased and robbed the First National Bank of Lawrence, Kansas, in an interview given decades after the event. The three overwhelmingly inexperienced holdup men—himself, Barrow, and Hamilton, whose only successes in the past netted either nothing or not more than a few hundred dollars in any single job—supposedly came away from this one with more than $33,000 ($396,000 today), although no record of such a robbery has been found to date.[32]

Barrow and Fults now chose Denton, Texas, as a fertile recruiting spot, as had the infamous train robber Sam Bass some sixty years before. They were still intent on raiding Eastham Prison camp and found five recruits, including Ted Rogers, who bore a resemblance to Raymond Hamilton. Barrow also enlisted "Red," identified by one writer as John Otis.[33]

The gang decided to rob two Denton banks at the same time on April 11, 1932. Fults took a stroll around the town square, where the banks were located. The street was occupied by a few horse-drawn wagons, pedestrians, and cars lined up along the curbs.

At first Fults was not worried by what he saw, but when he looked again, he noticed that every single car except one was parked facing the curb. He crossed the street in the direction of the backed-in car and observed two occupants. As Fults drew near, he recognized two formidable Texas Rangers, Tom Hickman and M. T. Gonzuales.[34]

The bandits regrouped at their hideout at Lake Dallas and concluded that more men were needed. After a futile trip to Amarillo for more recruits, Fults, Barrow, and another man, identified as Otis,[35] pointed their vehicle toward Denton, but experienced car trouble in Electra.

Oil and gas agent A. F. McCormick watched them peering beneath the raised hood of their disabled car. An avid newspaper reader who devoured every word printed about Charles Arthur "Pretty Boy" Floyd, he was suspicious. He called Electra police chief James T. Taylor, who responded by hitching a ride with one J. C. Harris.

Taylor and Harris happened upon the three men walking down the road that morning, just after nine o'clock on April 14, 1932. Harris pulled over and Taylor began questioning the trio, but Red bolted across a field.[36] Soon, McCormick joined the conversation, but instead of watching an arrest, he was kidnapped in Harris's car, along with Chief Taylor and his driver. When the captives were dumped eight miles outside of Electra near the Lazy J Ranch, Fults assured Taylor that he would take very good care of the police chief's fancy service revolver with engraved grips.

The bandits ran out of gas near Fowlkes, but fortunately for them, W. N. Owens soon drove up while following his regular mail route. Fults and Barrow jumped on his sideboards and managed to hijack the car. Taking the mailman hostage, they headed southeast toward Wichita Falls. They spent several hours driving the back roads of north Texas around Wichita Falls, far away from Owens' normal mail route.

Finally they turned north. On U.S. Highway 277/281, they drove very near the Red River border town of Burkburnett. When a toll bridge leading into Oklahoma came into view, Fults yelled, "Don't stop!" Clyde pressed pedal to metal and broke the chain-gate barrier. Two agents stepped from their booth and fired a few rounds toward the speeding vehicle, but missed. Traveling at a high rate of speed in a time when seventy miles per hour was considered suicidal, Clyde raced northward, through Randlett, Geronimo, and Lawton, where the road turned right.

Owens was scared of Fults, who spent most of the trip riding in the backseat with him in silence. While Fults shimmied up a telephone pole to cut the line and disrupt police communications, Clyde tried to comfort the hostage, with little effect. Clyde took Fults aside and counseled him. "Talk to this guy. He's nervous about you being so quiet." Fults put the man at ease by telling him, "My dad's a mailman. I couldn't hurt no mailman."

About ten miles northeast of Fletcher, once the home of the outlaw Frank James, they deposited Owens on the road, perhaps reacting to an earlier radio broadcast announcing a roadblock. When Clyde assured the man that his car would be found in good condition by the authorities in a day or so, Owens had a better idea.

"You guys would be doing me a big favor if you would just burn it," he said, explaining that the government would have to buy a new one.[37] And so they did, after returning to Denton, where the rest of the Lake Dallas gang waited.

Now the gang prepared to free the Eastham prisoners from the horrendous conditions that journalist Harry McCormick had reported in the *Houston Press*. On April 17, 1932, Fults and Barrow proceeded to Eastham with Bonnie. She would pretend to be a cousin of Aubrey Skelly and alert him about the impending raid. Skelly was the building tender who helped Clyde kill Ed Crowder. The trio drove to within one mile of the prison camp, where the men got out as Bonnie drove into Eastham and visited Aubrey. He promised to inform Barrow friends Henry Methvin and Joe Palmer of the planned raid and breakout.[38] After Bonnie returned to their hiding place, the three of them sped back to Dallas, arriving at night.

The next day, Fults, Barrow, and Bonnie Parker drove to Tyler to steal a couple of fast cars to use in the Eastham raid, stopping in a Kaufman hardware store to purchase ammunition. When Fults mentioned the large variety of weapons in the store as he climbed back in the car, they decided to commit a nighttime burglary there on the return trip from Tyler.[39]

The search for fast cars in Tyler was a success. Fults took possession of someone's new Buick while Clyde selected a pre-owned Chrysler. The trio drove their new rides back to Kaufman. The two cars slowed to a stop at the rear of the hardware store where Fults purchased ammunition earlier. As Fults worked the padlock on the shop's back door, Clyde watched for police and Bonnie waited in the Chrysler.

Many small towns across America during the depression

were unable to employ an entire police force. The county sheriffs' offices were also often undermanned, making routine patrols nearly impossible. During these hard times, the role of town police was often conducted by a part-time night watchman supported by citizen volunteers. Tom Jones was the night watchman the night Fults, Bonnie, and Clyde pulled up behind the Kaufman hardware store.[40]

While Fults bent over the store's padlock, a glimmer of light caught Clyde's eye, as Jones emerged from the shadows with a chrome-covered revolver. Clyde fired on Jones instantly. Using the Chrysler as cover, the night watchman returned fire, as Barrow advanced toward him then vanished into the darkness.

Jones ran as fast as he could to the fire bell, which alerted the Kaufman citizenry to emergencies. As the bell tolled, more and more citizens emerged and began gathering on the town square.

Suddenly, two large cars burst into the open and sped past the crowd collected on the square. Bonnie still hugged the floorboard, as she had when the shooting started back in the alley. The large Buick and Chrysler each glistened in the light and zoomed by, as the locals watched in astonishment.

Barrow and Fults maneuvered their vehicles north on Highway 40 in the direction of Dallas, but suddenly Clyde's headlights revealed several armed men using two road graders as a roadblock. Clyde stomped on the brakes, turned the steering wheel, and skidded through a 180-degree turn, prompting Fults to do likewise.[41] Once again, they roared past the Kaufmanites gathered on the square. Now headed southeast, they encountered another roadblock of heavy machinery. Once again, they whipped the cars back around in the direction they just came from, perhaps giving the local sporting crowd an opportunity to place their bets.

On this third run past the town square, Barrow caught a

glimpse of another escape route. An unpaved county road with a clay bed turned east and appeared to be unguarded. At last, the bandits sped along on a road toward easy freedom in the darkness, or so they probably thought. But within a very short time, the road became so slippery with rain that both cars had to be abandoned to its gooey, unrelenting grip.

Now the fugitives were forced to tramp through the rain and across a pasture to a farmhouse, where they began pounding on the door. Mr. Rogers awoke at about one in the morning and answered the door, only to have a pistol thrust in his face with a demand for his car.[42] There was one problem. Rogers owned no cars but offered the fugitives a pair of mules from his corral. "We'll take them," Fults said, no questions asked. Clyde mounted first, with Ralph lifting Bonnie up behind Clyde. Ralph then swung a leg over the bare back of his mule and steadied himself. Ralph felt a sudden rise followed by a forward pitch, just as he went airborne. Rogers had failed to mention that the animals in question were prizewinning bucking mules. Fults picked himself up out of the mud and they all rode into the rainy night.

On the Run

As morning broke on April 19, 1932, Dr. Scarsdale in nearby Kemp found that his car had been stolen, although the thieves had thoughtfully left two rain-soaked mules in its place. Even then, the bandits were burning blacktop on Highway 40 (175) toward Athens, Texas.

The stolen car soon ran out of gas. Between Kemp and Athens stood the small Texas town of Mabank, where the fugitives hoped to find another car to steal. City Marshal Knute Barnes had been alerted, assumed the gunsels were coming his way, and called for volunteers to form a posse. Soon, men and boys unable to work the fields because of the rains cheerfully joined the hunt. One of the younger participants was Walter M. Legg, Jr. (Junior Legg), who was sixteen at the time, eager to help and inexplicably absent from school.[43]

The banditos traversed the uninviting terrain of briars, vines, and thicket as far as Cedar Creek. With daylight approaching and the shotgun-wielding locals closing in, they dared go no farther. Apparently, everyone in the rural community surrounding Kemp knew about the car theft. The locals who were not in the posse remained vigilant, even as the outlaws hid quietly in the weeds.

Although they were nearly discovered several times, by early evening Fults, Bonnie, and Clyde were confident enough to move again. That decision would prove to be disastrous.

They broke cover at about five o'clock and crossed the main road, hoping to find another vehicle. They could not have known that 500 yards south of their crossing, the occupants of a lone farmhouse were on the lookout. A quick call from the farmhouse soon brought a small army of armed men to the location. A shot rang out and Fults took a slug to his ankle. He dove, or more likely tumbled, into a ditch for cover. Bonnie and Clyde quickly joined him as the ground nearby was ripped apart by bullets.

Clyde and Ralph showed uncharacteristic restraint and shot over the posse. However humane, the tactic did not work. "Boss" Ballard took a position behind the pinned-down bandits, hiding behind a thin tree that did not conceal his bulky girth. Fults ignored him, at least until his elbow was exploded by a .3220 slug. Clyde promptly improvised a tourniquet, declared, "I'm gonna make a run for it," and promised he would come back.[44]

Barrow sprang from the ditch and began a mad dash

to freedom, directly toward two posse men. Clyde never slowed his pace as he darted between them and was gone. Neither man realized that Barrow had run right between them, as they were reloading their weapons.

Meanwhile, Ballard crept toward Ralph and Bonnie. Before he reached them, Bonnie jumped to her feet, with hands raised. Just then Fults heard someone behind him say, "Hands up!" Fults raised his uninjured arm.[45] For the moment, at least, it was all over for Bonnie Parker and Ralph Fults, although Clyde had made good his escape.

Twelve hours later, a doctor treated the shattered arm. The first doctor summoned to render aid refused. This was no surprise, since Dr. Scarsdale was the very man who found two mules where his car should have been the day before. Soon, Ralph and Bonnie were confined to a cramped, stuffy, one-room jail, which still stands in Kemp, awaiting transportation to a more substantial facility in Kaufman. Meanwhile, Clyde had roared out of town in a gas truck, but soon came upon a more practical ride—an unattended Ford V-8. He slipped into Dallas long enough to inform family members about the Kemp troubles, and then sped north toward Lewisville and Lake Dallas.

Clyde found Ted Rogers and Johnny Hays,[46] but two others he looked for were nowhere to be found. They drove to Celina, where the others were supposed to have robbed a hardware store of guns and ammunition but had failed to do so. The trio now planned to rectify the situation and do it themselves, but if Barrow had learned anything about competent burglary, it was not apparent that night in Celina.

The gang arrived just before midnight on April 20, 1932, and caught the attention of a night watchman as they wandered around. When Floyd Perkins quizzed them, Clyde claimed he was looking for a cousin. Meanwhile, Ted positioned himself behind Perkins and delivered a crashing blow to the watchman's skull.[47] Perkins fell to his knees, just as Mayor F. M. Francis arrived. The gang delivered the pair to an empty Frisco Railroad car east of Celina and locked them inside before returning to town.[48] As the yeggs returned to the business at hand, two more citizens arrived and quickly joined the dignitaries in the boxcar.

Finally able to proceed with the burglary, the three thieves broke into the targeted building but promptly discovered that the store they entered was a pharmacy rather than the hardware store.

After they found the right building, the burglars made off with a cache of weapons. However, as they returned to the store for ammunition, they heard a familiar yet disturbing sound. Celina used the same alarm system as had Kaufman. And it was the Lake Dallas gang for whom the bell tolled.[49]

Deputy Sheriff "Dutch" Stelzer responded to the alarm and glimpsed a Ford racing away. Then he discovered that Clyde Barrow had removed the keys from his own car prior to the burglary, according to the April 21, 1932, *McKinney Daily Courier-Gazette*.

The gang spent the next day back at the Lake Dallas hideout, modifying their new firearms and camouflaging an abandoned metal building used to stash their stolen goods. Soon, Denton County sheriff G. C. Cockrell appeared with a posse, responding to reports of gunfire. The sheriff recovered a few handguns and two vehicles from the metal building, but Clyde Barrow had slipped away.

The sheriff also arrested two gang members. Jack and Fuzz chose the wrong time to rejoin Clyde and the gang. Sheriff Cockrell and his posse of lawmen were standing where Clyde Barrow was supposed to be.[50]

Four days after the Celina robbery, the mayor and other citizens whom Barrow stuffed into a railroad car arrived in Denton. Traveling with them were Electra police chief James T. Taylor, himself a Barrow kidnap victim, along with two special agents of the U.S. Bureau of Investigation. Taylor had been relieved of his service revolver at the time of his abduction. The weapon was recovered and now was in Denton. Upon his arrival, Taylor identified the fancy chrome-covered pistol as his.

Sheriff Cockrell knew then that he was on the right track. The Kemp shootout, Dr. Scarsdale's stolen car, the Celina heist, and the Electra kidnapping were all pieces of a single puzzle. Next, Cockrell stopped at the Kaufman jail for a friendly visit with Ralph Fults.

Fults was then whisked away to Wichita Falls to face kidnapping charges, but the first stop was the McKinney jail for a reunion with Fuzz and Jack, formerly of the Lake Dallas gang. Fults did not let on that he knew either man, or they him.[51] Fults also saw Red, the young braggart who sported a .44 pistol but fled at an antelope's pace during the Taylor kidnapping near Wichita Falls.

Clyde and his sister-in-law Blanche Barrow drove into Kaufman the next day, April 25, 1932, intending to free Ralph Fults. They were too late, however, since Ralph was already on his way to Wichita Falls. The pair returned to west Dallas.

Ralph's stay at the Wichita Falls jail was an eventful one. He bunked with Hilton Bybee, a two-time killer facing the electric chair who refused to accept his fate. Bybee and Fults promptly sawed one of the cell's window bars free. On May 10, the two desperadoes made a daring escape attempt. Bybee crawled from the cell and stationed himself atop the wire cage, waiting for jailer Sid Johnson, who would soon conduct his regular rounds.

When Johnson arrived, Bybee pounced, then managed to wrest away the jailer's service revolver. Bybee struck Johnson with the man's own weapon, then took his cell-block keys and released Fults. From the third floor where they were kept, Fults and Bybee made a mad dash down the stairs. They made the sharp turn at the second-floor landing and continued their flight. Downward they ran toward the first floor and the open door. Racing headlong, they dashed toward the opening but instead ran into Deputy Sheriff Pat Allen.

Bybee instantly pointed Johnson's firearm at Allen and pulled the trigger twice, but nothing happened. Since Allen now had his own weapon aimed right at them, Fults and Bybee gave up.[52] Bybee was immediately removed to the Tarrant County Jail in Fort Worth and eventually transferred to Eastham. Fults was sent to Huntsville following his May 11, 1932, armed-robbery conviction.

In the meantime, Clyde busied himself gathering funds and munitions for his on-again, off-again Eastham raid. He decided to visit the parents of a former friend, or at least their Hillsboro jewelry store. On the evening of April 30, 1932, shortly after ten o'clock, a car parked down the street from the jewelry store owned by John N. Bucher. The jeweler and his wife lived upstairs. Clyde's partners Ted Rogers and Johnny Hays rousted the Buchers out of bed by repeatedly banging on the door.

Bucher came to the door, probably a little sleepy-eyed and more than a little perturbed. The men claimed they needed a guitar string at once. Bucher actually had one on hand and asked for twenty-five cents. One of the men handed Bucher a $10 bill, knowing that he would have to open a safe to make change. Mrs. Bucher was summoned from upstairs to open the safe, but before Bucher could close it, Rogers produced a .45 and demanded the contents. The jeweler produced his own weapon but never had a chance to use it, as Rogers fired a round into the old man's chest. Mrs. Bucher grabbed the pistol from her husband's dying hand and aimed at the robbers. Rogers wrested the weapon from her before she could fire. John N. Bucher was dead. The bandits got away with $40 in cash and an estimated $1,500 in jewelry, today worth about $21,000.[53]

Mrs. Bucher later identified Ray Hamilton as the trigger man. Hamilton bore a strong resemblance to Ted Rogers, who later assured his associates that he would confess to the crime should Hamilton receive the death sentence. When Hamilton was convicted but handed a life sentence, Rogers remained silent. Rogers was later killed by another convict in prison.[54]

Barrow and his crew rampaged on through the spring and summer of 1932. Bonnie was "no-billed" (released) by a grand jury in early June. After a few weeks, she rejoined Clyde but returned home in early August.[55]

On August 5, while traveling through Stringtown, Oklahoma, Barrow, Hamilton, and a third man who later used the name Everett Milligan stopped at a country dance.[56] While the third man went inside, Sheriff C. G. Maxwell and his deputy Eugene Moore noticed Barrow and Hamilton drinking whiskey in the car. Maxwell announced they were under arrest, but before the lawmen could ask any questions, the bandits shot them both, killing Moore instantly and seriously wounding the sheriff. About two months later, Barrow murdered Howard Hall, an elderly store manager in Sherman, Texas, for nothing more than complaining about being robbed.

Yet another victim was a young family man who recently purchased a fancy new car that Barrow and his new sidekick, William Daniel Jones,[57] wanted. Doyle Johnson was gunned down while clinging to the running board and Barrow's scrawny neck on Christmas Day 1932. Jones fired the shot that sent the twenty-seven-year-old new father sprawling into the street in front of his own home and family. After all this, Jones and Barrow abandoned the car about two blocks away. Johnson died the next day.[58]

On January 1, Richard Allen "Smoot" Schmid, the owner of Schmid's Cycle Company, was sworn in as the sheriff of Dallas County, having been elected the prior November.[59]

Schmid persuaded twenty-nine-year-old postal employee Ted Hinton to join him that very day. Hinton was reluctant at first. After all, the pay was considerably lower than what he was making at the post office, and the job security was as fickle as the next election cycle. "Hell, Smoot. I don't want to arrest anybody," Hinton told Schmid during one recruitment attempt.[60] Still, Hinton's loyalty toward Schmid was not to be denied. The cycle-shop owner had taken Hinton under his wing and even provided him with a bike on easy terms when Hinton became a Western Union messenger boy at age eleven. Hinton considered Smoot to be the father he no longer had.[61] Ironically, Hinton was offered a contract with the Cleveland Indians a week earlier. He turned that down because it did not offer financial security.[62]

Eventually, Smoot Schmid convinced Hinton to join him as a deputy who acted as a process server, using his post-office experience to find the hapless debtors constantly served with legal papers in those depression days. He did not have to be trained as a lawman in order to work as a process server. Taking the job would allow Hinton to repay the kindness Schmid had shown him all those years, without facing the risks most lawmen faced. Or so he thought.

On Friday, January 6, 1933, just after midnight, Tarrant County deputy Malcolm Davis was gunned down on the front porch of a house at 507 County Avenue, in west Dallas.[63] Davis was there to help Dallas authorities set a trap for Odell Chambless, who was suspected with Les Stewart in the Tarrant County robbery of the Home Bank of Grapevine, Texas, eight days before.

The robbery netted the thieves $2,850 ($43,000 today), but Stewart was caught and pressured to name his accomplices. He promptly gave up Chambless, who often hid at the home of Raymond Hamilton's two sisters, Lillie McBride and Maggie Fairris.[64]

Chambless never arrived, but Clyde Barrow made an

unexpected visit. Mrs. Fairris warned Clyde about the stakeout and he began shooting through the windows. When Davis stepped around the corner from the left of the house, Clyde warned him to get back, but the lawman kept coming. After several warnings from Barrow, a shotgun blast caught the deputy in the heart, throwing him across the front porch, mortally wounded.[65] Before the sun rose that morning, Hinton was summoned to the sheriff's office for a new assignment.

In the Papers

The Barrow gang was soon in the papers again. Twenty days after the Davis murder, Bonnie, Clyde, and W. D. Jones kidnapped a Springfield, Missouri, motorcycle patrolman who pulled them over for questioning. Six hours later, they released Patrolman Persell but only after forcing him to steal a car battery and install it in their own stolen vehicle.[66]

Buck Barrow was paroled from Huntsville in March 1933, then drove north with Blanche in a car that he actually purchased with his own money, meeting Bonnie and Clyde in Fort Smith. The two couples and W. D. Jones moved on to Joplin, Missouri, where they rented a garage apartment, which still stands at 3347½ Thirty-fourth Street.

The family reunion continued until lawmen appeared on April 13 to investigate their suspicious behavior. Clyde Barrow or W. D. Jones murdered two lawmen as Blanche chased her dog Snowball down the street. Snowball at least had the sense to quit the gang. In their hasty escape, the Barrows left behind undeveloped film that soon made them the most famous criminals in America. Many of the photographs would be difficult to distinguish from the vacation snapshots of other twenty-something motorists of the day. Other images were more sinister, displaying the weaponry necessary for their murderous occupation. One gag photograph showed Bonnie with a cigar in her mouth and a pistol in her right hand. Naturally, all of this was grist for the newspapers.[67]

While on the run, Clyde drove one of their stolen cars right into a ravine seven miles north of Wellington, Texas, on June 10, seriously injuring Bonnie, whose right leg was covered with battery acid.[68] After a daring escape from a county sheriff nearby, and the kidnapping of more law officers, the gang toured western Oklahoma and Kansas before finding a hideout on the northern outskirts of Fort Smith, Arkansas.

While Bonnie recovered, the Barrow brothers attempted to contact Charles Arthur "Pretty Boy" Floyd through his family near Sallisaw, Oklahoma, according to Cumie Barrow. Floyd was no fan of Bonnie and Clyde, having told family members that "those two give us all a bad name." He not only declined to meet them but suggested that after a few days his kinsmen should notify the authorities. Bonnie and Clyde were "trigger-happy punks," Floyd reportedly once said.[69] They murdered yet another lawman in Alma, Arkansas, on June 23 and soon headed north.[70]

Buck Barrow was mortally wounded during a dramatic shootout near Platte City, Missouri, on July 19, and then captured with Blanche in Dexfield Park, Iowa. He died on July 29. And still the killings continued.

Although the surviving members of the Barrow gang did not know it, January 16, 1934, would be a momentous day, destined to be a turning point in their ill-fated criminal careers. By the end of that day, Clyde, Bonnie, and assorted gang members were responsible for killing ten men, six of whom were lawmen.[71] Law-enforcement authorities across the nation knew all about Bonnie and Clyde. Even the U.S. Bureau of Investigation tracked the north Texas youths who were only too ready to blast the life out of any lawman luckless enough to cross them.

Perhaps no one was more incensed by all this than Lee Simmons,[72] director and later superintendent of the Texas State Prison System. For it was on that day in January that Clyde Barrow finally helped some prisoners escape from Eastham Prison Farm. Raymond Hamilton was freed, as were Joe Palmer, Henry Methvin, Hilton Bybee, and J. B. French.[73] During the escape, Palmer shot and killed a guard whose given name was Major Joseph Crowson.

Lee Simmons was fed up. He convinced the Board of Prisons and the governor to hire a man whose sole purpose would be to catch or kill the Barrow gang. Simmons was granted permission to appoint a special investigator. Simmons soon found the man for the job. "I knew . . . that Barrow had made up his mind never to be taken alive and that Bonnie Parker was determined to go down with Clyde. That was the kind of game we had to hunt; it was my task to find a hunter of the kind to handle it."[74]

Francis Augustus Hamer was born at the Welch ranch in San Saba County, Texas on March 17, 1884, the second of eight children. He was called Frank, like his father. The elder Hamer joined the U.S. Cavalry in the late 1860s as a blacksmith, then married Lou Emma Francis.[75]

Young Frank attended a country school through the sixth grade and was highly proficient in math. He began the twentieth century in a sharecropping venture with his twelve-year-old brother, Harrison, and Dan McSwain. Regrettably, McSwain soon wanted Frank to resolve a dispute with a neighboring rancher by killing him. When Hamer refused, McSwain shot Hamer, prompting the wounded teenager to leave that country on horseback for west Texas.

"I thought I'd finished you," McSwain said when he later saw Hamer mounted on his favorite horse in front of the McSwain porch.

"Not by a damned sight," Hamer responded. "I've come to settle accounts."[76]

Both men went for their pistols, and down went Dan McSwain in a dead heap.

Six years later on April 21, 1906, the six-foot three-inch Frank Hamer was sworn in as a private in the Texas Rangers.[77] His no-nonsense reputation grew rapidly. A little more than two years after he joined the Texas Rangers, the lawless town of Navasota was begging for his help. On December 3, 1908, Frank Hamer was named its city marshal.[78] When he resigned in April 1911, he left behind a reformed town.

Hamer was lured to Houston by Mayor H. B. Rice to work as a special officer charged with identifying and capturing the killer or killers of several of the city's police officers. Hamer apprehended many of these thugs as well as one police officer accused of mercilessly beating a suspect in front of the man's wife and children.[79]

Three years later, Hamer was recruited to again become a Texas Ranger. The beginning of World War I brought threats of Germany enlisting Mexico as an ally. Hamer and other rangers commanded by Capt. E. H. Smith guarded the Texas border with Mexico and intercepted arms and ammunition crossing into Mexico from the north.[80]

Then in 1916, Hamer was assigned to assist the Texas Cattle Raisers Association, investigating rustling operations throughout the state.[81] Soon, Hamer was marked for assassination by murder-case defendants against whom he was to testify.

The former Gladys Johnson had been his wife less than half a year when on October 1, 1917, they drove into Sweetwater, Texas, with her brother Emmet and his brother Harrison Hamer. They stopped there to have a flat fixed. Gladys stayed with the car as Frank searched for a repairman. Suddenly, a man later identified as Gee McMeans ambushed Hamer from behind a doorway and shot him in the left shoulder. Hamer was left-handed and the shot disabled his gun hand. After a second shot slammed downward into Hamer's leg, Hamer used his good hand to wrest McMeans' gun from him.

In the meantime, Gladys spotted H. E. Phillips sneaking behind Hamer to get a clean shot. Gladys produced her own pistol and began firing at Phillips, who sought cover behind a car. Gladys's defensive tactic worked, at least until she ran out of bullets. Phillips then hurried to where Hamer and McMeans had been wrestling and fired his shotgun at the lawman's head. The blast was close enough to cut the brim from Hamer's hat, but Hamer managed to plant a bullet into McMeans' heart with his uninjured hand. This encouraged Phillips to scamper away.[82]

Through the years that followed, Hamer left the Rangers several times, usually for political reasons, he later said. And while some men left law enforcement altogether, Hamer never did. He was a man hunter and a damned good one. Hamer left the Rangers once again in 1933, to work as an investigator for an oil company based in Houston. At the same time, he maintained a home with Gladys and their two girls in Austin.[83]

He was still an oil-company investigator when Lee Simmons arrived at the Hamer home unannounced in early February 1934, asking Hamer to find Bonnie and Clyde. Simmons did not beat around the bush. "I want you to put Clyde and Bonnie on the spot and shoot everyone in sight."[84] On February 10,[85] Frank Hamer became the murderous couple's worst and final nightmare, setting in motion the second effort to ambush Bonnie and Clyde. They had escaped the first attempt in Sowers, Texas, on November 22, 1933, although both fugitives were injured. Dallas County sheriff Schmid and deputies Alcorn, Castor, and Hinton peppered Clyde's stolen vehicle with gunfire before the couple sped away.[86] The identity of the informant is yet unknown.[87]

The historical record includes three versions of the intensified search for Bonnie and Clyde that the authorities began in January 1934, one for each of the three law-enforcement organizations represented on the ambush team. Harmonizing the three versions of events is difficult and, in some regards, impossible.[88] The following account reflects one effort to reconcile the various accounts.

After February 10, Hamer left his south Texas home and drove to Dallas, where he met County Sheriff Smoot Schmid and his man hunters, Deputies Ted Hinton and Bob Alcorn, both of whom were said to be personally acquainted with Bonnie and Clyde.[89] On February 19, Hamer and Alcorn met with Louisiana's Bienville Parish sheriff Henderson Jordan. Bonnie and Clyde had been seen in his parish. Hamer wanted to meet with the Methvin family there, whom Jordan knew.[90]

Jordan's cooperation was needed not only because he knew the territory, but to make the whole thing legal. Jordan represented Louisiana law enforcement and provided the jurisdiction on which the entire operation depended.

Ivy T. Methvin was a logger who made regular hauls on "The Big Road," as Ringgold Road near the Methvin place was known. No doubt, Henry Methvin visited his family home, even while on the run. The Texas officers were interested in meeting the Methvins.

Instead they met with John Joyner, a Methvin friend and intermediary, on March 1. The meeting in Jordan's Arcadia office included Hamer, Alcorn, Department of Justice Special Agent Lester Kendale, and Joyner. Joyner's message was to the point. Henry Methvin was with Bonnie and Clyde, and he alone could convince them to come to Louisiana. Once they arrived, Henry would help the authorities capture them, in exchange for a signed agreement from the Texas governor exonerating him from any and all past crimes committed there, including, but not limited to, robbery, burglary, auto theft, prison escape, and murder.[91] The lawmen consented and signed an agreement for Joyner to take to Henry Methvin. The agreement was later signed by Governor Ferguson. After Joyner left Sheriff Jordan's office, nothing was heard from the Methvins in March.[92]

However, during the first six days of April 1934, Methvin and Barrow murdered three lawmen.[93] The events of April 1, 1934, made Lee Simmons and other Texas officials more determined than ever to bring Bonnie and Clyde to justice.

On that sunny Easter Sunday, veteran Highway Patrolmen Polk Ivy and Edward Bryan Wheeler were training a rookie fresh from boot camp. He was twenty-two-year-old Holloway Daniel Murphy,[94] from Alto, Texas. The three men started their Harley Davidsons and left the Tarrant County courthouse in Fort Worth for a day's work. The Texas Highway Patrol was established three years earlier to enforce traffic laws, assist stranded motorists, and protect highways by enforcing load limits on large trucks.

The officers were also looking for some particularly dangerous suspects that day. Raymond Hamilton had resigned from the Barrow gang after a dispute over money and the gang status of his new love, Mary O'Dare.

Soon, Hamilton was pursuing other interests, notably including two bank robberies in north Texas between March 19 and 31. Hamilton, his brother Floyd, and accomplices John Basden and Mary O'Dare netted more than $3,400 ($54,000 today) from these efforts.[95] And now, Wheeler, Ivy, and their young protégé, Murphy, had a description of the getaway car and were told to be on the lookout for the thieves.

Raymond Hamilton was in the news that day. An armed man had walked into the State National Bank in West, Texas,[96] the day before and stolen nearly $2,000. Clyde Barrow thought the robbery had all the earmarks of a job pulled off by his former partner.

Although it was Easter, Clyde, Bonnie, and Henry Methvin waited in a field, just off of State Highway 114 near Grapevine. They had used the site to meet family members in the past, but certain anonymous sources within the Barrow family have suggested that this time the trio was waiting to ambush Ray rather than meet their family.[97] No doubt there was bad blood between former partners Barrow and Hamilton. Nine days after Easter, a letter Hamilton had written to his Dallas attorney denouncing Clyde as a desperado, and describing himself as "a gentleman bandit," was published.[98]

Grapevine

Historians, chroniclers, and witnesses differ as to what exactly happened near Grapevine that morning. According to one account, Bonnie had been exercising her pet rabbit, Sonny Boy, and now sat in the front seat of the Ford V-8 as Clyde slept in the backseat and Henry Methvin stood guard outside.[99] Clyde apparently had no idea that the car Hamilton used in the bank heist matched perfectly with his own stolen vehicle, right down to the canary-yellow wheels. Thus, it is little wonder that two of the motorcycle patrolmen turned toward the car to investigate. Patrolman Wheeler took the lead, with Murphy behind him. There was no radio communication among the officers, and Ivy did not notice when the others turned onto the road leading to the parked Ford.

Bonnie Parker noticed. She turned to Clyde in the backseat and woke him up. "It's the law," she whispered.[100]

Clyde looked at the officers and turned to Methvin, saying, "Let's take them."

Clyde had kidnapped unsuspecting lawmen before and usually released them unharmed. Years later, some

Barrow family members said this is what Clyde intended to do near Grapevine and claimed he was furious at what happened next.[101] Methvin was new and was not involved in the prior kidnappings. To him, the command to "take them" meant only one thing. Methvin leveled his Browning automatic rifle (BAR) at Wheeler and blasted him from his motorcycle. Wheeler died instantly, leaving only Murphy to face the killers.

Murphy was a cautious man, and that probably cost him his life. He carried a shotgun but did not load it for fear of an accidental discharge. Murphy was found dying later, next to his unfired shotgun with a few shells scattered around him.

Accounts of the Grapevine murders were controversial, to say the least. William Schieffer claimed, for example, that he first spotted the car as he drove from his farm to deliver a load of rocks. When he returned, the black Ford sedan was still parked in the same place. Schieffer claimed that later, from the front porch of his house, he saw the motorcycle officers pull up to the Ford. Perhaps he did, but the distance from which he witnessed the murders was too great for a positive identification. Yet, Schieffer also told investigators that he saw a man and a woman both dressed in riding breeches exit the car and start shooting at the lawmen. After the lawmen were on the ground, according to Schieffer, the smaller of the two shooters (the woman, according to Schieffer) walked up to Murphy, rolled him over, and fired repeatedly into his body.[102] Mr. and Mrs. Fred Giggal reported, on the other hand, that the taller of the two shooters shot into a body on the ground.[103]

Ted Hinton, for one, bristled at Schieffer's story. Hinton's book, *Ambush: The Real Story of Bonnie and Clyde* (as told to Larry Grove), written in 1977 and published two years later, stated, "[Schieffer's] identifications would prove embarrassing."[104] And while there is no disagreement about

Bonnie's presence near Grapevine, the smaller of the two shooters may well have been Clyde, since he stood nearly a head shorter than Henry Methvin. Methvin later claimed he killed both patrolmen.[105]

Still, at the time, the Schieffer tale of a petite young woman blasting away at the patrolman lying on the ground was sensational and widely accepted. And so, the chances of Bonnie and Clyde being taken alive were rapidly decreasing. This was evidenced by a reward offered by Leslie G. Phares, then the Texas Highway Patrol acting director, who later became chief.[106] The slain men were his officers and he had no interest in splitting hairs over the details of their senseless murders. Phares offered a $1,000 reward ($16,000 today) for the killers' bodies—not their capture, but their bodies.[107]

Five days after the Grapevine murders, Barrow and Methvin killed Commerce, Oklahoma, constable Cal Campbell, kidnapped Commerce police chief Perry Boyd, and dropped him near Fort Scott, Kansas. Bonnie Parker insisted that Boyd clear up one public-relations issue before the gang departed. Boyd was to inform the press that she did not smoke cigars, in spite of the gag photograph that fell into the hands of the authorities at the Joplin apartment where they killed two brave law officers.

Frank Hamer was not amused. He had studied the Barrow gang's buying habits, rest routines, and escape routes. He concluded that because they were wanted for murder in both Texas and Missouri prior to the April 6 killing of Constable Cal Campbell, they would likely make Louisiana their hideout, since they had killed no one there.[108]

"I soon learned that Barrow played a circle from Dallas to Joplin, Missouri, to Louisiana, and back to Dallas," Hamer wrote, noting the occasional forays into Indiana, Iowa, and New Mexico, " . . . but like wild horses, they would circle to their old range."[109]

Within two weeks of the Grapevine murders, Hamer, Ben F. "Manny" Gault,[110] Hinton, and Bob Alcorn were on the trail of the Barrow gang. They began at some point to live as Bonnie and Clyde lived, sometimes sleeping in the woods or in cars or not sleeping at all for days. The team subsisted on whatever food did not spoil in the sweltering heat of the Louisiana backcountry. Once they established the hideout area of their prey, namely a ten-mile stretch of gravel logging road from Gibsland to Sailes, the officers planned an ambush. Bienville Parish sheriff Henderson Jordan was contacted again.[111]

Bonnie, at least, understood her predicament. On Sunday, May 6, Bonnie and Clyde met with family members east of Dallas. Bonnie asked her mother not to criticize Clyde if they were killed in the days to come, and left a poem that predicted their death.[112]

Meanwhile, the net was closing. Joyner came to Arcadia on May 21,[113] saying that Henry was eager to help the authorities. Methvin would get away that evening on some excuse, Bonnie and Clyde would eventually look for him at his father's house, and the posse could trap them.[114] Joyner told the posse that Methvin would try to get away that very night at the Majestic Café in Shreveport.[115]

Methvin, Bonnie, and Clyde stopped there as expected. Henry went inside for a carryout order, but while Bonnie and Clyde waited, a police car on routine patrol drove by, prompting Clyde to speed away. Henry Methvin now had the chance he was looking for. He simply got up and walked into the Louisiana night, leaving sandwiches, sodas, and a mystified waitress inside the eatery.[116]

The officers had not recognized Clyde, but now they gave pursuit. The patrolmen were unable to catch the fleeing car and later reported the incident to Police Chief Bryant back at the Shreveport police headquarters. Bryant in turn told Hinton and Alcorn, who understood why Henry Methvin had abandoned the food. They interviewed the waitress the next day, just to make sure. "That's him. Same eyes, same pimply face. There's no mistake,"[117] she said, singling out Methvin's photograph without hesitation.

The posse positioned itself on a knoll above Ringgold Road, eight miles south of Gibsland, at about nine o'clock on the night of Monday, May 21, 1934.[118] That particular spot was secluded from passing traffic and near the home of Henry's father, Ivy Methvin. Hamer later recalled that this location was near where Clyde regularly looked for messages under a board used as a "post office." He described the ambush site in detail, although he misidentified the location. He did not mention Methvin at all, most likely to protect his sources.[119]

The officers were certain Bonnie and Clyde would eventually drive by, but the stakeout was hardly idyllic. The posse spent two miserable nights fighting with swarming mosquitoes, creeping chiggers, and clinging ticks. "Seldom have I ever been in such a nest of vindictive mosquitoes," Hinton wrote later. "They attacked the ears and neck and even the mouth."[120] Tuesday evening, there was only one passing vehicle, a logging truck, but not the one that belonged to Ivy Methvin. Bonnie and Clyde never appeared. The men grew weary from lack of sleep during the long, hot, insect-infested stakeout. "By nightfall, our eyes were red rimmed and our lids were heavy," Hinton wrote. "We were dirty and unshaven; the night and day in the underbrush had left every exposed part of our face and arms crimson with smeared blood from the niggling bugs."[121]

Early on the morning of Wednesday, May 23, Ivy Methvin arrived at the ambush site driving his Model-A Ford logging truck.[122] The truck was parked facing the direction from which Clyde was expected to approach, and the right front tire was removed. When Clyde eventually appeared, he would see Ivy Methvin's disabled truck and might at least slow down to investigate. This would put Clyde and Bonnie in a vulnerable position, looking away from the blind that was hiding the lawmen and toward the truck, which sat no more than thirty feet from the closest gun barrel.

About 8:45 that morning, a school-bus driver rolled to a stop and offered his assistance. Ivy Methvin waved him off, saying he was just about to put the wheel back on and get on his way.[123]

Around that time, Bonnie and Clyde had stopped at Canfield's Café in Gibsland for breakfast. Before leaving, they ordered sandwiches to go. Back inside the tan Ford he was now driving, surrounded by enough weaponry to equip an infantry squad, Clyde removed his shoes as usual and placed a sixteen-gauge shotgun between his left leg and the driver's door and a twenty-gauge shotgun at his right leg. Bonnie placed a nickel-plated .45 semiautomatic pistol in her lap and covered it with a magazine.[124] Clyde pointed the Ford V-8 south and barreled toward the fork that split Highways 89 and 418 in Mount Lebanon. Then they drove past Sailes, Louisiana, toward the Methvin place.

The six lawmen at the ambush site were beyond tired. They had not slept indoors since the previous Sunday. Their food supply was nearly exhausted—and much of their zeal with it. "We looked like the wrath of God—unshaven, eyes bloodshot, and feeling the wear of no sleep since Sunday. . . . We agreed to give it another thirty minutes," Hinton later wrote.[125]

They were lined up about ten feet apart along the top of the knoll that ran parallel to the road. Hinton and Hamer anchored each end, with the others in between. Sheriff Henderson Jordan and his deputy Prentis Oakley, Bob Alcorn, and Manny Gault were among them.[126]

Frustration ran high, since they could not predict when this stakeout would end. The men rubbed and scratched at the sore and bleeding bites; sweat dripped into tired,

The Ringgold Six. Standing: Ted Hinton, Prentis Oakley, Ben F. "Manny" Gault. Seated: Bob Alcorn, Henderson Jordan, Frank Hamer. *(From the collections of the Texas/Dallas History and Archives Division, Dallas Public Library)*

burning eyes; and not one vehicle had passed by after the school bus some thirty minutes earlier.

Hinton and Hamer each said later that the first thing they heard was the unmistakable whine of an engine being pushed to its limits. In the distance, two people could be seen inside the Ford driving toward them. Bonnie and Clyde could not have known that they were speeding toward death, shortly after 9:15 in the morning, Wednesday, May 23, 1934.

"This is it." Alcorn whispered. "It's Clyde."[127]

CHAPTER TEN

Joe Palmer:
The Deep, Dark Woods

Houston Press reporter Dick Vaughan hoped to find a good story that day. Although the letter was probably a hoax, the map with it might actually lead to something newsworthy. Coming all this way from Houston for nothing would be a real disappointment, but the possibility of getting a big scoop was worth the trip.

Vaughan believed that the map directed him to a location on the Louisiana side of the border, so he began his hunt in Shreveport. At 243 miles from Houston, this was a formidable drive in April 1934. Caddo Parish sheriff T. R. Hughes was very skeptical, but he directed Deputy R. A. Shaw to take Vaughan to the site pinpointed on the map.[1] About thirty miles northwest of Shreveport, north of Highway 80, Vaughan asked Shaw to stop. He exited the patrol car and took off on foot, saying only, "I'll do the hunting."[2]

Even to someone brave enough to struggle through it, the terrain was intimidating. Pines towered above the Texas-Louisiana border, shutting out most of the sunlight. Worse yet, the ground that stretched beneath bristled with tightly woven briar thickets, prickly berry bushes, and menacing thorn trees. Fighting off the army of swarming, biting insects in the near-darkness distracted the intruder just long enough to plunge him face first into spider webs as taut as guitar strings.

Soon, Vaughan was lost, fighting the constant pull and tear of the barbed underbrush. Using his wits rather than the map, he managed to find his way back to the patrol car. Although he was tempted to assume that the unsigned letter was just a cruel joke, Vaughan suggested that Shaw turn the car around toward the direction from which they came.

"Just another nut letter,"[3] the sheriff had said. Perhaps he was right, but as Deputy Shaw waited on that Tuesday, April 3, Vaughan plunged back into the woods.

The letter had arrived on April Fool's Day. Editor Marcellus E. "Mefo" Foster handed the letter and map to Vaughan. "I thought it was a joke," Vaughan said later. Still, there was a hint of authenticity, especially the reference to the "carcass of [the Texas prison system's] chief rat."[4] So Foster gave Vaughan the assignment and Hughes gave Vaughan Deputy Shaw.

Several months earlier, Joe Palmer was a thirty-two-year-old convict serving his fourth term at Eastham, about two hundred miles away near the small community of

Joe Palmer prison mug. (*Courtesy of the Texas Ranger Hall of Fame and Museum, Waco, Texas*)

Weldon. He suffered from numerous ailments, including asthma, stomach ulcers, and perhaps even tuberculosis.[5] Despite these frailties, Palmer was no weakling. He was a man who kept accounts in his head. According to his own testimony, after a prison guard named Major Crowson beat him severely, Palmer decided he would settle one account as soon as possible.

On January 16, 1934, Palmer got his chance to square things with Major Crowson.[6] During a daring early-morning prison break arranged by Clyde Barrow, Bonnie Parker, and others, Palmer shot Crowson off his horse. Crowson died the next day, but not before he made a deathbed apology to Lee Simmons, the Texas prison system director, for failing to maintain his position out in the field.[7]

Once Palmer was on the outside, his enthusiasm for squaring injustice intensified. First, however, he had to help the other escapees pay James Mullens, alias Jimmy LaMont, a convict on the verge of parole. Mullens had served as a messenger between Ray Hamilton at Eastham and his brother Floyd in west Dallas, facilitating the escape.[8]

Palmer and the escapees became the second Barrow gang, consisting of Clyde, Raymond "Ray" Hamilton, Henry Methvin, and Hilton Bybee, a convicted killer who had escaped in the place of Barrow crony Ralph Fults. This was a motley crew indeed. Only two survived to old age.

Raymond Elzie Hamilton was one of six children born to John and Alice. John deserted the family twice in four years before Alice married Steve Davis in 1927.[9]

Davis had his own problems. He was convicted of stealing turkeys and argued constantly with Ray, prompting the boy to hit the mean streets of west Dallas. Ray occasionally returned home, but soon found he could make enough for meals and the occasional room by selling stolen bicycles to a local shop. Richard Allen "Smoot" Schmid[10] operated a bicycle shop in Dallas, where Hamilton and others would

Clyde Barrow (left) poses with Henry Methvin (center) and Raymond Hamilton. *(Courtesy of the Texas Ranger Hall of Fame and Museum, Waco, Texas)*

sell bicycles they had stolen. Schmid in turn would sell the bicycles, presumably ignorant of their provenance. His customers included Ted Hinton and Clyde Barrow.[11] Years later, when Schmid became sheriff of Dallas County, he hired Hinton and eventually ordered him to track down Clyde Barrow.

Hamilton joined the Barrow gang in early 1932 but also planned and committed robberies on his own. One of his outside jobs that year was the robbery of the First State Bank of Cedar Hill, Texas, on November 25.[12] He was assisted by Gene O'Dare, who was caught, convicted of armed robbery, and sentenced to ninety-nine years in a Texas prison.

Ralph Fults did not escape with the others in January, but he had already escaped once from Eastham by the time Barrow met him in Bud Russell's prisoner transport truck in 1930.[13] The transport was affectionately dubbed Uncle Bud's One-Way Wagon.[14] Fults had been captured in St. Louis attempting to burglarize a business. Clyde was sentenced to two seven-year terms for burglaries and auto thefts. Clyde received a parole in 1932 but had to hobble home on crutches. He had persuaded a fellow prisoner to cut off two of his toes so he could avoid certain work crews.[15]

On April 19, 1932, Clyde, Bonnie, and Ralph had been surrounded by a posse near Mabank, Texas, after a robbery, and Fults sustained a gunshot wound. Clyde got away, leaving Ralph and Bonnie behind. They spent one night in a tiny one-room brick jail before they were moved to Kaufman.[16] Eventually Fults was sent to Texas State Prison in Huntsville.

Henry Methvin was a poorly educated Louisianan who was serving a ten-year stretch in Refugio County, Texas, for stealing a 1929 Ford and trying to kill its owner.[17] Hilton Bybee had been serving a life sentence for a murder conviction in Stephens County, Texas.

And so, in January 1934, the new Barrow gang avoided

capture by a circuitous route that soon brought them to Iowa. They chose a bank in Rembrandt to rob on January 23. Palmer was willing enough to help in the robbery, but all he could do was lie on the rear floorboards of the getaway car, due to a recurring, severe sick spell.[18] Apparently he slept through the whole thing, but Barrow insisted he get a share anyway, much to the consternation of Ray Hamilton.

Perhaps sensing trouble, Bybee took his share and left. Two weeks later he was nabbed in Amarillo, Texas. He escaped Eastham for the last time in 1937, but in July of the following year, he was gunned down by police in Monticello, Arkansas, after robbing the Texas National Guard Armory in Jacksboro.[19]

Forty-eight hours after the Rembrandt job, on Thursday, January 25, 1934, Palmer, Barrow, and the others robbed the Central National Bank in Poteau, Oklahoma. Palmer talked with the others about returning to Eastham for some revenge against the guards, but quit the gang and had Clyde drop him at the Conner Hotel in Joplin, Missouri. Palmer was a very lucky man to have quarreled with Ray Hamilton and survived.

Ray Hamilton never really got along with Palmer at Eastham and he had not been happy when Barrow awarded the guy a share of the Rembrandt bank loot, just for sleeping through the robbery. Sometime before the gang dropped Palmer in Joplin, Hamilton had attempted to murder him as he slept in the backseat of their current stolen car. Clyde saved Palmer by backhanding Hamilton from the driver's seat, but then lost control of the getaway car, which crashed and broke an axle.[20]

Now that he was on his own, Palmer started to formulate a plan. He had left the gang just in time. Soon thereafter, Clyde Barrow had serious troubles of his own.

The problems started when Hamilton introduced his new girlfriend to the gang in February. She was Mary O'Dare, the former wife of onetime Hamilton associate Gene O'Dare, who was now serving time for the bank robbery in Cedar Hill, Texas.[21]

No one in the Barrow gang cared for Mary at all. Bonnie immediately began calling her "washerwoman" to her face. Raymond's older brother Floyd had little regard for Mary and at one time said she used enough makeup to be able "to grow a crop."[22] O'Dare also tried to convince Bonnie that they should drug Clyde, take whatever they could carry, and find a new life. She was totally oblivious to the strong relationship between Bonnie and Clyde.

There were more problems. "I just saw that stool pigeon Mary O'Dare," Clyde's mother said to Bonnie's mother, Emma Parker, in a phone conversation that the Dallas Police Department was listening in on. "She tried to get the kids [Bonnie and Clyde] caught when she was with them and finally got Raymond caught." Emma said that if "that woman" ever came too close, she would assault O'Dare with one of her irons.[23]

O'Dare was no more popular with the rest of the Barrow gang than with Bonnie and Clyde's mothers. Raymond's own brother Floyd described her as a "prostitute" and a "gold digger."[24] Still, she stayed with the gang as Hamilton's bed partner, while the rest of the gang tried to agree on what to do.[25]

The outlaws thought she was an informant and discussed killing her.[26] Finally, O'Dare went too far when she argued for a cut of the loot taken in the R. P. Henry and Sons Bank heist in Lancaster, Texas, on February 27, 1934.[27] Barrow and the rest could tolerate treachery but were not ready to include her in the divvy. Ray Hamilton was forced to choose between Mary and the gang after he handed her part of his own loot. He stole a car and left with Mary on March 6.[28]

Hamilton now achieved some brief success without Bonnie and Clyde. He robbed a bank in north Texas on March 19 and a bank in West, Texas, the day before Barrow

Raymond Hamilton poses in his Sunday best.
*(From the collections of the Texas/Dallas History
and Archives Division, Dallas Public Library)*

and Methvin killed two policemen near Grapevine for no reason at all. Hamilton robbed a bank in Lewisville on April 25, of about $1,000 ($16,000 today), with the help of new Hamilton gang associate Teddy R. Brooks.[29] Town constable D. H. Street and good citizen Tom Bullock Hyder[30] gave chase, along with other Lewisville residents. Soon Hamilton and Brooks topped a hill on the road to Howe, south of Sherman, and realized they were trapped.

"Don't shoot, boys. I'm fresh out of guns, ammo, whiskey, and women!" Hamilton yelled, just after he stopped a few feet from the end of the gun barrels leveled at them.[31]

Raymond and Mary eventually became guests of the Dallas County Jail, where they were housed separately after their arrests.[32] They had last seen each other during an early April tryst at the Lafayette Hotel de Luxe in New Orleans.[33] Mary had been captured on April 23 in Amarillo.[34]

Following a federal trial in February 1935, O'Dare was convicted of harboring Bonnie and Clyde. She was sentenced to one year and a day at the Alderson Federal Prison for Women in West Virginia.[35] After her release, she was arrested and convicted on a drug-trafficking charge in 1938. Mary O'Dare received a five-year sentence and disappeared from the pages of history.

Methvin was one of the few Barrow gang members to survive the depression. Shortly after the January 16, 1934, prison break, Methvin may have held a joyous reunion with his father and mother. However, by January 23, he was back on the road with Bonnie, Clyde, and Raymond Hamilton, robbing banks, killing lawmen, kidnapping citizens, and stealing cars across Iowa, Oklahoma, and Texas. Soon, they became celebrity outlaws.[36]

Today, it is widely accepted that Ivy Methvin made a deal with the Texas lawmen who ambushed Bonnie and Clyde in late May 1934. Consequently, Texas pardoned his son for the crimes he committed there.[37]

Henry was low on money by August and unable to get a pay advance for work at his brother's sawmill. His brother, Terrell,[38] also refused Henry a personal loan. Suddenly, a Shreveport collector expressed an interest in a gun Henry carried during his time with Bonnie and Clyde. However, the collector could not come to Bienville Parish and Henry was told to bring the merchandise to Shreveport. The buyer brought a few other gun enthusiasts, all of whom were Oklahoma policemen. They had a John Doe warrant charging Methvin with the April 6, 1934, death of Constable William Calvin "Cal" Campbell in Commerce.[39] Methvin was convicted of murdering Campbell and received the death penalty, but his sentence was commuted to life in prison. Even so, he served less than eight years and was paroled on March 18, 1942.[40]

Ivy Methvin died four years later under mysterious circumstances. Henry inexplicably crawled under a Southern Pacific train in a rail yard near Sulphur, Louisiana, on April 19, 1948, and was nearly cut in half.[41]

Floyd Hamilton was convicted of a robbery he committed with his younger brother Ray. He occupied an Alcatraz cell next to Robert "Bird Man" Stroud until he was paroled in 1958.[42]

Floyd eventually established a halfway house for former convicts, read a great deal of Eastern philosophy, and once said he believed he had been a wicked priest in a former life.[43] The misdeeds and misfortunes of his current life, he said, were payback. He died in Dallas on July 24, 1984.[44]

James Mullens arranged the great Eastham escape, but he could no more stay away from trouble than a hog can stay away from slop and was soon arrested.[45] Prison records show that Mullens, using the alias Muller, was sentenced to up to fifteen years in 1954, for armed robbery in Texas. He was sixty-nine years old.[46]

Ted Rogers, the real killer of Hillsboro shop owner John

N. Bucher, never confessed to the crime for which Ray Hamilton received a life sentence. Generous to a fault, Rogers told some intimate inmates that he had killed Bucher and would have confessed had Hamilton received the death penalty.[47] Rogers was serving time behind "the Walls" at Huntsville for an unrelated crime when he was stabbed in the back and killed by fellow inmate Pete McKenzie.[48]

William Daniel "Deacon" Jones was yet another Barrow gang associate. In 1932, he began his criminal career at age sixteen with Bonnie and Clyde. Jones idolized Clyde, thought the world of Bonnie, was keenly aware of the reputation surrounding both, and was eager to be a member of the Barrow gang.

He quickly proved this on Christmas Day in Temple, Texas, by killing a young father for no reason at all, right in front of his family. "It all seemed pointless as to why Clyde wanted that car,"[49] Jones said in an interview more than thirty years later. After the murder, Jones and Barrow abandoned the car two blocks away, leaving the doors wide open. Bonnie picked up the pair in the car they originally arrived in.[50]

Jones ran with Bonnie and Clyde for nearly eight months, quitting the gang in Mississippi. He was arrested when he returned to Houston, and he learned about the death of his mentors while he was in jail.[51] Jones was released during the 1950s, married, and settled in Houston. After his wife died, Jones began mixing a drug containing morphine with whiskey and became an addict.[52] He checked into a rehabilitation center in 1971.

Three years later, he met a young woman in a Houston bar and agreed to drive her home. Undoubtedly, he was surprised to learn that she shared her home with her former boyfriend, George Arthur Jones,[53] who was no relation to the retired bandit. When the woman began arguing with George, W. D. heard the yelling and knocked at the door.

George produced a twelve-gauge shotgun and blew the aging gangster right off the porch and into the next world.[54] George killed himself later with the same shotgun rather than go to jail.

When Ralph Fults was paroled in 1935, Raymond Hamilton insisted on a reunion. The two conducted robberies in Mississippi before they parted, according to Fults. Hamilton was captured in April and electrocuted in May of the same year.[55]

Fults was also recaptured and spent time in Mississippi state prison.[56] He received a conditional Mississippi pardon in 1944 and later went to work in the shipyards in Pascagoula[57] during World War II. He had attempted to enlist, but the army doctor took one look at his bullet-riddled body and rejected him.

He met his future wife[58] in Pascagoula and married her in a local Baptist church. After he retired from the shipyards, Fults began to work at the Buckner Home for Boys[59] near Dallas, using his personal experiences to motivate the students there. He led the school boxing team to two Golden Gloves titles. In 1960, the publicity-shy Fults helped establish a locally televised program called *Confessions*.[60]

Fults was living in Dallas when, in 1992, he was diagnosed with terminal cancer. "I can't be concerned about that. The way I see it, I lived sixty-some-odd years longer than I should have. I was given a second chance, and I've had a really great life."[61]

Fults died a grandfather of three on March 17, 1993.[62] Perhaps he thought of the murderous Joe Palmer when he mentioned how lucky he had been to get a second chance.

During the high tide of the Barrow-gang era, there had been no second chance for Wade Hampton McNabb. Perhaps his fate had been decided right after Joe Palmer left the gang in January 1934.[63]

Wade Hampton McNabb began serving a twenty-five-year

stretch for armed robbery in Longview, Texas, at the Eastham
Prison Farm in 1932. McNabb made his time of forced labor
a little easier by ingratiating himself with the prison guards.
Their harsh methods of discipline were exposed a few years
later by the iconoclastic newsman Harry McCormick.[64]
Cruelties of all kind were practiced upon prisoners, and
perhaps to avoid this, McNabb became a "tender," that is, a
prisoner who "tended to" work production and other issues
at the behest of the guards. Tenders were known in other
prisons as trustys. They were permitted, if not encouraged,
to use brute force to keep productivity at the levels set by
the warden. Since the prisoners considered the tenders to
be rats or worse, tenders were allowed to carry knives or
sticks, but not guns. Clyde Barrow killed one such tender at
Eastham the same year McNabb entered prison.[65] Even so,
McNabb did not hesitate to do what the guards expected.

Palmer was one inmate whom McNabb repeatedly
beat[66] in his efforts to produce the results the guards
wanted. McNabb was gratified but not surprised when he
was awarded a sixty-day furlough, apparently as a reward
for his success. He used that furlough in late February or
early March 1934[67] to visit his parents in Greenville, Texas,
northwest of Dallas. According to Fults, this had all been
arranged by Joe Palmer, using his share of the bank money
stolen after the Eastham breakout.[68]

Palmer was not the only escapee who may have held a
grudge against McNabb. Henry Methvin and Clyde Barrow
himself were said to also be looking for a chance to get
to him.[69] One or both may have been involved in the
murder.[70]

"He [McNabb] was in the car with us at Gladewater
[Texas] on Thursday," McNabb's sister-in-law, Florence
McNabb, told Dick Vaughan of the *Houston Press* in April.
"He must have seen somebody he knew or someone called
him, for he jumped out and rushed into a domino parlor,"

she continued. "Then he ran out and went into another. That was the last we saw of him."[71]

Earlier, Wade and Florence had breakfasted at a restaurant. She later told Vaughan that she listened intently as her brother-in-law talked about doing things "he hated to do" at the direction of the guards.

S. T. McNabb told Vaughan that his son did those things out of fear for his own safety. "I can give you a break, young man. You had better take it . . . or else,"[72] a prison guard had reportedly said. McNabb simply had no choice, or so he claimed. And since beginning his furlough, McNabb had worried about meeting one of his fellow inmates on the outside. One prisoner in particular told him after a brutal beating that some day the two would meet on the outside, where there were no guards to protect McNabb. Apparently, Florence did not know who the inmate was.

On April 3, 1934, as Vaughan searched the piney woods, a rise suddenly appeared in a clearing, illuminated with dappled sunlight. "I came to a glade where birds were winging and the scent of dogwood blossoms filled the air. No place for a murder I thought," Vaughan wrote in an article.[73]

He saw something astride the knoll as he came closer. The unmistakable shape of a human body, hunched face down in the clearing, told him that Sheriff Hughes was wrong this time. Vaughan broke out in the sweat that fear alone produces. "I felt like I had been standing in a warm shower and someone had suddenly turned on ice water. A sponge seemed to have been crammed down my throat," Vaughan later wrote.

It was McNabb. The reporter did not spend any time contemplating the situation. "I was alone and needed company. Deputy Shaw was waiting in the car and I crashed back through the thorns and underbrush, not running, but wanting to."[74]

Later it was determined that the body was actually in

Texas. Vaughan notified the authorities in Waskom, and the case was turned over to Sheriff John Sanders[75] in Marshall. Vaughan wrote that McNabb had been deliberately if not forcefully led along the path to the knoll, "probably pleading for his life." He also wrote that the dead man lay face down with his head in his hat as though he had been kneeling. And both hands were "clasped under him as if in prayer."[76] McNabb's skull had been pierced by no fewer than two slugs, perhaps more, fired at close range from a .45 pistol.[77]

The letter that Vaughan carried to the death scene contained clues about the identity of the murderer and indicated he was not acting alone.[78] It was penciled on blue-lined, yellow note paper, and said McNabb was killed because of his cruelty to prisoners. The author said he could "go on for hours reciting cases of inhuman treatment that has been meted out to the unfortunates of the Texas prison at the hands of Wade McNabb and other building tenders."[79] The letter acknowledged the *Houston Press's* fight against corruption and "inhuman slaughters" inside the Texas prison system and said, "We are contributing our bit by sending you a map which will lead to the carcass of [the Texas prison system's] chief rat."[80]

The reason given in the letter was virtually identical to Palmer's statement at his sentencing hearing, where he took all the blame for killing Major Crowson.[81] Palmer told the court that he killed the prison guard because of his mistreatment of inmates, and "I am making this statement for the sake of my own conscience."[82] Conscience or not, he did not mention McNabb.

Palmer was strapped into the electric chair at 12:04 A.M. on May 10, 1935.[83] He was pronounced dead just four minutes later. Earlier, he consoled the man who once tried to kill him and even agreed to die first. Raymond Hamilton was originally scheduled to die just before Palmer was to be executed at 12:19.[84]

Raymond Hamilton sits with his mother moments before his execution at Texas State Prison, Huntsville. *(From the collections of the Texas/Dallas History and Archives Division, Dallas Public Library)*

Thus some believed then, as others do now, that in late March 1934, Palmer had killed the man who savagely beat him again and again. Clyde Barrow and Henry Methvin may have been there too. However, none of the circumstantial evidence or theories put forward at the time convinced the authorities to charge anyone.

And so, the murder of Wade Hampton McNabb in a lonely place beneath the towering pines of East Texas remains unsolved to this day.

Notes

Chapter 1

1. Crouch and Brice, 152-53.
2. Orr, 49.
3. Mack, *Texas Information for Immigrants*, 141, 143.
4. Crouch and Brice, 6.
5. Ibid., 153.
6. Ibid.
7. Crouch, 97.
8. Crouch and Brice, 13.
9. Ibid., 20.
10. Ibid., 24.
11. Sonnichsen, *I'll Die Before I Run*, 35.
12. Crouch and Brice, 24, 25.
13. Ibid., 25, 26.
14. Ibid., 29.
15. Orr, 6.
16. Taylor, 5-6.
17. *Weekly Harrison Flag*, January 28, 1869.
18. Orr, 11.
19. Crouch and Brice, 4.
20. Ibid., 42, 60.
21. Ibid., 45.
22. Ibid., 106.
23. Orr, 15-16
24. Crouch and Brice, 48.
25. Vestal, 25.
26. Crouch and Brice, 50.
27. Vestal, 25.
28. Crouch, 12 .
29. Ibid., 13.
30. Smallwood, Crouch, and Peacock, 40.
31. Crouch, 95.
32. Richter, 329.
33. Crouch and Brice, *Cullen Montgomery Baker*, 38.
34. Sonnichsen, 9.

35. Crouch and Brice, 60.
36. Ibid., 60-64.
37. Orr, 23.
38. Crouch and Brice, 64.
39. Breihan, 73, 75.
40. Orr, 29.
41. Eason, 10-11.
42. Crouch, 69-101.
43. Crouch and Brice, 75, 76, 78.
44. Ibid., 80 n. 50.
45. Ibid., 83-84.
46. Ibid., 92.
47. Orr, 37-39.
48. Crouch and Brice, 92.
49. Ibid., 94.
50. Orr, 40.
51. Crouch and Brice, 92, 97.
52. Ibid., 112, 115.
53. Ibid., 105.
54. Smallwood, Crouch, and Peacock, 73.
55. Crouch and Brice, 117.
56. Clayton, 15.
57. Crouch and Brice, 117-18.
58. Crouch, 92-94.
59. Crouch and Brice, 128.
60. Ibid., 126.
61. Orr, 42.
62. Breihan, 81.
63. Orr, 126.
64. Crouch and Brice, 137.
65. Ibid., 140.
66. Breihan, 82, 83.
67. Crouch and Brice, 141.
68. Ibid., 145.
69. Ibid., 146.
70. Orr, 46.
71. Crouch and Brice, 149, 153-54.
72. Taylor, 144-45.
73. Crouch and Brice, 158-59.

Chapter 2
1. Metz, *John Wesley Hardin: Dark Angel of Texas*, 1.
2. Ibid., 2.
3. Ibid.
4. Hardin, 7.

5. Ibid., 8.
6. Ibid., 5.
7. Ibid., 6.
8. Ibid., 7; Metz, 7; Boggs, 6.
9. Metz, 11-13.
10. Ibid., 15-16.
11. Ibid., 19-20.
12. Ibid., 22-23.
13. Ibid., 28-32; Hardin, 30, 32.
14. Metz, , 36.
15. Ibid., 38-39.
16. O'Neal, *Encyclopedia of Western Gunfighters,* 129; Hardin, 48; Metz, 57-60.
17. Metz, 81-83, 94.
18. Utley, *Lone Star Justice,* 64-66, 172-73.
19. Gammel, 8:561.
20. Utley, 172.
21. Webb, *Handbook,* 693-94.
22. Metz, 97-99; Tise, 157.
23. Metz, 102-4.
24. Ibid., 109-10.
25. Ibid., 111.
26. Webb, 693-94.
27. Metz, 69.
28. *Denison (TX) Daily Herald.*
29. Hardin, 58.
30. Ibid.; Metz, 67.
31. Hardin, 58.
32. Ibid.
33. Ibid., 69.
34. *Abilene Chronicle,* August 10, 1871.
35. *Topeka Daily Commonwealth,* August 10, 1871.
36. *El Paso Daily Times,* August 21, 1895.
37. Metz, 74.
38. Boggs, 77.
39. Parsons, 49.
40. Ibid., xii.
41. *Western Chronicle,* June 8, 1877.
42. Parsons, 49, 50.
43. Ibid., 51.
44. Ibid.
45. Boggs, , 55.
46. Marohn, 132.
47. Ibid., 180.
48. O'Neal, 276-77.

49. Ibid., 277.
50. Ibid.
51. Cunningham, 103.
52. O'Neal, 276-79.
53. Cunningham, 113.
54. Ibid., 128.
55. Marohn, 222.
56. Ibid., 223; Haley, 232.
57. *El Paso Daily Herald*, "What Knocked Him," July 9, 1895; *Pecos Valley Weekly Argus*, "Martin Mrose Killed," July 5, 1895.
58. Marohn, 215.
59. O'Neal, 113.
60. Ibid.
61. Ibid., 223.
62. Marohn, 230.
63. *El Paso Daily Times*, July 2, 1895.
64. Metz, *John Selman, Gunfighter*, 179.
65. Ibid.
66. Ibid., 179-80.
67. Devereaux, 10.
68. *El Paso Daily Times*, August 21, 1895; Metz, *John Wesley Hardin*, 265; Cunningham, 64-65.
69. *El Paso Daily Times*, April 7, 1896.
70. Metz, *John Selman, Gunfighter*, 229.
71. Ibid., 203.
72. Metz, *John Wesley Hardin*, 278-79.

Chapter 3
1. Boggs, 97.
2. Miller, "Boastful Bill Longley."
3. Bartholomew, 5.
4. Ibid., 6.
5. Ibid., 10.
6. Thrapp, 873.
7. Miller.
8. *St. Louis Daily Globe-Democrat.*
9. Miller.
10. Metz, *John Wesley Hardin*, 191.
11. *Galveston Daily News*, October 12, 1878.
12. Boggs, 101; Miller; Thrapp, 873.
13. Miller; Boggs, 101; Bartholomew, 28-29.
14. Boggs, 101; Tyler, 1:344.
15. Thrapp, 873.
16. Boggs, 103-4; O'Neal, 194.
17. Boggs, 103; Miller.

18. Miller, *Bloody Bill Longley*, 80.
19. Metz, *John Wesley Hardin*, 26, 190-91.
20. *Daily Austin Republican*, December 28, 1868.
21. Miller, *Bloody Bill Longley*, 15; Boggs, 99.
22. Miller, *Bloody Bill Longley*, 15.
23. Evans, December 30, 1868.
24. *Galveston Daily News*, September 16, 1877.
25. Miller, *Bloody Bill Longley*, 17.
26. Woods; Boggs, 102.
27. Miller, *Bloody Bill Longley*, 25.
28. *South Pass (Wyoming Territory) News*.
29. Miller, *Bloody Bill Longley*, 41.
30. Ibid.
31. Delo.
32. Tyler, 4:282; Boggs, 105; Miller, *Bloody Bill Longley*, 90.
33. Thrapp, 873; O'Neal, 194; Miller, *Bloody Bill Longley*, 95-96, 98; Boggs, 105.
34. Fuller, 17.
35. Boggs, 105; O'Neal, 194-95; Miller, "Boastful Bill Longley"; Miller, *Bloody Bill Longley*, 105-6; Tyler, 4:282.
36. *Galveston Daily News*, October 5, 1877.

Chapter 4
1. O'Neal, *The Bloody Legacy of Pink Higgins*, 18 n. 16.
2. Nolan, *Bad Blood*, 1.
3. Ibid., 5.
4. Nichols.
5. Nolan, 6.
6. O'Neal, *Bloody Legacy*, 27.
7. Nolan, 7.
8. Nichols.
9. Nolan, 10.
10. Nichols.
11. *Santa Fe New Mexican*, January 21, 1869.
12. O'Neal, *Bloody Legacy*, 28.
13. Nichols.
14. Fehrenbach, *Comanches*, 499.
15. Nolan, 13.
16. Ibid., 14.
17. Ibid.
18. O'Neal, *Bloody Legacy*, 28.
19. Nichols.
20. Nolan, 17, 28.
21. Tise, 319.
22. Nichols.

23. O'Neal, *Bloody Legacy,* 35.
24. *Norton Union Intelligencer,* February 15, 1873.
25. O'Neal, *Bloody Legacy,* 29.
26. Redmon, February 28, 1873.
27. Nolan, 22.
28. Redmon.
29. Gillett, *Fugitives from Justice,* 74; Nolan, 24.
30. Gillett, 74.
31. Nolan, 26; *Norton Union Intelligencer,* March 29, 1873.
32. *San Antonio Daily Herald,* March 25, 1873.
33. Gillett, 76.
34. Nichols.
35. Nolan, 29.
36. *Santa Fe New Mexican,* February 19, 1873.
37. Ibid.
38. Fulton and Mullin, 10.
39. Nolan, 50.
40. Ibid., 51.
41. Ibid., 51-52.
42. Nolan, *Lincoln County War,* 51.
43. Ibid.
44. Ibid., 52.
45. William Casey.
46. Nolan, *Lincoln County War*, 52.
47. Klasner, 102.
48. Nolan, *Bad Blood,* 80.
49. William Casey.
50. Nolan, *Lincoln County War*, 52.
51. Ibid., 53.
52. Klasner, 106.
53. Nolan, *Bad Blood,* 81.
54. Price.
55. Nolan, *Bad Blood,* 82-83.
56. Nolan, *Lincoln County War,* 53.
57. Ibid.
58. Klasner, 106, 107.
59. Nolan, *Lincoln County War,* 53.
60. Price.
61. Nolan, *Bad Blood,* 87.
62. Sonnichsen, 103.
63. *Santa Fe New Mexican,* March 13, 1874.
64. Gillett, 76-77.
65. Nolan, *Bad Blood,* 96.
66. Ibid.
67. Ibid., 94.

68. *Lampasas Dispatch*, March 19, 1874.
69. Nolan, *Bad Blood*, 99.
70. Gillett, 77.
71. Nolan, *Bad Blood*, 99.
72. Ibid., 102.
73. O'Neal, *Bloody Legacy*, 44.
74. *Lampasas Leader*, January 26, 1889.
75. Nichols.
76. O'Neal, *Bloody Legacy*, 8.
77. Coffey, 70.
78. O'Neal, *Bloody Legacy*, 15.
79. Ibid., 19.
80. Ibid., 20.
81. Ibid., 25.
82. Nolan, *Bad Blood*, 105.
83. O'Neal, *Bloody Legacy*, 37-38.
84. Nichols.
85. Ibid.
86. Nolan, *Bad Blood*, 108.
87. Nichols.
88. Ibid.
89. Nolan, *Bad Blood*, 112.
90. Sonnichsen, 107.
91. Nolan, *Bad Blood*, 115.
92. *Lampasas Leader*.
93. Sonnichsen, 138-39.
94. Nolan, *Bad Blood*, 116; O'Neal, *Bloody Legacy*, 45.
95. *Lampasas Leader*.
96. Nichols.
97. *Lampasas Leader*.
98. Sonnichsen, 109.
99. Nolan, *Bad Blood*,123.
100. Gillett, 79, 80.
101. Nolan, *Bad Blood*, 129-31.
102. Sonnichsen, 114.
103. O'Neal, *Bloody Legacy*, 56.
104. Nolan, *Bad Blood*, 140.
105. Nichols.
106. Sonnichsen, 148-49.
107. Ibid., 117.
108. Nolan, *Bad Blood*, 143.
109. Nichols.
110. Nolan, *Bad Blood*, 143.
111. Ibid., 145.
112. O'Neal, *Bloody Legacy*, 57.

113. *Waco Weekly Examiner,* December 27, 1878.
114. Nolan, *Bad Blood,* 149.
115. O'Neal, *Bloody Legacy,* 58.
116. Nolan, *Bad Blood,* 150.
117. Jackson.
118. O'Neal, *Bloody Legacy,* 59.
119. Tise, 319.
120. O'Neal, *Bloody Legacy,* 61.
121. Ibid., 67.
122. Charles Adams Jones
123. O'Neal, *Bloody Legacy,* 149.

Chapter 5
1. Shirley, vi.
2. Ibid., 8.
3. Sonnichsen, *Ten Texas Feuds,* 200.
4. Shirley, 9.
5. Ibid.
6. *Miller v. State.*
7. Shirley, 20.
8. Ibid., 21-22; Richard C. Marohn, 203.
9. O'Neal, *Encyclopedia,* 231; Shirley, 25.
10. Marohn, 210; Shirley, 27.
11. Metz, *The Shooters,* 156; Grand jury indictment of M. Clements.
12. Sonnichsen, *Ten Texas Feuds,* 202; Shirley, 29-30.
13. Marohn, 204; Shirley, 30-32; *State v. G. A. Frazer.*
14. Wilkins, 201.
15. O'Neal, *Encyclopedia,* 113; Harkey, 113-14.
16. Shirley, 34.
17. O'Neal, *Encyclopedia,* 113; Shirley, 36; Metz, *The Shooters,* 157.
18. Sonnichsen, *Ten Texas Feuds,* 205; Cunningham, 57.
19. Metz, *John Selman, Gunfighter,* 175; *El Paso Herald,* August 20, 1895; Shirley, 41-42.
20. Marohn, 210; *Eddy (NM Territory) Current,* September 19, 1896; El Paso *Daily Times,* October 15, 1896.
21. Hardin, 10.
22. Sonnichsen, *Ten Texas Feuds,* 207; Marohn, 207; Shirley, 45-46.
23. Ibid.; *El Paso Times,* May 18, 1899; Harkey, 177.
24. Shirley, 49-51; O'Neal, *Encyclopedia,* 232.
25. Shirley, 51-52.
26. Ibid., 58; O'Neal, *Encyclopedia,* 232.
27. Shirley, 60; O'Neal, 233; Metz, The *Shooters,* 157.
28. Shirley, 64-65.
29. Ibid., 72-73; O'Neal, *Encyclopedia,* 233.
30. O'Neal, *Encyclopedia,* 115, 199.

31. Anderson, 35.
32. Shirley, 78; O'Neal, *Encyclopedia,* 118.
33. Metz, *Pat Garrett,* 294; Shirley, 84.
34. Shirley, 81, 87; *El Paso Herald,* May 5, 1909.
35. Metz, *Pat Garrett,* 292.
36. *New Mexico Sentinel,* April 23, 1939.
37. Ibid.; Shirley, 83.
38. Metz, *Pat Garrett,* 294 n. 5.
39. Curry, 217.
40. Ibid., 218.
41. Shirley, 89.
42. Ibid., 90; Harkey, 183-89.
43. Hervey; Metz, *Pat Garrett,* 299.
44. Metz, *Pat Garrett,* 297 n. 18.
45. Curry, 216-17.
46. Shirley, 88.
47. Metz, *Pat Garrett,* 303.
48. Ramon F. Adams, *Burrs Under the Saddle,* 220; Adams, *More Burrs Under the Saddle,* 146, 150.
49. Curry, 218.
50. Anderson, 37-38.
51. Sonnichsen, interview.

Chapter 6
1. Gamel, 30-31.
2. Gillett, *Six Years,* 47.
3. Menardville changed its name to Menard at the request of the Fort Worth and Rio Grande Railroad Company and Rio Grande Railroad in about 1919. Wilkins, 73.
4. O'Neal, *Encyclopedia,* 73-74.
5. Johnson, *The Mason County "Hoo Doo War,"* 13.
6. Ibid., 140, 240.
7. Ibid., 5-6.
8. Johnson, *John Ringo,* 55.
9. Johnson, *The Mason County "Hoo Doo War,"* 5-6, Tise, 357.
10. Fehrenbach, *Lone Star,* 363-64.
11. Tise, 357.
12. Johnson, *The Mason County "Hoo Doo War,"* 30.
13. Ibid.
14. Roberts, 92.
15. Johnson, *The Mason County "Hoo Doo War,"* 30.
16. *West Texas Free Press,* April 11, 1874.
17. Johnson, *The Mason County "Hoo Doo War,"* 35.
18. Ibid. Anglicized versions of German names, with the original spellings in parentheses, have been used where possible, to minimize

confusion and facilitate comparison with prior works, which often use anglicized spellings, for example referring to Johann Anton Wohrle as *John Worley.*
19. Rose and Sherry, 37-44.
20. Johnson, *The Mason County "Hoo Doo War,"* 40.
21. Ibid., 48.
22. Sonnichsen, *Ten Texas Feuds,* 90, 92; Johnson, *John Ringo,* 68.
23. Johnson, *John Ringo,* 64.
24. Holmes, February 17, 1875.
25. Sonnichsen, *Ten Texas Feuds,* 88.
26. Johnson, *The Mason County "Hoo Doo War,"* 273.
27. Ibid., 53.
28. Holmes, March 7, 1875.
29. Sonnichsen, *Ten Texas Feuds,* 93.
30. Ibid., 94.
31. Doell.
32. Sonnichsen, *Ten Texas Feuds,* 95.
33. Ibid.
34. Ibid.; Hatley, 143.
35. Sonnichsen, *Ten Texas Feuds,* 95-96.
36. Ibid., 96.
37. Ibid.
38. Johnson, *The Mason County "Hoo Doo War,"* 80-81.
39. Roberts, 90.
40. Johnson, *The Mason County "Hoo Doo War,"* 82.
41. *Austin Daily Statesman,* January 4, 1876.
42. Gillett, *Six Years,* 47.
43. Sonnichsen, *Ten Texas Feuds,* 97.
44. *San Antonio Daily Herald,* August 17, 1875.
45. DeVos, 47.
46. Johnson, *John Ringo,* 74.
47. Johnson, *The Mason County "Hoo Doo War,"* 96.
48. Wilkins, 74.
49. Sonnichsen, *Ten Texas Feuds,* 99.
50. Gamel, 40.
51. Roberts, 91-92.
52. Gamel, 25.
53. Holmes to Coke, September 8, 1875, Coke Papers.
54. *Austin Daily Statesman,* November 14, 1875; *Austin Weekly Statesman,* November 18, 1875.
55. Johnson, *John Ringo,* 78-79.
56. Johnson, *The Mason County "Hoo Doo War,"* 105, 106.
57. Burnet County District Court Records.
58. Johnson, *The Mason County "Hoo Doo War,"* 175.
59. Ibid., 110.
60. Krueger, 108.

61. Johnson, *The Mason County "Hoo Doo War,"* 113.
62. Doell.
63. King, 169.
64. Special Order No. 47.
65. Johnson, *The Mason County "Hoo Doo War,"* 237.
66. Ibid., 134; Gamel, 21-22.
67. *Galveston Daily News,* November 23, 1875; *San Antonio Daily Express*, November 23, 1875.
68. Johnson, *The Mason County "Hoo Doo War,"* 139.
69. Ibid., 141.
70. Johnson, *The Mason County "Hoo Doo War,"* 142.
71. *Austin Daily Statesman,* February 1, 1876.
72. Gillett, *Fugitives from Justice*, 78.
73. O'Neil, 135-36.
74. *Houston Daily Telegraph,* June 14, 1876.
75. Johnson, *The Mason County "Hoo Doo War,"* 165.
76. Ibid., 175.
77. *West Texas Free Press,* October 28, 1876.
78. *Daily Yellowstone Journal,* December 15, 16, 1888.
79. Johnson, "George W. Gladden," 1, 3-6.
80. O'Neil, 136.
81. Johnson, *John Ringo,* 109.
82. Johnson, *The Mason County "Hoo Doo War,"* 237-39.

Chapter 7

1. Hogg, 9-10.
2. Gard, *Sam Bass,* 7.
3. Gard, *Fabulous Quarter Horse*, 40-41; Miller, *Sam Bass and Gang*, 27.
4. Gard, *Sam Bass,* 49.
5. Miller, *Sam Bass and Gang,* 31.
6. Ibid., 32; *Hays City Sentinel,* September 28, 1877.
7. Miller, *Sam Bass and Gang,* 23-25; Hogg, 23-25.
8. Miller, *Sam Bass and Gang,* 25.
9. Ibid., 41; Metz, *The Shooters,* 34.
10. *Galveston Daily News,* April 27, 1878.
11. Miller, *Sam Bass and Gang,* 41; Metz, *The Shooters,* 34.
12. Miller, *Sam Bass and Gang,* 43.
13. Gard, *Sam Bass,* 58; O'Neal, *Encyclopedia,* 35.
14. Metz, *The Shooters,* 34; Miller, *Sam Bass and Gang,* 50.
15. Miller, *Sam Bass and Gang,* 50-51, 54, 108.
16. Birdwell, 7-8.
17. Miller, *Sam Bass and Gang,* 52.
18. Ibid., 55-57, 281, 320.
19. Ibid., 55-62.
20. Ibid., 50, 54.

21. Ibid., 62.
22. Webb, *Texas Rangers*, 2:373; Gillett, *Six Years*, 109.
23. Miller, *Sam Bass and Gang*, 73.
24. Ibid., 76-77.
25. Ibid., 80.
26. Gillett, *Six Years*, 113.
27. Miller, *Sam Bass and Gang*, 43, 46, 108, 124, 141, 142, 158.
28. Ibid., 115-16, 121.
29. Ibid., 127.
30. Ibid., 115.
31. Ibid., 152.
32. DeArment, *Deadly Dozen*, 35.
33. Yadon, 81-82; Metz, *Encyclopedia*, 56.
34. Gard, *Sam Bass*, 131; Hogg, 99.
35. Miller, *Sam Bass and Gang*, 145, 158.
36. Hogg, 100-101.
37. *Dallas Daily Herald*, April 11, 1878; Miller, *Sam Bass and Gang*, 164-65.
38. Gard, *Sam Bass*, 134.
39. Miller, *Sam Bass and Gang*, 167.
40. Parsons, 69.
41. Horan, 30.
42. Gard, *Sam Bass*, 138.
43. Ibid., 39; Miller, *Sam Bass and Gang*, 144.
44. Ibid., 178; Webb, *Texas Rangers*, 2:376.
45. Miller, *Sam Bass and Gang*, 293-96, 298.
46. Gard, *Sam Bass*, 145; *Dallas Daily Herald*, April 23, 1878.
47. Miller, *Sam Bass and Gang*, 188-89.
48. Ibid., 175; Gillett, *Six Years*, 115.
49. Miller, *Sam Bass and Gang*, 172.
50. Ibid., 22.
51. Webb, *Texas Rangers*, 2:378; *Galveston Daily News*, June 5, 1878.
52. Hogg, 129-30.
53. DeArment, *Jim Courtright of Fort Worth*, 74-77.
54. Gard, *Sam Bass*, 167-68; O'Neal, *Encyclopedia*, 36; Gillett, *Six Years*, 116.
55. Miller, *Sam Bass and Gang*, 224.
56. Gillett, *Six Years*, 117.
57. Ibid., 118; Webb, *Texas Rangers*, 2:383.
58. Webb, 228-29.
59. Miller, *Sam Bass and Gang*, 279-80.
60. Ibid., 233; Gillett, *Six Years*, 118; Cunningham, 292.
61. Gard, *Sam Bass*, 194.
62. Webb, *Texas Rangers*, 2:280; Gillett, *Six Years*, 119.

63. Gard, *Sam Bass*, 196; Webb, *Texas Rangers*, 2:280.

64. Miller, *Sam Bass and Gang*, 241.

65. Webb Collection, box 2M275.

66. Gillett, *Six Years*, 121.

67. Ibid., 122; Miller, *Sam Bass and Gang*, 244; Gard, *Sam Bass*, 204.

68. Miller, *Sam Bass and Gang*, 242.

69. Parsons, 69.

70. Ibid.; Gillett, *Six Years*, 124; Miller, *Sam Bass and Gang*, 250.

71. Miller, *Sam Bass and Gang*, 251; Gard, *Sam Bass*, 208-9; Gillett, *Six Years*, 124.

72. Webb, *Texas Rangers*, 2:387; Cunningham, 293.

73. Miller, *Sam Bass and Gang*, 253.

74. Gillett, *Six Years*, 125; Webb, *Texas Rangers*, 2:387.

75. Webb, *Texas Rangers*, 2:390.

76. Gard, *Sam Bass*, 214.

77. *Life and Adventures of Sam Bass*, 83.

78. Miller, *Sam Bass and Gang*, 257; Webb, *Texas Rangers*, 2:389; Gillett, *Six Years*, 126; Cunningham, 294.

79. *Life and Adventures of Sam Bass*, 83.

80. Miller, *Sam Bass and Gang*, 258; Gard, *Sam Bass*, 216.

81. *Galveston Daily News*, July 25, 1878; Miller, *Sam Bass and Gang*, 259.

82. Preece, 102.

83. *Life and Adventures of Sam Bass*, 84; *Galveston Daily News*, July 24, 1878; Wilkins, 166.

84. Miller, *Sam Bass and Gang*, 264; Gard, *Sam Bass*, 223.

85. *Galveston Daily News*, July 24, 1878.

86. Records of the Adjutant General of Texas, box 401-379-9.

87. August 14, 1878.

88. Miller, *Sam Bass and Gang*, 270.

89. *State of Texas v. Frank Jackson*; Gard, *Sam Bass*, 232.

90. *Galveston Daily News*, June 8, 1879; Gard, *Sam Bass*, 235; Cunningham, 296-97.

91. Miller, *Sam Bass and Gang*, 300.

92. Gard, *Sam Bass*, 231.

93. Miller, *Sam Bass and Gang*, 266.

94. Ibid., 285.

95. Ibid., 386 n. 37.

96. Ibid., 302.

97. Sterling, 491-95.

98. *State of Texas v. Frank Jackson*.

Chapter 8

1. Greene, 41-44. This account is based largely on Greene's work.

2. Ibid., 46.
3. Utley, *Lone Star Lawmen*, 127-28.
4. Greene, 48.
5. Tise, 165.
6. Greene, 52.
7. Ibid., 54.
8. Alexander, 130-31.
9. Gatton, 135.
10. Alexander, 143-44.
11. Smith, *Daltons!*, 47-48, 102-5, 117, 121, 122, 171-73, 174.
12. Smith, *Last Hurrah of the James-Younger Gang,* 184-85.
13. Greene, 58-59.
14. Ibid., 60. Carmichael died of his wounds on January 17, 1928.
15. Ibid., 61.
16. Ibid., 64.
17. Ibid., 70.
18. Ibid., 71.
19. Ibid, 80.
20. Ibid., 71.
21. Ibid., 85.
22. Ibid., 135.
23. Tise, 557; Rathmell, 63-65.
24. Greene, 142.
25. Ibid., 159-60.
26. Ibid., 164.
27. Alexander, 138-39.
28. Ibid., 192.
29. Ibid., 193.
30. Ibid., 205.
31. Tise, 165.
32. Greene, 210.
33. Ibid., 220.
34. Ibid., 223.
35. Ibid., 228.
36. Ibid., 233.
37. Ibid., 244.
38. Ibid., 247.

Chapter 9
1. Hinton, 167-68.
2. Knight, *Bonnie and Clyde,* 166, 167.
3. Ibid., 161-62. Some writers list as Henry's father Iverson T. Methvin. Iverson was his uncle and brother of Ivy T., Henry's father. Iverson T. died in 1952.
4. Ibid., 6.

5. Barrow, 207.
6. Knight, 207.
7. Ibid., 36-37; Barrow, 207; Phillips, 52-53.
8. Barrow, 206.
9. Phillips, 169; *Houston Chronicle*, January 16, 1934; *Dallas Morning News*, January 17, 1934; Hinton, 118.
10. Knight, 15.
11. Phillips, 43.
12. Barrow, 228 n. 5; Knight, 40, 145.
13. Knight, 182.
14. Ibid.
15. Ibid., 16-17, 25.
16. Ibid., 22.
17. Phillips, 82.
18. Barrow, xxxv.
19. Ibid., xxxvii. See also Knight, 186.
20. Knight, 23; Barrow, xxxvii.
21. Barrow, 149.
22. *Waco Times-Herald*, March 12, 1930.
23. Knight, 32.
24. Ramsey, 35.
25. Ibid., 33, 37.
26. *Middletown Journal*, March 18, 1930.
27. Phillips, 32.
28. Knight, 44.
29. Phillips, 64-65.
30. *McKinney (TX) Daily Courier-Gazette*, January 28, 1932.
31. Phillips, 67; Knight, 43.
32. Knight, 43, 203.
33. Phillips, 282-84.
34. Ibid., 74.
35. Ibid, 75, 76, 97, 282-84.
36. Ibid., 76.
37. Knight, 45.
38. Ramsey, 44.
39. Ibid., 44-45.
40. *Kaufman Daily Herald*, April 20, 1932. The article identifies the hardware store as the H. Bock store in Mabank rather than Kaufman.
41. Phillips, 87.
42. *Kaufman Daily Herald*, April 20, 1932.
43. Phillips, 89.
44. *Dallas Evening Journal*, March 18, 1935.
45. *Kaufman Daily Herald*, April 20, 1932.
46. Phillips, 95 .
47. *McKinney (TX) Daily Courier-Gazette*, April 21, 1932.

48. Ibid.
49. Ibid.
50. Knight, 47.
51. Phillips, 97-98.
52. Ibid., 98-99.
53. *Hillsboro Evening Mirror,* May 1, 1932.
54. Knight, 52, 188.
55. Frost and Jenkins, 188.
56. Some writers identify Milligan as Ross Dyer. "Milligan" was later arrested but not charged, suggesting that he became an informant. Knight, 54, 55.
57. Phillips, 110-11.
58. *Temple Daily Telegram,* December 27, 1932; Ramsey, 80-85.
59. Hinton, 4-5; Tise, 147; *Dallas Dispatch,* December 30, 1932.
60. Ibid., 5.
61. Ibid., 1.
62. Ibid., 5.
63. *Dallas Morning News,* January 7, 1933.
64. Barrow, 212.
65. *Dallas Morning News,* January 7, 1933; Frost and Jenkins, 191.
66. Ramsey, 92-94.
67. Ibid., 100-114.
68. Knight, 87.
69. Ibid., 90-91; Wallis, 327.
70. Phillips, 138-39.
71. Knight, 200.
72. Frost and Jenkins, 202.
73. Simmons, 126.
74. Ibid., 207.
75. Frost and Jenkins, 1-7.
76. Ibid., 9, 15.
77. Ibid., 24; Simmons, 22.
78. *Navasota (TX) Examiner-Review,* December 3, 1908.
79. Frost and Jenkins, 44, 47.
80. Ibid., 56-57.
81. Ibid., 66.
82. Ibid., 66, 67, 70-72.
83. Ibid., 177.
84. Simmons, 132; Webb, *Texas Rangers,* 2:539.
85. Knight, 141. Confusion exists over the exact date, as later Hamer said he and Deputy Bob Alcorn were in Bienville Parish no later than February 19. Phillips, 202. Avie Methvin and the family intermediary, John Joyner, said the date was perhaps the first of March (*Methvin v. Oklahoma*).
86. Ramsey, 193.

87. Knight, 116-22.

88. Knight, *Three Ambushes*. Frank Hamer was interviewed in July 1934 by Walter Prescott Webb for his book, *The Texas Rangers*, published the following year. Bienville Parish sheriff Henderson Jordan was also interviewed in 1934 for an article published that year in *True Detective* magazine. Twenty-three years later, Lee Simmons wrote *Assignment Huntsville*, which was compatible with the Hamer interview in many respects. The Hamer biography, *I'm Frank Hamer*, was published in 1968. The Ted Hinton memoir, *Ambush: The Real Story of Bonnie and Clyde*, was written in 1977 and published two years after his death. Each of the published late-life memoirs added new facts to the story, in some instances directly contradicting prior accounts.

89. *Dallas Evening Journal*, June 6, 1934. Dallas County deputy sheriff Bob Alcorn (1897-1964) had been assigned to the Barrow case in early 1934. He died on the thirtieth anniversary of the ambush. Ted Hinton (1904-77) began working full time on the Barrow case in April 1934. He was the last surviving member of the ambush team. Ramsey, 241; Knight, *Three Ambushes*, 191.

90. Phillips, 202.

91. Ibid., 354 n. 23; *Methvin v. Oklahoma*.

92. *Methvin v. Oklahoma*.

93. *Dallas Morning News*, April 2, 1934; *Miami Oklahoma News-Record*, April 6, 1934.

94. Murphy's age is listed variously as twenty-two and twenty-four on April 1, 1934. Barrow, 221; *Dallas Morning News*, April 2, 1934.

95. Knight, *Bonnie and Clyde*, 142, 144-45; *Dallas Daily Times Herald*, April 1, 1934.

96. *Dallas Daily Times Herald*, April 1, 1934.

97. Hinton, 136-37; Knight, *Bonnie and Clyde*, 216 n. 19.

98. Frost and Jenkins, 212; Ramsey, 230.

99. Ramsey, 218-23.

100. Other accounts say that it was Bonnie who was asleep in the car and Clyde who first noticed the arriving patrolmen. Hinton, 137.

101. Knight, 147.

102. *Dallas Morning News*, April 2, 1934; *Dallas Evening Journal*, April 2, 1934.

103. Knight, 146.

104. Hinton, 137-38.

105. *Dallas Morning News*, April 2, 1943; *Dallas Evening Journal*, April 2, 1934.

106. Leslie G. Phares left the Texas Highway Patrol four years to the day of the Grapevine murders—April 1, 1938—when he retired as chief. Chief Phares died in 1957. This information was obtained through the Texas Department of Public Safety Human Resources Division in Austin.

107. *Dallas Evening Journal,* April 2, 1934; *Dallas Daily Times Herald,* April 2, 1934.

108. Frost and Jenkins, 210.

109. Ibid.; Webb, *Texas Rangers,* 2:540.

110. Ben F. "Manny" Gault (1886-1947) of the Texas State Police joined the pursuit after the Grapevine murders. Knight, *Bonnie and Clyde,* 191.

111. Ibid., 164; Hinton, 161.

112. Knight, 158-60.

113. The date May 21, Monday, is considered accurate according to the case file in *Methvin v. Oklahoma,* but Hinton listed the date as May 19, 1934, a Saturday, saying it "had to have been about the time we were checking in to the Inn Hotel." See Hinton, 158.

114. In both Frost and Jenkins' and Hinton's books, the lethal lovebirds are continuously referred to as Clyde and Bonnie, whereas in most other works, including movies, newspapers, etc., they are referred to as Bonnie and Clyde.

115. Hinton, 158; Phillips, 203.

116. *Methvin v. Oklahoma.*

117. Hinton, 159.

118. Ibid.; Frost and Jenkins, 222. Hamer is quoted as saying they took up the vigil at the ambush site about midnight on May 22.

119. Frost and Jenkins, 222. Sheriff Jordan mentions Henry Methvin but maintains he was stopped by the officers and helped with the ambush. Hinton stated in his late-life memoirs that Ivy Methvin was stopped, handcuffed to a tree, and then promised leniency for his son Henry in order to keep him quiet. Hinton, 168.

120. Hinton, 163.

121. Ibid., 164.

122. Ibid., 165-67; Knight, *Bonnie and Clyde,* 165, 218 n. 14; Phillips, 204; *Ringgold Record,* April 26, 1968.

123. Knight, *Bonnie and Clyde,* 165.

124. Ibid.

125. Hinton, 167.

126. Hinton's and Frost and Jenkins' versions of the lineup of lawmen vary slightly. See Frost and Jenkins, 231; Hinton, 165. Hamer later claimed that fair warning was given the criminals before any shooting began and that the officers were forced to open fire after the two pointed their weapons at him. "At the command, 'Stick 'em up!' both turned, but instead of obeying as we hoped, they clutched the weapons." Hamer said when Bonnie pointed her gun at him, it was "like looking down the Holland Tunnel." Jordan claimed in his 1934 *True Detective* interview (Waers) that he himself called upon Clyde to surrender.

127. Ramsey, 246, 248; Hinton, 168. Although Hinton claimed in his 1977 manuscript that he was the one who identified Barrow, the warning

that Clyde was approaching is usually attributed to Alcorn. Phillips, 205.

Chapter 10

1. *Houston Press,* April 3, 1934.
2. Ibid.
3. Ibid., April 4, 1934.
4. Ibid.
5. Knight, *Bonnie and Clyde,* 126; Simmons, 165.
6. *Dallas Dispatch,* April 9, 1935; Phillips, 279.
7. Simmons, 116-17; *State of Texas v. Joe Palmer.* Palmer stated at a different time that there was no intention to shoot any of the guards. J. B. French also escaped but ran in a different direction. Knight, *Bonnie and Clyde,* 127-28.
8. Phillips, 167-72; Knight, *Bonnie and Clyde,* 124, 128. James Mullens' last name is variously spelled Mullins, Mullin, or Mullen, depending on the source.
9. Underwood, 3.
10. Ibid., 5.
11. Hinton, 177.
12. Underwood, 19.
13. McCormick, 118.
14. Associated Press.
15. Ramsey, 41; Phillips, 54-55.
16. *Kaufman Daily Herald,* April, 20, 21, 1932.
17. Refugio County Court Records #831; McConal, 97.
18. McConal, 104.
19. Ibid., 115.
20. *State of Texas v. Joe Palmer,* 172-73; Knight, *Bonnie and Clyde,* 202; Simmons, 167.
21. Underwood, 19.
22. Hamilton, 33.
23. Barrow, 297 n. 63.
24. Phillips, 173.
25. Simmons, 167.
26. Ibid.
27. Barrow, 182.
28. McConal, 107; Phillips, *178.*
29. Underwood, 52, 73; *State of Texas v. Joe Palmer,* 190.
30. Underwood, 74.
31. Ibid.
32. Ibid,. 73-74; Knight, *Bonnie and Clyde, 154.*
33. Ramsey, 230.
34. Ibid., 231.
35. Phillips, 311.

36. Yadon, 180-82.

37. Ramsey, 240-41; *Methvin v. Oklahoma*; Hinton, 158.

38. Knight, *Bonnie and Clyde,* 189.

39. *State v. Clyde Barrow, Bonnie Parker, and John Doe*; Barrow, 222.

40. Knight, *Bonnie and Clyde,* 190.

41. Ibid.

42. Hamilton, 156.

43. Floyd read the Bible while in prison. This may have motivated him to spread the word to others about the futility of a life of crime. He remarried his long-past divorced wife, set up his halfway house for ex-cons, and by 1967 had received paroles from both Texas and the federal government. Ted Hinton was instrumental in arranging Floyd's full-time employment at car dealership in Dallas. Hamilton stayed with that employer until his retirement. Phillips, 308-9.

44. *Dallas Morning News,* July 25, 1984.

45. Ibid., 115-16. Mullens turned tail and ran, but unfortunately for him, he ran into a policeman.

46. Knight, *Bonnie and Clyde,* 190.

47. Ibid.

48. Simmons, 153.

49. *Temple (TX) Daily Telegram,* December 27, 1932. As late as November 1968, Jones maintained that it was Clyde who killed Doyle Johnson. See W. D. Jones.

50. *Temple (TX) Daily Telegram,* December 27, 1932.

51. W. D. Jones.

52. Phillips, 309.

53. Knight, *Bonnie and Clyde,* 189.

54. Ramsey, 287.

55. Phillips, 258-74.

56. *Houston Press,* June 30, 1935.

57. While serving time in the Mississippi prison, Fults became religious and began a personal transformation. McCormick, 124; Knight, *Bonnie and Clyde*, 187.

58. McCormick, 124.

59. Phillips, 316.

60. Ibid. The program featured state officials in panel discussions that addressed the needs of paroled convicts. Often this helped parolees find gainful employment instead of reverting back to careers in crime. The program was so successful that for a time it was broadcast nationally.

61. Ibid.

62. *Dallas Morning News,* March 18, 1993.

63. Phillips, 172.

64. Ibid., 51; McConal, 144.

65. Phillips, 53.

66. Knight, *Bonnie and Clyde,* 144.
67. *Houston Press,* April 4, 1934; Barrow, 219-20. The furlough began either on February 24 or March 1.
68. Phillips, 172.
69. Underwood, 57.
70. Refugio County Court Records #831; McConal, 97.
71. *Houston Press,* April 4, 1934.
72. Ibid.
73. Ibid.
74. Ibid.
75. Underwood, 57.
76. *Houston Press,* April 4, 1934.
77. While many authors and historians believe that Palmer set up the entire kidnapping and murder scheme with the help of others, at least one writer attributes the deed to Methvin and Barrow alone. Perhaps Methvin saw a way back into Clyde's good graces after the "stupid" murder of the two motorcycle patrolmen the previous Easter Sunday. Underwood wrote that Methvin knew Clyde had been victimized by McNabb while at Eastham and heard that McNabb had even bragged about Clyde being his "wife." Of course, McNabb was killed *before* the Easter Sunday murders near Grapevine. Methvin told Clyde he knew McNabb's whereabouts, and the revenge-filled Clyde demanded that information. Methvin told him and, as Underwood wrote, "away they went." After a few queries, they turned up their prey walking down the street. Underwood stated they "ordered him into the car" and drove him to a point near Waskom, Texas. Underwood wrote that, after telling McNabb to say his prayers, Methvin whacked him in the head with the butt of a shotgun. Clyde then pumped two rounds into him. Underwood, 57.
78. *Houston Press,* April 3, 1934.
79. Ibid., April 4, 1934.
80. Ibid.
81. Barrow, 220.
82. *Dallas Dispatch,* April 9, 1935.
83. Underwood, 215.
84. Ibid.

Bibliography

Books

Adams, Ramon F. *Burrs Under the Saddle: A Second Look at Books and Histories of the West*. Norman: University of Oklahoma Press, 1964.

———. *More Burrs Under the Saddle: Books and Histories of the West*. Norman: University of Oklahoma Press, 1979.

Alexander, Bob. *Lawmen, Outlaws and SOBs*. Vol. 2. Silver City, NM: High Lonesome Books, 2007.

Anderson, Dan. *100 Oklahoma Outlaws, Gangsters, and Lawmen: 1839-1939*. With Laurence Yadon. Gretna, LA: Pelican, 2007.

Barrow, Blanche Caldwell. *My Life with Bonnie and Clyde*. Edited by John Neal Phillips. Norman: University of Oklahoma Press, 2004.

Bartholomew, Ed. *Wild Bill Longley: A Texas Hard Case*. Houston: Frontier Press of Texas, 1953.

Birdwell, J. W. *The Life and Adventures of Robert McKimie*. Houston: Frontier Press of Texas, 1955.

Boggs, Johnny D. *Great Murder Trials of the Old West*. Plano: Republic of Texas Press, 2003.

Breihan, Carl W. *Great Gunfighters of the West*. South Yarmouth, MA: Curley, 1978.

Clayton, Powell. *Aftermath of the Civil War in Arkansas*. New York: Neale, 1915.

Coffey, Michael. *The Irish in America*. New York: Hyperion, 1997.

Crouch, Barry A. *The Freedmen's Bureau and Black Texans*. Austin: University of Texas Press, 1992.

Crouch, Barry A., and Donaly E. Brice. *Cullen Montgomery Baker, Reconstruction Desperado*. Baton Rouge: Louisiana State University Press, 1997.

Cunningham, Eugene. *Triggernometry: A Gallery of Gunfighters*. 1941. Reprint, Norman: University of Oklahoma Press, 1996.

Curry, George. *George Curry, 1861-1947: An Autobiography*. Albuquerque: University of New Mexico Press, 1958.

DeArment, Robert K. *Alias Frank Canton*. Norman: University of Oklahoma Press, 1996.

———. *Deadly Dozen: Forgotten Gunfighters of the Old West*. Vol. 2.

Norman: University of Oklahoma Press, 2007.

———. *Jim Courtright of Fort Worth: His Life and Legend*. Fort Worth: Texas Christian University Press, 2004.

DeVos, Julius, ed. *One Hundred Years of the Hilda Methodist Church and Parent Organizations, 1856-1955*. Mason, TX: Hilda United Methodist Church, 1973.

Fehrenbach, T. R. *Comanches: The Destruction of a People*. New York: Alfred A. Knopf, 1974.

———. *Lone Star: A History of Texas and the Texans*. New York: Macmillan, 1968.

Fisher, O. C. *It Occurred in Kimble*. San Angelo, TX: Talley Press, 1984.

Fortune, Jan I. *Fugitives: The Story of Clyde Barrow and Bonnie Parker, as Told by Bonnie's Mother and Clyde's Sister*. Dallas: Texas Ranger Press, 1934.

Frost, Gordon F., and John H. Jenkins. *I'm Frank Hamer: The Life of a Texas Peace Officer*. 1968. Reprint, Austin: Pemberton Press, 1980.

Fuller, Henry C. *The Adventures of Bill Longley*. Nacogdoches, TX: Baker Printing, n.d.

Fulton, Maurice Garland, and Robert N. Mullin, ed. *History of the Lincoln County War*. Tucson: University of Arizona Press, 2004.

Gamel, Thomas W. *The Life of Thomas W. Gamel*. Mason, TX: privately printed, 1933.

Gammel, Hans Peter Nielson, comp. *The Laws of Texas, 1822-1897*. 10 vols. Austin: Gammel, 1898.

Gard, Wayne. *Fabulous Quarter Horse: Steel Dust*. New York: Duell, Sloan and Pearce, 1958.

———. *Sam Bass*. Lincoln: University of Nebraska Press, 1969.

Gatton, Harvey T. *The Texas Bankers Association: The First Century*. Austin: Texas Bankers Association, 1984.

Gillett, James B. *Fugitives from Justice: The Notebook of Texas Ranger James B. Gillett*. 1921. Reprint, Austin: State House Press, 1997.

———. *Six Years with the Texas Rangers, 1875 to 1881*. New Haven: Yale University Press, 1925.

Greene, A.C. *The Santa Claus Bank Robbery*. New York: Alfred A. Knopf, 1972.

Haley, J. Evetts. *Jeff Milton: A Good Man with a Gun*. Norman: University of Oklahoma Press, 1948.

Hamilton, Floyd. *Public Enemy No. 1*. Dallas: Acclaimed Books, 1978.

Hardin, John Wesley. *The Life of John Wesley Hardin as Written by Himself*. 1896. Reprint, Norman: University of Oklahoma Press, 1961.

Harkey, Daniel R. "Dee." *Mean as Hell: The Life of a New Mexico Lawman*. Albuquerque: University of New Mexico Press, 1948.

Hatley, Allen G. *Bringing the Law to Texas: Crime and Violence in*

Nineteenth Century Texas. La Grange, TX: Centex Press, 2002.

Hinton, Ted, as told to Larry Grove. *Ambush: The Real Story of Bonnie and Clyde.* Bryan, TX: Shoal Creek, 1979.

Hogg, Thomas E. *Authentic History of Sam Bass and His Gang.* 1878. Reprint, Bandera, TX: Frontier Times, 1932.

Holmes, Lucia M. *The Lucia Holmes Diary, 1875-1876.* Mason, TX: Mason County Historical Commission, 1985.

Horan, James D. *The Pinkertons.* New York: Bonanza Books, 1967.

Johnson, David. *John Ringo.* Stillwater, OK: Barbed Wire Press, 1996.

——. *The Mason County "Hoo Doo" War, 1874-1902.* Denton: University of North Texas Press, 2006.

King, Irene Marshall. *John O. Muesebach: German Colonizer in Texas.* Austin: University of Texas Press, 1987.

Klasner, Lily Casey. *My Girlhood Among the Outlaws.* Edited by Eve Ball. Tucson: University of Arizona Press, 1972.

Knight, James R. *Bonnie and Clyde: A Twenty-First-Century Update.* With Jonathan Davis. Austin: Eakin Press, 2003.

Knight, Jim. *Three Ambushes.* Gibsland, LA: Bonnie and Clyde Museum, 2008.

Krueger, Max Amadeus Paulus. *Second Fatherland: The Life and Fortunes of a German Immigrant.* College Station: Texas A&M University Press, 1976.

Life and Adventures of Sam Bass. Dallas: Dallas Commercial Steam Print, 1878.

McConal, Patrick M. *Over the Wall: The Men Behind the 1934 Death House Escape.* Austin: Eakin Press, 2000.

McCormick, Harry, as told to Mary Carey. *Bank Robbers Wrote My Diary.* Austin: Eakin Press, 1985.

Mack, H. C. *Texas: Information for Immigrants.* Franklin, TN, 1869.

Marohn, Richard C. *The Last Gunfighter: John Wesley Hardin.* College Station: Early West/Creative, 1995.

Metz, Leon. *Encyclopedia of Lawmen, Outlaws, and Gunfighters.* New York: Checkmark Books, 2003.

——. *John Selman, Gunfighter.* 2nd ed. Norman: University of Oklahoma Press, 1980.

——. *John Wesley Hardin: Dark Angel of Texas.* Norman: University of Oklahoma Press, 1998.

——. *Pat Garrett: The Story of a Western Lawman.* Norman: University of Oklahoma Press, 1974.

——. *The Shooters: A Gallery of Notorious Gunmen from the American West.* New York: Berkley Books, 1996.

Miller, Rick. *Bloody Bill Longley.* Wolfe, TX: Henington, 1996.

——. *Sam Bass and Gang.* Austin: State House Press, 1999.

Nolan, Frederick. *Bad Blood: The Life and Times of the Horrell Brothers.* Stillwater, OK: Barbed Wire Press, 1994.

———. *The Lincoln County War: A Documentary History.* Norman: University of Oklahoma Press, 1992.

O'Neal, Bill. *The Bloody Legacy of Pink Higgins: A Half Century of Violence in Texas.* Austin: Eakin Press, 1999.

———. *Encyclopedia of Western Gunfighters.* Norman: University of Oklahoma Press, 1979.

O'Neil, James B. *They Die But Once.* New York: Knight, 1935.

Orr, Thomas. *Life of the Notorious Desperado Cullen Baker.* N.p.: Price and Barton, 1870.

Parsons, Chuck. *John B. Armstrong: Texas Ranger and Pioneer Ranchman.* College Station: Texas A&M University Press, 2007.

Phillips, John Neal. *Running with Bonnie and Clyde: The Ten Fast Years of Ralph Fults.* Norman: University of Oklahoma Press, 1996.

Preece, Harold. *Lone Star Man.* New York: Hastings House, 1960.

Ramsey, Winston G. *On the Trail of Bonnie and Clyde Then and Now.* London: Battle of Britain International Ltd., 2003.

Rathmell, William. *Life of the Marlows: A True Story of Frontier Life of Early Days.* Edited with an introduction and annotations by Robert K. DeArment. Denton, TX: University of North Texas Press, 2004.

Roberts, Dan W. *Rangers and Sovereignty.* San Antonio: Wood Printing and Engraving, 1914.

Rose, Peter R., and Elizabeth E. Sherry, ed. *The Hoo Doo War: Portraits of a Lawless Time.* Mason, TX: Mason County Historical Commission, 2003.

Shirley, Glenn. *Shotgun for Hire: The Story of "Deacon" Jim Miller, Killer of Pat Garrett.* Norman: University of Oklahoma Press, 1970.

Simmons, Lee. *Assignment Huntsville: Memoirs of a Texas Peace Officer.* Austin: University of Texas Press, 1957.

Smallwood, James A., Barry A. Crouch, and Larry Peacock. *Murder and Mayhem: The War of Reconstruction in Texas.* College Station: Texas A&M University Press, 2003.

Smith, Robert B. *Daltons! The Raid on Coffeyville, Kansas.* Norman: University of Oklahoma Press, 1996.

———. *Last Hurrah of the James-Younger Gang.* Norman: University of Oklahoma Press, 2001.

———. *Tough Towns: True Tales from the Gritty Streets of the Old West.* Guilford, CT: Globe Pequot Press, 2007.

Sonnichsen, C. L. *I'll Die Before I Run.* New York: Harper and Brothers, 1951.

———. *Ten Texas Feuds.* Albuquerque: University of New Mexico, 2000.

Sterling, William Warren. *Trails and Trials of a Texas Ranger.* Norman: University of Oklahoma Press, 1959.

Thrapp, Dan L. *Encyclopedia of Frontier Biography.* Spokane, WA: Arthur H. Clark, 1990.

Tise, Sammy. *Texas County Sheriffs.* Halletsville, TX: Tise Genealogical Research, 1989.

Tyler, Ron, ed. *The New Handbook of Texas*. Austin: Texas State Historical Association, 1996.

Underwood, Sid. *Depression Desperado: The Chronicle of Raymond Hamilton*. Austin: Eakin Press, 1995.

Utley, Robert M. *Lone Star Justice: The First Century of the Texas Rangers*. Oxford: Oxford University Press, 2002.

———. *Lone Star Lawmen: The Second Century of the Texas Rangers*. Oxford: Oxford University Press, 2007.

Vestal, Yvonne. *The Borderlands and Cullen Baker*. Atlanta, TX: Journal, 1978.

Wallis, Michael. *Pretty Boy: The Life and Times of Charles Arthur Floyd*. New York: St. Martin's Press, 1992.

Webb, Walter Prescott. *The Texas Rangers: A Century of Frontier Defense*. 2 vols. 1935. Reprint, Austin: University of Texas Press, 2005.

———, ed. *The Handbook of Texas*. Austin: Texas State Historical Association, 1952.

Wilkins, Frederick. *The Law Comes to Texas: The Texas Rangers, 1870-1901*. Austin: State House Press, 1999.

Yadon, Laurence J. *200 Texas Outlaws and Lawmen: 1835-1935*. With Dan Anderson. Gretna, LA: Pelican, 2008.

Articles

Delo, David M. "Camp Stambuagh . . . The Miner's Delight." *Wind River Mountaineer* 3, no. 4 (October-December 1987).

Devereaux, Jan. "Jagville. *National Association for Outlaw and Lawman History Quarterly* 27, no. 1 (January-March 2004).

Eason, Al. "Cullen Montgomery Baker--Purveyor of Death." *Frontier Times* 40 (August-September 1966).

Hervey, James Madison. "The Assassination of Pat Garrett." *True West Magazine* (March-April 1961).

Jackson, Jeff. "Vigilantes: The End of the Horrell Brothers." *Nola Quarterly* 16, no. 2 (April-June 1992): 13-19.

Johnson, Dave. "George W. Gladden, Hard Luck Warrior." *Nola Quarterly* 15, no. 3 (September 1991).

Jones, Charles Adams. "Pink Higgins: The Good Bad Man." *Atlantic Monthly* (July 1934).

Jones, W. D. "Riding with Bonnie and Clyde." *Playboy Magazine* 15, no. 11 (November 1968).

Miller, Rick. "Boastful Bill Longley: Cold-Blooded Killer." *Wild West Magazine* (February 2002).

Richter, William L. "The Revolver Rules the Day!: Colonel DeWitt C. Brown and the Freedman's Bureau in Paris, Texas, 1867-1868." *Southwest Historical Quarterly* 93 (January 1990).

Waers, C. F. "The Bloody Barrows." *True Detective* (November 1934).

Western Chronicle (June 8, 1877).

Manuscripts

Taylor, T. U. "Swamp Fox of the Sulphur, or Life and Times of Cullen Montgomery Baker" (typescript, Center for American History, University of Texas at Austin, ca. 1936).

Newspapers

Abilene Chronicle
Associated Press (filed from Blum, TX), May 28, 1944
Austin Daily Statesman
Austin Weekly Statesman
Daily Austin Republican
Daily Yellowstone Journal
Dallas Daily Herald
Dallas Daily Times Herald
Dallas Dispatch
Dallas Evening Journal
Dallas Morning News
Denison (TX) Daily Herald
Eddy (NM Territory) Current
El Paso Daily Herald
El Paso Daily Times
El Paso Herald
El Paso Times
Galveston Daily News
Hays City Sentinel
Hillsboro (TX) Evening Mirror
Houston Chronicle
Houston Daily Telegraph
Houston Press
Kansas City Star
Kaufman Daily Herald
Lampasas Dispatch
Lampasas Leader
McKinney (TX) Daily Courier-Gazette
Miami Daily Record
Miami (OK) News-Record
Middletown (OH) Journal
Navasota (TX) Examiner-Review

New Mexico Sentinel
Norton Union Intelligencer (Dallas, TX)
Omaha Republican
Pecos Valley Weekly Argus, July 5, 1895
Ringgold (LA) Record
St. Louis Daily Globe-Democrat, October 12, 1878
San Antonio Daily Express
San Antonio Daily Herald
Santa Fe New Mexican
South Pass News (WY Territory), April 9, 1870
Temple (TX) Daily Telegram
Topeka Daily Commonwealth, August 9, 1871
Waco Times-Herald
Waco Weekly Examiner
Weekly Harrison Flag (Marshall, TX)
West Texas Free Press
Wichita Daily Times (Wichita Falls, TX)

Letters

Evans, Alfred, to Gov. E. M. Pease, December 30, 1868. Lucie Price Collection, Center for American History, University of Texas at Austin.

Price, Maj. William Redwood, to Lt. J. P. Willard, January 25, 1874. District of New Mexico, Letters Received by Headquarters, Ninth Military District, 1865-90, Roll 23.

Other Sources

Burnet County District Court Records, Case 879.

Casey, Robert A. Interview by J. Haley. Haley History Center, Midland, TX.

Casey, William. Interview by J. Haley. Haley History Center, Midland, TX.

Coe, Frank. Interview by J. Haley. 1927. Haley History Center, Midland, TX.

Coke, Richard M. Papers. State Archives, Austin, TX.

Doell, Henry. Interview by C. L. Sonnichsen. July 12, 1944. University of Texas at El Paso.

Grand jury indictment of M. Clements. Reeves County District Court Records, Case No. 151, September term 1893.

Jones, Bill. Interview by J. Haley. Haley History Center, Midland, TX.

Methvin v. Oklahoma. A-9060 (1936).

Miller v. State. Case No. 3283, *Texas Criminal Appeals* vol. 18.

Nichols, John. Interview by J. Haley. 1927. Haley History Center, Midland, TX.

Records of the Adjutant General of Texas. 1870-76. State Archives, Austin, TX.

Redmon, State Police Sgt. J. M. Reports. February 13, 17, and 28, 1873. Records of the Adjutant General of Texas. 1870-876. State Archives, Austin, TX.

Refugio County Court Records, Case 831.

Sonnichsen, C. L. Interview by Inez Richmond, assistant librarian, Ada Public Library. June 5, 1953. Sonnichsen Papers, University of Texas at El Paso Archives.

Sparks, Capt. John C., Company C, Frontier Battalion. Reports. Records of the Adjutant General of Texas. 1870-876. State Archives, Austin, TX.

Special Order No. 47. October 7, 1875.

State of Texas v. Frank Jackson, Williamson County District Court Records, Case No. 1762.

State of Texas v. Joe Palmer.

State v. Clyde Barrow, Bonnie Parker, and John Doe, whose true name is unknown, Ottawa County District Court (OK) Records (October 3, 1934).

State v. G. A. Frazer, Reeves County District Court Records, Case No. 186.

Webb, Walter Prescott. Collection. Adjutant General Correspondence. Center for American History, University of Texas at Austin.

Woods, T. P. "Crimes Committed in Washington County." (Texas State Library, Austin) (July 12, 1870).

Index

Abernathy, Emory, 250
Abilene, 65-66
Ada, Oklahoma, 159
Adams, Ramon, 158
Adamson, Carl, 149, 151
Ake, Jeff, 182, 184
Alcatraz, 290
Alcorn, Bob, 272, 277, 279
Allen, Green, 43
Allen, Pat, 264
Alvord, Julius, 198
Anderson, Wilson, 90-91, 99
Applegate, Bill, 122
Arcadia, 277
Arkansas, 29, 35, 49
Armstrong, John B., 68, 210, 215

Babb, Bill, 132
Baccus, Pete, 168-69
Bader, Karl, 174, 176, 178
Bader, Pete, 172, 174-75, 177, 181-83
Baily, Wesley, 34
Baird, James A., 179
Baird, John, 167, 176-82
Baird, Moses, 174-77, 182
Baker, Cullen Montgomery, 29, 31, 37, 43, 45, 50-51, 88-89

Ballard, "Boss," 260
Bardsley, George W., 193
Barnes, Seaborn, 195, 205, 214, 219
Barrow, Blanche, 263
Barrow, Clyde Chestnut, 245-46, 262, 266-67, 269, 273, 283, 285-86, 293, 296
Barrow, Marvin Ivan "Buck," 248, 268
Barrymore, Drew, 197
Barrymore, Maurice, 197
Bartholomew, Ed, 85-86
Bass, Sam, 30, 185, 195-96, 199, 201, 205, 209, 215, 219, 255
Beasley, Joe, 146, 157
Bedford, G. E. "Bit," 226, 241
Bedino, Juan, 59
Berry, James F., 188-89, 191
Bickerstaff, Benjamin F., 29, 36-37, 43-44
Billy the Kid, 73, 114, 118, 149, 151
Bland, John, 64
Blasengame, Frances, 225
Bowen, Bill, 111-13
Bowen, Jane, 68
Bowen, Neill, 67-68

Bowen, Tom, 129, 132
Boyd, Perry, 276
Bradford, Cy, 240
Brady, William, 115
Brazil (Brazel), Wayne, 151-52, 155
Brice, Donaly E., 30
Brightstar, 29, 35, 42, 48-50
Britton, F. L., 110
Brooks, Teddy R., 289
Bucher, John N., 264, 290
Bureau of Refugees, 37
Bybee, Hilton, 263, 269, 283, 285

Campbell, William Calvin "Cal," 276, 290
Carmichael, George, 227, 229, 241
Carter, Charley, 203, 205
Celina, 261-63
Chamblee, John, 49-50
Chambless, Odell, 266
Cherry, Wesley, 112
Cheyney, Jim, 174, 177-78, 183
Chipley, William Dudley, 70
Cisco, 223-24, 227-28, 230-32, 235, 237-39, 243
Clark, John E., 162, 165-68, 175, 177-78
Clayton, Powell, 44, 47
Clements, Emmanuel "Mannie," 139-40, 146, 149
Clements, Gip, 66
Clements, Manning, 61, 66
Clements, Sarah "Sallie," 139
Clymer, John, 181
Cockrell, G. C., 262

Cody, Buffalo Bill, 136
Coe, Frank, 118
Coke, Bill, 178, 180
Collins, Ben, 148
Collins, Henry, 205-6
Collins, Joel, 187-88, 191, 194, 198
Cooley, Scott, 161, 173-74, 176-77, 179-81, 183-84
Coop, John, 137-38
Copeland, John N., 114
Cougar, Charles, 65-66
Courtney, John, 42
Courtright, "Long Haired" Jim, 204
Cox, Jim, 62-63
Crabtree, Bill, 132
Crockett, David, 32
Crompton, Zacharias, 117, 119-20, 122
Crouch, Barry A., 30
Crowder, Ed, 245, 247, 257
Cuero, 60, 63
Culp, Morgan, 34
Curry, George, 153, 156
Curry, Jim, 197
Custer, George A., 37

Dakota Territory, 188
Dallas, Texas, 245, 247-50, 253-54, 257-58, 261, 263, 266, 272, 274, 276-77
Daniels, T. M., 112
Davis, Jack, 187, 190, 193, 220
Davis, Joe, 48-50
Davis, Louis, 225, 231-33, 237, 241

Davis, Malcolm, 266
Davis, Steve, 283
Deadwood, Dakota Territory, 188-91
Dempsey, I. M., 48-49
Denson, John, 140-41, 145
Denson, Sam, 110
Denson, Shadrach T. "Shade," 108
Denton, 249-50, 255, 257, 262
Dexfield Park, 268
Dixon, John, 129, 132
"Doc's little Yankee," 173
Doddridge, 49
Doell, Henry, 169, 172, 180
Dolan, Jimmy, 121
Duncan, John Riley "Jack," 68
Dunlop, Bill, 43, 46

Earhart, Bill, 145
Earp, Joe, 146-47, 157
Earp, Wyatt, 184, 188
Eastham Prison Farm, 245-46, 253, 255, 257, 264, 269, 282-83, 285-86, 290, 293
Egan, William Franklin, 185
El Paso, 75-78, 80, 82, 122, 141, 144, 149, 158, 183
Englin, Doris, 235, 237
Englin, Rob, 235, 237
Evans, Alfred, 92-95
Evans, Green, 93-96
Evans, Henry, 94
Evans, Pryor, 93
Evergreen, 85, 87, 91, 93-96
Everheart, William C., 202

Fairris, Maggie, 266

Fields, W. C., 153
Finley, Tom, 197
Finney, J. J., 90
Floyd, Charles Arthur "Pretty Boy," 255, 268
Fore, Frank, 148
Fornoff, Fred, 153
Forrest, Nathan Bedford, 37
Foster, Belle, 48
Foster, Blue, 178
Foster, J. B. "Jim," 239
Foster, Marcellus E. "Mefo," 282
Foster, Mark, 100-101
Foster, Martha, 35
Foster, William, 29, 42, 48-50
Fountain, Albert J., 155
Frazer, George A. "Bud," 76, 138, 142, 157
Freedmen's Bureau, 37, 40-41, 43, 45
Fults, Ralph, 253-54, 261, 263, 283, 285, 292

Gamel, Tom, 170, 175, 182-83
Garrett, Patrick Floyd, 76, 153, 149, 155-57, 159
Gault, Ben F. "Manny," 277, 279
Gayne, Walter, 159
Gibson, Con, 141
Giddings, Texas, 87-88, 99
Gillett, James B., 113, 131, 212, 221
Gladden, George, 174, 177, 183
Glenn, W. H., 132
Grapevine, Texas, 266, 274-77, 289

Griffith, Ben, 41, 43, 46
Grimes, Ahijah W. "Caige,"
    213
Grizell, Jim, 112, 125
Grizell, Sarah Ann, 105
Gross, Henry, 101
Grove, Larry, 275
Gylam, Texas Jack "Jackito,"
    117, 122

Hall, Caleb, 170
Hall, Lee, 201-2, 210
Hamer, Francis Augustus, 221,
    228, 269-70, 276
Hamer, Harrison, 270
Hamilton, Floyd, 290
Hamilton, Raymond Elzie,
    253, 255, 265-66, 269, 273,
    283, 286-87, 289, 291-92,
    295
Harcourt, Charles "Doc," 173
Hardin, John Wesley, 51, 53-
    57, 59, 61-65, 67, 74-75, 76,
    79-80, 87, 92, 139, 144-45,
    201, 210
Hardin, Martin Quilla "Mart,"
    140-41
Harkey, Daniel R. "Dee," 146,
    157
Harris, Ellis, 231
Harris, J. C., 255
Hart, Edward "Little," 73,
    121-22
Hays, Johnny, 261, 264
Helm, John Marshall "Jack,"
    62, 64
Helms, Henry, 226, 232, 237,
    240, 242

Herndon, Albert G., 197, 201
Herold, George, 210, 214
Hervey, James M., 153
Hickman, Tom, 227
Hickok, James Butler "Wild
    Bill," 65
Higgins, John Calhoun
    Pinckney "Pink," 103-4,
    124-25, 127-28, 134-35
Highsmith, Henry Albert,
    213
Hill, Robert, 226-27, 232-33
Hilton, Paris, 224
Hinton, Ted, 266, 272, 275,
    285
Hoester, Dan, 166, 171, 174,
    177-78
Hogg, Thomas E., 202
Holmes, Henry M., 175
Horner, Joe, 187
Horrell, Benedict, 104, 106,
    108, 112, 117-18, 122
Horrell, John, 105-6
Horrell, Mart, 111-12, 119,
    128, 130-34
Horrell, Merritt, 111-12, 124,
    127, 129
Horrell, Sam, 105, 134, 136
Horrell, Tom, 106, 119, 128,
    130, 132-34
Horrell, William, 105
Horton, Joseph, 173
Hughes, John R., 141, 156
Hughes, T. R., 281
Hutchinson, William H., 70

Iowa, 268
Ivy, Polk, 273

Jack, Thomas P., 100-101
Jackson, Francis M. "Frank,"
    195, 197, 201, 204-6, 208,
    217, 219-21
Jackson, John S., 43, 46, 48
James, Frank, 256
James, Jesse, 136
Jarrott, James, 147, 157
Johnson, Arkansas, 195-96,
    204
Johnson, Charley, 168-70,
    172, 174, 180
Johnson, Doyle, 265
Johnson, Gladys, 270
Johnson, Sid, 263
Johnson, Walter, 205, 208
Jones, George Arthur, 291
Jones, Heiskell, 114, 120
Jones, John B., 131, 173, 177,
    199, 219
Jones, Tom, 242, 244, 258
Jones, William Daniel
    "Deacon," 265, 267, 291
Joplin, Missouri, 267
Jordan, Henderson, 272, 277,
    279
Joyner, John, 272

Kansas, 65
Kaufman, 257-58, 261-63, 285
Kemp, 259-61, 263
Kennedy, John, 42
Kilburn, E. P. "Pack," 242-43
King, C. W., 119, 121, 123
King Ranch, 62
Kirby, Matthew "Dummy," 29,
    41, 43, 49, 88
Kirkman, William, 40, 44

Koppel, Henry, 213
Krebs, Bernard J., 252
Ku Klux Klan, 29, 43, 86, 94,
    126
Kuykendall, William L., 97

Lampasas, 104, 106-8, 110-13,
    116-17, 122, 124, 126-31,
    133-36, 182, 210
Larn, John, 73
Law and Order League, 126
Lay, William Roland (Rolland),
    100
Leach, M. F., 191-92, 220
Leahy, Harry, 241
Lee, Robert Jehu "Bob," 29,
    37-38, 43-44, 51
Lehmberg, Karl "Charley," 171
Lewis, Callie, 66
Longley, Caleb, 90
Longley, Wild Bill, 37, 41, 51,
    83, 86, 91, 98-101, 110
Look, George, 78
Lucero, Felipe, 152

McAdams, Meredith, 42
McCormick, A. F., 255
McCormick, Harry, 293
McKemmie, Robert "Reddy,"
    188, 190
McKeown, John, 87, 93
McLaughlin, N. B., 42
McMeans, Gee, 270
McNabb, Florence, 293
McNabb, Wade Hampton, 292,
    295-96
McSwain, Dan, 269, 270
Mann, Jim, 70

Martin, Hurricane Minnie, 73
Martin, Juan, 117-18
Mason, James Polk, 181
Mason County, 161-73, 175,
    177-80, 183-84
Mason County "Hoo Doo" War,
    162
Maxwell, C. G., 265
Melville, Andrew, 112
Methvin, Henry, 257, 269,
    272, 274, 276-77, 283, 285,
    293, 296
Methvin, Ivy T., 245, 272, 278,
    289-90
Meusenbach, John O., 178
Middletown, Ohio, 252
Miller, J. P., 180
Miller, James B. "Killin' Jim,"
    76, 130, 137, 139, 144, 146,
    151-53, 156, 158-59
Mills, Alexander "Ham," 119-
    21
Milton, Jeff, 78, 82
"Minute Men" militias, 107
Missouri, 267
Mitchell, Bob, 126-28,
    130
Moore, Eugene, 265
Moore, Rance, 180
Morgan, James B., 61
Morose, Martin, 75, 77, 80
Moss, Mathew, 178
Mullens, James, 283, 290
Murph, Peyton, 43
Murphy, Daniel, 143
Murphy, Holloway Daniel, 273
Murphy, Jim, 199, 205-6, 209,
    214-15, 219

Murphy, Larry, 114-15, 118-
    19, 122

Nacogdoches, Texas, 36
Nevill, Charles L., 212
Nichols, John, 106, 108, 113
Nixon, Tom, 188-90, 194
Northington, Alex, 127

O'Dare, Gene, 285, 287
O'Dare, Mary, 273, 286-87,
    289
Ohio, 252
Oklahoma, 159
Olson, Marion, 229
Orr, Thomas, 38, 46, 48-51, 90
Otis, John, 255
Owens, W. N., 256

Palmer, Joe, 257, 269, 282,
    292-93
Paramore, Green, 67
Parker, Bonnie Elizabeth, 249,
    257, 261, 269, 274, 276,
    283
Patron, Juan, 115, 119-20, 123
Peacock, Lewis, 38
Peak, Junius, 202, 204
Pecos, 138-41, 143-45,
    157
Perkins, Floyd, 261
Petty, Mary Jane, 34
Phares, Leslie G., 276
Phillips, H. E., 271
Pinkerton, William, 199
Pipes, Samuel J., 197, 199
Poe, Jewell, 223, 226
Potts, Bill, 187

Pruitt, Clint, 149
Pruitt, Port, 148

Queen, Victor, 75, 77

Rames, John Howard "Seth," 42
Rames (Raines), Lee, 42, 48-
49, 90
Rames, Seth, 43, 46
Rand, Charles, 43
Ratliff, Marshall, 223, 231-32,
235, 238
Reagan, Richard "Dick," 60
Redies, R. T., 227, 230
Redmon, J. M., 110
Regan, Frank, 114, 120
Reynolds, N. O., 131, 179, 210
Richardson, Harry, 252
Riggs, Barney, 139, 143, 145-
46
Riley, John H., 114-15
Ringo, John, 174, 176-77,
181-84
Roberts, Allen G., 167, 183
Roberts, Dan, 166, 169, 175,
177
Rogers, Ted, 255, 261, 264-65,
290
Rollins, Frank, 51
Rollins, L. R., 41
Round Rock, 208-10, 212-15,
217, 219
Rountree, Robert F., 184

Salmon, James, 46
Salmon, John, 43
Scarborough, D. F. "Frank," 46
Scarborough, George, 78, 80

Schieffer, William, 275
Schmid, Richard Allen
"Smoot," 265-66, 272, 283
Scott, Jerry, 111-12, 117, 119-
20, 123-24, 127
Scott, Preston R., 42, 46
Selman, John, 72, 75, 78-80,
144
Shaw, R. A., 281
Sherman, William Tecumseh,
107
Shirley, Glenn, 158
Short, Marcus (Mark), 108,
112-13
Shreveport, 277
Shroyer, William "Lou," 99
Sie, Dan, 149
Simmons, Lee, 269, 271, 273,
283
Skelly, Aubrey, 246, 257
Slaughter, Johnny, 189-90
Slayton, A. M., 228
Sloter, Charles, 55
Smallwood, T. L., 228
Smith, Billy, 49-50
Smith, Howell, 42, 48-49
Smith, Van C., 122
Souther, W. L., 252
Sparks, Thomas, 108
Spears, Alex, 224, 229
Spell, Robert, 48-49
Spotswood, Tom, 196, 207
Standifer, Bill, 135
Stanford, Leland, 192
Sterling, William Warren, 221
Stewart, Les, 266
Stroud, Robert "Bird Man,"
290

Stull, John, 132
Sublett, Phil, 59
Sutton, William E., 62, 64
Swain, J. H., 68
Sweet, Albertus, 123, 135

Taylor, James T., 255, 262
Taylor, Jim, 61, 63-64
Taylor, Scrap, 63
Terrell, Zeke, 124
Thomas, George, 99
Thomas, Henry "Heck," 196, 207
Thompson, Mark B., 154
Tinker, Bill, 128
Todd, G. W., 181
Towle, James F. "Frank," 188-89, 191
Turley, Tom, 168-70
Turner, Ben C., 121-22

Underwood, Henry, 186, 195-97, 202-3, 205, 220

Vaughan, Dick, 281, 293
Vaughn, James Theodore "Dorrie," 131

Ware, John and Billy, 140
Warner, D. C., 117

Warthan, John F. and Mary E., 34
Washmood, Ahmed, 149
Webb, Charles, 61, 72
Webb, Jim, 99
Wheeler, Bryan, 273
Whitcraft, Joe (Allen), 112
Wichita Falls, 256, 263
Wiggins, Abe, 168-69
Wilburn, Aaron O., 122
Williams, Eleanor Bee, 249
Williams, Jim, 177, 183
Williams, John, 43, 46
Williams, Thomas G., 110
Williamson, Tim, 161, 166, 168, 171, 173, 175, 178
Willis, Hiram F., 41
Wilson, John W., 96
Wilson, Vernon, 210
Withers, Clay, 203, 205
Woods, T. P., 96
Woody, George, 252
Worley, John, 171-73
Wren, W. R. "Bill," 126, 128, 130
Wylie, R. C., 238

Zarate, Guadalupe, 74
Zurn, Jake, 198